Praise for
PARTY OF CONSCIENCE

"*Party of Conscience* is a sophisticated re-examination of the past and present of Canada's party of the left, which is both timely and long overdue. Drawing from a wide array of academics, activists, and party stalwarts the essays here give all concerned much to think about as progressive democrats everywhere seek new ways to replace the social, political, and economic injustices of twenty-first-century capitalism with a more just socially democratic order."

— Kevin Brushett, Department of History, Royal Military College of Canada

"*Party of Conscience* is an important addition to the current conversation about the left and electoral politics. The book feels like a conversation around a kitchen table; both a dialogue and a reflection on where we have been and where to go from here."

— Sheri Benson, MP for Saskatoon West, NDP

"*Party of Conscience* is a thought-provoking intellectual history of the CCF/NDP from its origins to present day, which provides a captivating overview of the debates that have animated its history. It is a must-read for citizens looking for a critical perspective on the CCF/NDP and for anyone who wants to understand where Canada's left has been and where it might go in the future."

— David McGrane, professor of political studies, St. Thomas More College, University of Saskatchewan and author of *Remaining Loyal: Social Democracy in Quebec and Saskatchewan*

"The history and practice of socialism and social democracy in Canada has long needed this kind of wide-ranging, multi-dimensional analysis. This collection of essays brings together fascinating insights into the roots of the CCF/NDP, its ideological distinctiveness, and the political diversity and complexity that have run through the party. *Party of Conscience* sheds light on how to move forward into a world of greater social justice."

— Craig Heron, Department of History, York University and author of
   Lunch-Bucket Lives: Remaking the Workers' City

"*Party of Conscience* provides an insightful analysis of the important role played by the CCF/NDP in Canadian politics. Drawing on Canada's leading experts in the field, the book fills what was too long a gap in our understanding of Canada's social democratic parties."

— David Docherty, President, Mount Royal University and author of
   Mr. Smith Goes to Ottawa: Life in the House of Commons

PARTY OF CONSCIENCE

THE CCF, THE NDP,
AND SOCIAL DEMOCRACY
IN CANADA

EDITED BY ROBERTA LEXIER,
STEPHANIE BANGARTH, AND JON WEIER

BETWEEN THE LINES
TORONTO

Party of Conscience
© 2018 Roberta Lexier, Stephanie Bangarth, and Jonathan Weier

First published in 2018 by
Between the Lines
401 Richmond Street West, Studio 281
Toronto, Ontario M5V 3A8
Canada
1-800-718-7201
www.btlbooks.com

Library and Archives Canada Cataloguing in Publication

Party of conscience : the CCF, the NDP, and social democracy in Canada
    / edited by Roberta Lexier, Stephanie Bangarth, Jonathan Weier.

Includes bibliographical references and index.
Issued in print and electronic formats.

ISBN 978-1-77113-392-0 (softcover).--ISBN 978-1-77113-393-7 (EPUB).--
ISBN 978-1-77113-394-4 (PDF)

        1. Co-operative Commonwealth Federation--History. 2. New Democratic Party--History. 3. Political parties--Canada--History. 4. Socialism--Canada--History. I. Lexier, Roberta, 1977-, editor II. Bangarth, Stephanie, 1972-, editor III. Weier, Jonathan, editor

JL197.N4P37 2018   324.27107   C2018-902800-9
                                                           C2018-902801-7

Cover illustration and cover and text design by Maggie Earle
Printed in Canada

We acknowledge for their financial support of our publishing activities: the Government of Canada; the Canada Council for the Arts, which last year invested $153 million to bring the arts to Canadians throughout the country; and the Government of Ontario through the Ontario Arts Council, the Ontario Book Publishers Tax Credit program, and the Ontario Media Development Corporation.

CONTENTS

FOREWORD

Writing in *Prison Notebooks*, Antonio Gramsci remarks that "the config-
uration of the state" varies from state to state, "which is precisely why an
accurate reconnaissance on a national scale was needed." "Reconnaissance"
means an accurate, rigorous, and historically informed analysis of each
country that socialists hope to transform—and implied by this Gramscian
metaphor, far too often dismissed as the revolutionary Sardinian's com-
monsensical call for good historical analysis, is in fact an entire view of
the world, at once sober, realistic, and hopeful, which maintains that actual
humans can work to better humanity. The great value of this innovative
and invaluable collection of essays on the CCF/NDP tradition is that,
at its best moments, it begins a new reconnaissance of the party and the
Canada it sought to reform. Here are scholars and activists respectful of
complexity, aware of contradiction, and always attentive to political and
historical context.

At their best, CCFers and NDPers have been acutely aware of the terrain on which they operated, and they have debated openly among themselves about how it might be transformed. In the 1930s, CCFers, some
of them partisans of "labour socialism," alongside middle-class members
aspiring to a planned economy and society in which their expert knowledge would be honoured, undertook systematic analyses of the country
they sought to transform. (They were often locked in agonistic relations
with the communists, from whom they derived many lessons on party
organization and even political thought.) In the 1940s, having achieved
hegemony on the left and political power in Regina, they strove to build
a "pocket edition" of the New Jerusalem and to instantiate a new form of
politics in Canada. Their successors, the New Democrats, beginning in
part as CCFers chastened by the Cold War and tamed by liberal order,
underwent a significant mid-1960s transformation, turning some of them

into New Left advocates of anti-militarism, Canadian sovereignty, and workers' self-management. From the 1970s to the 1990s, many of these New Democrats attended closely to socialist feminism, environmentalism, human rights, and national self-determination for Québec and First Nations. And, after riding a roller-coaster taking them from near electoral extinction in 1993 (7 percent of the vote) to near-victory in 2011 (31 per cent and official opposition status), many New Democrats demonstrated both left-wing potential and left-wing vulnerability: entranced by Parliament and starring as liberal muckrakers par excellence of scandals nobody now remembers, they overlooked, often even disparaged, the need to mount a comprehensive challenge to the neoliberal order in which we live. Their return to third-party status in 2015 was the ultimate reward of their single-minded pursuit of the chimera of a purified liberal order centred upon Parliament and their neglect of the hard work of building a counter-hegemonic movement and a party capable of generating an alternative worldview. The world passed them by. Perhaps, some of these essays suggest, they can catch up to it.

Within the labour socialism that inspired many CCFers, there was a close link between the organic working-class intellectuals and the party. In the 1960s and 1970s, many New Democrats threw themselves into the organization of oppositional ways of thinking and being, as reflected in countless newspapers, community organizations, and radical movements. In the 1980s and 1990s, socialist feminists in the unions and in the party championed a vision of an alternative gender order. Throughout, such counter-hegemonic challenges to the conventional wisdom failed to generate a homogeneous, co-ordinated, expansive, and sustained network of cultural institutions through which an alternative future might be imagined and debated. Perhaps the most telling weakness of today's NDP is the absence of a powerful mass media articulating its viewpoint.

I am a life long New Democrat—a consistent voter and, for the most part, a constant member. (One significant exception: I could not, as a gay man, stomach the Ontario party's scandalous back-down on civil rights with respect to sexual minorities in the 1990s.) I suspect I will be an NDPer until I die. Yet, it often seems to me that, far from being a rich relationship characterized by democratic dialogue and debate, my relationship with the NDP is now mediated most powerfully by those two deeply political institutions in our culture— i.e., Visa and MasterCard. Democracy, as Sheldon Wolin once wrote, is not so much about where the political is located but how it is experienced. I suspect many other New

Democrats will share my perception that from the CCF, which featured so many ardent supporters pouring over the dense text of *Social Planning for Canada* in their church basements in the 1930s, to today's NDP, something in the experience of party members has dramatically changed. From Tommy Douglas to today's telemarketers, something important has been lost. Rarely, if ever, consulted by the party, I feel both strongly attached to it (because it represents a vulnerable and precious legacy of oppositional thought, brings together many of the people who might make a progressive future possible, and stubbornly constitutes a communitarian outlier on a continent saturated with possessive individualism) and just as strongly alienated from it (because of its perpetual pursuit of respectability, middle-class moderation, and Parliamentary prestige distracts it from the serious system-challenging tasks at hand). The NDP represents a perpetual, at best partially realized, radical possibility. It has, unquestionably, mitigated the untrammeled individualism of North American liberalism at its most abusive. It has also succumbed to, and in fact perpetuated, the liberal passive revolution whereby all genuinely democratic and radical currents are reduced to their lowest common electoral denominators—and absorbed by the ever-adaptive Liberal party. How strong has been the pull of the liberal order and its privileges for New Democrats—from Hazen Argue to Bob Rae!

Five great contradictions shape our contemporary world. The first is pitting ruling classes against ruled classes, and this is now active on both national and global scales. It is epitomized by the extreme social makeover of all the advanced industrial countries, as economic inequality attains astounding levels. The second is that of opposing the social relations of production, distribution, and circulation against the social forces of production: our entire social order is placed at risk by saturated markets for consumer commodities, as the symbolic value of goods comes to overshadow their use-value. The third is the vastly accelerated displacement of workers by machinery, rendering vast swaths of the world's working population redundant. The fourth is the contradiction between social reproduction and accumulation, manifested in the crisis of the male breadwinner role, declining real wages, and a weakening of the traditional family without any coherent, adequate, or plausible "Plan B." And finally, there is the global environmental crisis: capital necessarily relates to the natural world as a vast storehouse of potential commodities, as even fish swimming in the ocean, the air we breathe, the space humans individually or collectively occupy, even the cells within our own bodies, can be monetized and sold.

All five contradictions are subsumed in a vast ideology of "property," that vast practice and ideal—the "fibre of our entire civil and moral structure," as one authority that Gramsci quoted had it—that thinkers and activists close to the CCF/NDP tradition have, from the 1930s to today, problematized. For all their contradictions and failings, the architects of the Regina Manifesto, the Wafflers of the 1970s, the feminists of the 1980s, and the authors of the Leap Manifesto grasped that, at its core, socialism committed to radical democracy must place property in question and challenge its hegemonic dominion.

Neoliberalism's makeover of the socio-economic order is correlated with an equally radical revision of the relationship of state and civil society. Market obligations overwhelm political citizenship. The very nature of the democratic state is redefined in ways that bestow total power upon the "world market" and envisage the state to be not the manager of the economy but an active presence educating members of the public on their proper deportment and subjectivity: citizens are reconceptualized as customers and performance indicators in public institutions mimic those in the private sphere. Socialists confront a neoliberalism that is at once sweepingly total in its ambitions and minute and "capillary" in its day-to-dayness. The "new democracy" can only be imagined as its antithesis.

Readers will find in this volume of original essays many intimations of how earlier socialists dealt with the parallel structural contradictions of their own time. They will find in them much that is inspiring—in, for example, the grounded (and perhaps inadvertently radical) practicality that constructed, albeit imperfectly and partially, Canada's health system. They will also find much that is disquieting. All these essays confirm, in my view, that rather than seeing the NDP as the "Nearly Dead Party" (the putdown of the 1990s) or the "Newly Dynamic Party" (the optimistic marketing slogan of 2011), we might learn to see it as one important "Node in a Democratic Project"—one particular front within a much wider people's struggle for human flourishing and human survival. There is in this book, sometimes fragmentary and often more fully developed, the beginnings of an exciting new reckoning with—and indeed a full reconnaissance of—our country's major left-wing party.

Ian McKay
McMaster University

INTRODUCTION

Roberta Lexier, Stephanie Bangarth, and Jon Weier

July 2018 marks the eighty-fifth anniversary of the drafting of the Regina Manifesto. The authors of this pivotal document explained their intention to use political action to bring about a social and economic transformation that would

> replace the present capitalist system, with its inherent injustice and inhumanity, by a social order from which the domination and exploitation of one class by another will be eliminated, in which economic planning will supersede unregulated private enterprise and competition, and in which genuine democratic self-government, based upon economic equality, will be possible.[1]

They would achieve this goal by founding a new political party, the Co-operative Commonwealth Federation (CCF), which "[aimed] at political power in order to put an end to this capitalist domination of our political life."[2] The CCF transitioned to the New Democratic Party (NDP) in 1961. Canadian politics has been shaped by a multi-party system with the CCF/NDP on the political left.

However, despite this long history, relatively little attention has been paid to the contributions of the CCF/NDP in Canadian politics. If one were to survey the field of political history in Canada, it would appear as though there is no left in Canada and that the politics of the nation have been shaped solely by the Liberal and Conservative parties. The CCF/NDP is consistently presented as a fringe party, always confined to the opposition and with little influence over Canadian policies and perspectives. The analyses that do exist frequently emphasize the importance of particular (white, male) leaders, including J. S. Woodsworth, Tommy Douglas, and Jack Layton, but fail to acknowledge the broader contributions of the social democratic party on Canadian life. The impression this instills, that the left has made no contribution to Canadian politics and history, is blatantly false; the left has molded this country in significant ways. The CCF/NDP has been a key force in the development of many of the ideas that Canadians hold dear in the present, including health care, public education, and peacekeeping/pacifism. As well, the CCF/NDP has played a leadership role in diversifying Canada's political culture, and supporting women, members of racialized communities, and LGBTQ+ Canadians as they sought inclusion and leadership in mainstream politics. It is critical, on the eighty-fifth anniversary of the founding of the CCF, to remedy this imbalance and critically examine the place of social democracy in Canadian history and politics.

Remarkably, little scholarly attention has been paid to the history and development of social democracy in Canada and specifically to the CCF/NDP. Fifty years ago, Walter Young wrote a book about the origins of the CCF.[3] Since then, monographs by Desmond Morton (1974, 1986), Ivan Avakumovic (1978), Norman Penner (1992), and Alan Whitehorn (1992) have chronicled the existence of socialism in Canada, the emergence of the NDP, and the evolution of the party.[4] As well, there are biographies and autobiographies of varying quality on many of the major players in the NDP that provide further insight into the evolution of social democracy in Canada.[5] However, all of these works are exceptionally limited. The authors are mostly party members and participants in the events under discussion; there is, therefore, inadequate opportunity for critical scholarly assessments in most of these published works. These monographs are also extremely dated, with almost nothing written by historians on the party since the 1990s. The only recent historical work is a biography of the first leader of the NDP, Tommy Douglas, who remains a revered political figure in Canada because of his work to initiate universal health care.[6] Additionally, political scientists have recently published monographs about social democracy more broadly: David McGrane examines the emergence and evolution of social democracy in Saskatchewan and Quebec,[7] while essays in an edited collection by David Laycock and Lynda Erickson reassess the developments that led to the Orange Wave success in 2015.[8]

This current collection of articles emerges from a conference held in Calgary in May 2017 titled "Social Democracy and the Left in Canada:

Past, Present, and Future." The choice of Calgary was significant, because the very first meeting of labour, socialist, and farmers' political organizations who would, the following year, draft the Regina Manifesto and found the Co-operative Commonwealth Federation was held at what is now the Royal Canadian Legion #1 in Calgary in 1932. The 2017 conference therefore celebrated the eighty-fifth anniversary of the first meeting of the CCF, just as this collection commemorates the anniversary of the official founding of the party. Moreover, holding the conference in Calgary recognized the second anniversary of the provincial NDP's defeat of the Progressive Conservative Party of Alberta after close to forty-four years in office and Alberta's status as the only province at the time governed by the NDP.

This conference brought together graduate students, emerging and established scholars, politicians, think tank activists, union members, and the general public in an important discussion about social democracy and the left in Canada. We had keynote lectures, which are included in this collection, from: Avi Lewis, grandson of former NDP leader David Lewis and son of former Ontario NDP leader Stephen Lewis and co-author of the Leap Manifesto; Bill Blaikie, former NDP Member of Parliament from Manitoba; and Jonathan Sas, then Director of Policy at the Broadbent Institute. Panel discussions included papers reassessing the written history of the CCF/NDP, examining the theory and practice of social democracy, assessing the role of particular leaders in the past and present of the CCF/NDP, exploring the contributions of the party to foreign policy and government programs, discussing the differing role of the CCF/NDP in the regions, evaluating the role of unions and activists in the party, considering the influence of neoliberalism on party policies, and debating the potential of the leadership candidates who were running to replace Tom Mulcair. Many of these papers are included in this collection.

Together and separately, the chapters in this collection offer an opportunity to reassess the contributions and value of the CCF/NDP in Canadian politics and history. In particular, this collection is notable for the inclusion of many voices and perspectives. Our contributors are drawn from a variety of sectors: academia, labour, political life, and non-governmental organizations (NGOs). The papers in this collection, organized in a roughly chronological order, include: scholarly articles, grounded in primary research and critical analysis; personal reflections based on years of political service; and speeches analyzing past and present currents within the political left.

The collection begins with a piece by foremost CCF historian James Naylor, which reassesses the role of Canada's social democracy in the origins of the party; he argues that social democracy was only incorporated into the platform in the 1940s and 1950s rather than, as is usually assumed, at the founding in the 1930s. The second chapter, by lawyer and politician John Brewin, examines the role of religion in the CCF/NDP, arguing that many prominent individuals, including his father, Andrew, were attracted to the party because of its ideological connections with the socially conscious churches. While many have emphasized the role of religion in the CCF, Brewin provides a unique, personal assessment of the important ways the CCF attracted those with a broader social mission. Chapter 3, by United Steelworker staff member Jennifer Hassum, examines the often-overlooked role of labour activists in the formation of the CCF. Her chapter demands a reassessment of the relationship between intellectuals and the labour movement in the past and the present. The fourth chapter, by Atlantic Canadian historian Corey Slumkoski, evaluates the role of Clarence Gillis, the first CCF MP from the area, and his efforts to advance a particular regional agenda rather than social democracy. This chapter complicates traditional analyses of the party as a western Canadian phenomenon and highlights the importance of regional issues to those involved in governance.

Chapter 5, by human rights historian Stephanie Bangarth, re-evaluates the role of the NDP in foreign policy issues throughout the Cold War period. She challenges traditional interpretations that emphasize the role of the Liberal and Progressive Conservative parties in the development of foreign policy positions and inserts the Canadian left into foreign policy directives. In the sixth chapter, Robert McDonald, an historian of British Columbia, explores the middle-class influences on the CCF/NDP and argues that Fabian socialist influences remain constant in the thinking of influential progressives in the province. His article challenges current assumptions about the relationship between ideas and partisanship in the British Columbia CCF/NDP. In the seventh chapter, David Blocker examines the history of the Waffle movement in Winnipeg and London, Ontario, and demonstrates that New Left activists sought to achieve profound and transformative social and political change through both mainstream partisan politics and extra-parliamentary social movements. This adds an important layer to the story of the controversial Waffle movement and to our understanding of sixties activism in Canada. In Chapter 8, Peter Graham examines the history of NDP and New Left activism at the municipal level, including the role of Jack Layton in these events.

Since municipal politics are often overlooked in the history of the CCF/ NDP, this article adds nuance to our understanding of the past. Chapter 9, by emerging scholar Christo Aivalis, explores debates about the historical trajectory of the NDP via an intellectual analysis of three NDP leaders: Tommy Douglas, David Lewis, and Ed Broadbent. Aivalis argues that, while the contemporary NDP has not wholesale abandoned their legacy, there remains a stark difference between the party now and the NDP during the 1968–84 period. This analysis complicates the history of the NDP and its most influential leaders.

In Chapter 10, Roberta Lexier, an historian of social movements in Canada, explores the conflictual relationship between the NDP and extra-parliamentary activists. Using three examples, the Waffle, the NPI (New Politics Initiative), and the Leap Manifesto, she argues that, while social movements and the NDP need each other to be successful, tensions persist between different forms of political participation. Chapter 11, the keynote speech given by former NDP MP Bill Blaikie, discusses how four issues—neoliberalism, the constitution, the culture wars, and social movements—helped to thwart the hopes that the federal NDP had for itself in the late 1970s and early 1980s. By examining internal and external tensions, Blaikie complicates our understanding of the failures of the NDP and provides some potential ways forward for the left party in Canada. The next chapter, by Matt Fodor, examines the evolution of NDP election platforms and demonstrates the important ways that party policies evolved from a focus on social democracy to an embrace of "Third Way" politics. It makes important contributions to an analysis of why the party initially resisted, but then succumbed to, the Third Way.

In Chapter 13, Karl Bélanger, former national director of the NDP and current president of the Douglas-Coldwell Foundation, gives us an overview of the history of the party in Quebec. He provides tremendous insight into the challenges the NDP faces in the province and offers some important suggestions for how it might succeed in the future. The following chapter, by Murray Cooke, examines the concept of populism and the CCF/NDP's relationship to left and right populism. He argues that, in the current context, an embrace of populism is the best possible option for the future success of the NDP. In Chapter 15, esteemed historians Erika Dyck and Greg Marchildon consider the ways in which social democrats fiercely defend a reified medicare rather than taking the lead on its reform. Medicare, they argue, was successful because it was outward looking, pragmatic, creative, and flexible, and social democrats need to find ways to move forward in a similar way, rather than blindly defending the program that was implemented in the past.

In Chapter 16, Jonathan Sas, former policy director for the Broadbent Institute, provides an overview of the "Change the Game" project, which "invites a critical look at the history of social democracy in Canada so that we can learn from the successes and challenges of the past in order to build the best possible path forward." The goal of the project, and this article, is to encourage a rethinking of the possibilities for social democracy in the modern Canadian context. Chapter 17, by former NDP candidate Jillian Ratti, assesses the most recent leadership campaign and shares some important insights into the future direction of the party. This campaign, she argues, highlights the unique features of the party and offers some positive opportunities for electoral success in the 2019 federal election. Finally, the collection concludes with a speech by Avi Lewis on the past, present, and future of the CCF/NDP. Lewis delves into his grandfather's speeches and writings and finds that proposed social democratic solutions to past problems are still relevant in today's context. However, Lewis also argues that, with climate change as a particular threat to human survival on the planet, a bold new program, or "Leap," must be embraced by the NDP and all political parties. Together, these chapters provide a complex and nuanced reassessment of the history and potential future of the CCF/NDP and left politics in Canada.

It is, however, necessary to acknowledge the limits of this collection. At the end of the conference, we held a session intended to identify the gaps in the topics and perspectives presented in order to address these in the publication that was to follow. We are willing to acknowledge that our collection falls short in a number of areas. We were unable to include articles on the NDP and Indigenous peoples or other racialized minorities, or any research analyzing the relationship of the NDP with race. We could not get anyone to write on the environment or other current policy issues. We also were unable to include any articles that specifically address gender and its role in the party and in Canadian politics more broadly. The relationship between the party and communism is also another significant area that warrants inclusion. We attempted, but largely failed, to fill these holes. These are significant limitations in our collection, and they highlight the state of academic scholarship on the left and the CCF/NDP; until scholars and others undertake research into these issues, any understanding of the CCF/NDP's role and place in Canadian history will be incomplete. We see this collection as an important step in encouraging and promoting future research that will address some of these areas and hope that it will inspire future research and publication.

The left has frequently allowed outsiders, especially Liberals and Conservatives, to offer assessments on the past, present, and future of the CCF/NDP. As long as this continues, the left will be defined by those committed to the marginalization and defeat of a social democratic option in Canadian politics. It is essential to provide a critical, academic analysis of the past that can remind Canadians of the important contributions the CCF/NDP and its forerunners made to the idea of Canada and the creation of a progressive, compassionate, and caring country and polity. This collection provides an initial contribution to this important conversation.

CHAPTER 1

THE CO–OPERATIVE COMMONWEALTH FEDERATION IN THE 1930S

"NOT REFORM, BUT THE REPLACING OF CAPITALISM"[1]

James Naylor

"Return the NDP to its roots!" There is probably no hardier perennial in the Canadian political garden. It sprouts particularly in New Democratic Party (NDP) leadership races where such rhetorical summonses serve to rally the membership to by-gone—but presumably only dormant—ideals. What those ideals may be appear self-evident and unquestioned. The New Democratic Party and, by extension, the Co-operative Common-wealth Federation (CCF) before it are the "good" and eminently Canadian socialists (in distinction, in particular, to the communists): humane and thoughtful, solidly on the side of progress and the downtrodden, respectful of the constitutional order and civil rights. Their innate morality descends, according to this tale, from Protestant social gospellers such as James Woodsworth and Stanley Knowles; their intelligence was established at the outset by intellectuals from the nest of Rhodes Scholars that was the League for Social Reconstruction (LSR); and their commitment to the underdog was supplied by the ranks of ordinary farmers and workers who rallied to their banner, hoping for a more rational and egalitarian society.[2] All of this was codified in the Regina Manifesto of 1933, considered the founding document of this entire tradition. If a criticism were to be made, it would be that they were dreamers, the conscience of Canadian society, winning moral victories (medicare notwithstanding) but somehow out of sync with the harsh realities of the modern world.

This origin story was readily adopted by the CCF and NDP. It painted the movement as nonthreatening and increasingly a party that fit

well within Canada's emerging post-World War II image of itself, particularly in relation to the United States. Although not without a grain of
truth, this is poor history. Certainly, the CCF and NDP have been more
complicated than this; most commentators recognize the movement has
struggled with its identity. In periods of intense reaction, during the Cold
War and again in the long phase of neoliberalism since the late 1970s,
the party has made—in different ways and in different places—considerable political concessions.[3] Hence, the call for a "return." Still, there
is a tendency to categorize the CCF and NDP under a single rubric—
social democracy—implying a degree of continuity that effaces historical
changes. I would argue that it is particularly problematic when we look
at the decade that gave birth to the CCF, the 1930s. The Depression era
spawned a very different flower.[4]

The image we have of the CCF and NDP as social democratic is
one that, in fact, dates from the 1940s and 1950s. It is of a party of reform
that sought to regulate the economy through such measures as Keynesian
fiscal policies to avoid economic calamities like the Depression; it sought
to introduce an array of social welfare measures to ensure a level of material and social security; and it supported legislation that forced employers
to recognize and negotiate seriously with labour unions. Very little of this
was, in any meaningful way, on the agenda in Canada in the 1930s. Even
had such a program to reform capitalism been on the minds of those who
met in Calgary to found the CCF, this particular route to social change
would have appeared fanciful. Canadian capitalism seemed immovable.
Amid soaring unemployment and collapsing wages, governments were
pleading poverty and supplying relief to as few recipients as they could,
and with onerous requirements and minimal rates; demands for anything
better, or for a more comprehensive reform of the social order was met
with stony silence at best, or repression at worst.[5] What we think of as a
"social democratic" strategy was not really in the cards.

Such a program was not on offer for an even more fundamental reason: those who formed the backbone of the CCF in the 1930s did not
really think like this—they thought about society and the state in quite
different ways. It is useful to remember some other elements of the inter-
war period. The formative events for this generation were World War I and,
in Canada, the labour uprising at the end of the war. Across the country
and, indeed, across much of North America and Europe, working people
seemed to be in open revolt. Strikes spread from industry to industry; by
1919 they had tended to become general, spreading throughout commu-

nities. Working-class parties were formed and were making new electoral breakthroughs. Industrialization, immigration, and war had brought a host of challenges; most notably, it was the workers' movement—in unions and small and localized political parties—that rose to meet them.[6] What is distinctive about this moment, and the worldview it reflected and nurtured, was the role that social class played. Resistance to the status quo was, fundamentally, focused on labour.

The Winnipeg General Strike was but one episode in this encounter—among the most dramatic—and is worth considering as a barometer of workers' attitudes and assumptions in the period. The dispute started with the demand by workers in the metal trades and the building trades industries that employers bargain with federations of the various unions in their trades. Because of the source of the general strike, it has historically been painted as a precocious fight for a modern collective bargaining system and for other kinds of reform that a future CCF or NDP would pursue. The crucial question, though, is why did so many workers take part? Why did it turn into an epic six-week battle that effectively shut down the prairie metropolis? Certainly, some Winnipeg workers felt such solidarity could be repaid when they entered their own battles with employers. But many of them had little to gain. Many simply put themselves at risk, such as the city's postal workers, who were famously victimized by the federal government. They had no history of collective action, but they did not buckle when the government threatened to (and did) fire them.[7] Astoundingly, half of Winnipeg strikers or more were not members of unions; huge numbers were immigrants from eastern Europe who were, with a few exceptions, quite marginal to the organized labour movement. For the most part, the unions were comprised of skilled workers of British birth or ancestry, and non-British immigrants were overwhelmingly unskilled and subject to considerable prejudice. Operating in quite a different labour market, such immigrants had little bargaining power and little chance of organizing stable unions and forcing employers to negotiate with them. The war had fueled anti-immigrant sentiments and the end of the war promised increasing rivalry over a reduced number of jobs; indeed, the months before the strike had witnessed anti-immigrant riots in the city. Nonetheless, vast numbers of these immigrants joined the "British"-led strike. Similarly, returned soldiers, who, one might think, felt alienated from—and even resentful of—those who spent the war in Canada, supported the strike in large numbers. Indeed, the attempt by the city's elite, organized in the Citizens' Committee of One Thousand, to paint the strike as a plot by "enemy aliens" to subvert British values, largely fell flat as it failed to dent returned soldiers' support for the walk out.[8]

This astounding solidarity is even more remarkable given the unclear goals of the strike. While ostensibly about collective bargaining rights, there was clearly much more motivating many of those who struck. One theme of the literature on the strike is to ask whether it was a "strike or revolution"; employers attempted to paint it as the latter in order to delegitimize and defeat it. And the strikers, particularly in its aftermath, attempted to limit its definition to one that focused on trade union issues. They did so, however, defensively. They wanted to avoid military intervention during the strike and played down its radicalism during the show trials that followed.[9] Clearly, this is an inadequate dichotomy. It was much more than a strike in the narrow way that we traditionally define it; many of those who joined in were fighting for something both vaguer and broader than collective bargaining. Yet, it was not a revolution; there was no intent nor plan to overthrow the existing order though this one action.

Then what was it? David Bercuson's overly pat declaration that "the strikers were not revolutionaries" dismisses their social hopes and even social vision.[10] The strike is perhaps best seen as an urban revolt, where vast numbers of people incensed at various consequences of the industrial-capitalist order gained a voice. But to say what? There was no political platform, *per se*—except that there seemed to be some common notion that labour—the working-class—was the force that could challenge the multiple inequities that faced modern society. As was the case around the industrial world in this era, the alternative to the status quo was, in some form or other, labour. In Winnipeg after the strike, the mantle was passed, in essence, to the parties of the working-class, the Independent Labour Party, and, to a lesser extent, the communists, who, defeated on the streets, took up the battle at city hall and in the legislatures.

What is the link between these post-war struggles with the emergence of the CCF almost a decade-and-a-half later? In many cases it was quite direct; those who played leading roles in the events of 1919 in Winnipeg and elsewhere were central figures in this new organization. In the 1920s, those who had played leading roles in the post-war labour revolt had built local and provincial labour parties. Western Canadian labour parties began to meet annually and, in 1932, it was this group that founded the CCF; the CCF's roots in Ontario were in similar working-class parties such as the Labour Party of Ontario. All these labour and socialist parties embodied the sentiment of 1919 that only the working class could rescue society. In fact, it was their social identity as workers, more than their political program, that drew them together. Nonetheless, a shared evolution in their thinking had taken place, away from the vague labourism of the past and toward a more conscious socialism.[11] The experiences of the post-war labour revolt, the repression that followed, and the deep crises of capitalism that became apparent after 1929 combined to push these labour parties in a more clearly defined socialist direction. As well, by 1932, they recognized two things: that labour had to be more effectively organized to fight the economic and political ravages of the Depression, and that other social classes were also dramatically affected by the Depression and were seeking a voice. Farmers, of course, had long been seen as an oppressed class with its own interests but with whom labour could ally, although the two groups had generally remained organizationally independent of each other. Labour parties had been sympathetic to the agrarian-based Progressive Party that had peaked in the 1920s; by the 1930s, there was a sense that the formerly vague alliance with farmers had to be reconstructed and solidified within a new political vessel.[12]

More pressing than the farmers, though, were the urban middle class—variously defined as white-collar workers, clerks, small business people, professionals, and the like. They represented both a promise and a deep threat. Labour activists saw this often-hard-hit social layer, as it was in Europe, as the potential social basis for fascism; if labour did not win them as allies, they could be the most dangerous of enemies.[13] It was precisely on this understanding that the idea of building a multi-class political organization took shape. The trick, though, was to maintain working-class control, since alien social classes, particularly the nebulous middle class, were seen as incapable of articulating a clear alternative to capitalism. The federated structure of the CCF was key here. Individuals could only join the CCF by joining one of the affiliated parties. This allowed the labour parties to maintain their structure and identity and, in turn, provide the necessary political and ethical leadership to the wider organization. The apex of this thinking, perhaps, took place at the Labour Conference, the Ontario labour affiliate to the CCF (made up of dozens of unions and socialist groups), over whether middle-class members of the CCF should be allowed to vote on points of principle.[14] It was axiomatic to the Labour Conference that, while some form of alliance was necessary, non-working-class affiliates were without the experience in the labour movement, had no record of perseverance in the struggle, and lacked any real education in socialism; they would, therefore, be incapable of understanding and defending working-class principles, the basis of any socialism movement.

Not surprisingly, as middle-class people joined the socialist CCF, such attitudes turned to conflict—a conflict explicitly understood as a kind of class struggle within the party, and an important one.[15] If labour-identified socialists were unsuccessful in holding the CCF to what they saw as working-class politics, the new movement would be incapable of fending off the existential challenges of the decade: fascism and war. This conflict in the CCF existed on several levels. Interestingly, some of the most explosive conflicts were over identity and symbols rather than a political platform. And working-class credentials were the trump card played to win more than a few debates, as in the famous Connell Affair in British Columbia, which saw the departure of the BC CCF house leader in the province's legislature from the party. The issue appeared to be one of political program: Rev. Robert Connell, who led the party's caucus, expressed his disagreement with the financial plank of the CCF. But, as it turned out, this was a minor issue; once he left the party, the BC CCF abandoned the policy. Programmatic differences were, in fact, secondary here; the real issue was between those who, like Ernest Winch, had "learned his socialism, not merely from books, but from the bitter experiences of life" and a middle-class preacher and botanist who could make no such claims.[16]

In Manitoba, the labour CCF affiliate, the Independent Labour Party (ILP), was wary of what they saw as the vague class character of the national CCF and hesitated to join the broader federation at first.[17] And in the late 1930s, the Manitoba ILP, the party of J. S. Woodsworth, walked out of the CCF on just such grounds.[18] Ontario, though, provides the most examples. To the ears of the farmers and the intellectuals of the League for Social Reconstruction, the language and iconography of the labour affiliate—appeals to comradeship and red flags—made them indistinguishable from the communists. The farmers and LSRers could not understand why, despite clear differences with the communists, their labour colleagues in the CCF insisted on defending the communists and marching with them on May Day, the international working-class holiday. But these were working-class duties—duties that had no resonance among "middle-class" CCFers.[19]

Exasperated, Woodsworth and the LSR, with the backing of the farmers, organized a purge of the Ontario labour affiliate that had founded the provincial CCF. As a curious footnote, Graham Spry, who had helped organize the purge and who, as editor of the CCF weekly paper, emerged as the main provincial spokesperson, soon realized that labour was more or less correct: without a working-class anchor the provincial CCF was set adrift. He promptly initiated a campaign against "reformists" in the CCF, by which he meant those susceptible to any number of palliatives circulating during the decade that fell short of socialism. An inadequate number of the remaining members, it seems, had much of an understanding and appreciation of the rudiments of socialism. Following the purge, in fact, the provincial council took pains to explain to the provincial convention that the "C.C.F. is primarily based upon the urban working class with some support from the middle class and so-called intellectuals and the rural population on the farms."[20] Indeed, the federation set about increasing its day-to-day participation in industrial struggles in order to rebuild its working-class base.

So, what does all this say about the politics of the CCF in the 1930s? First, one should place much less emphasis on the Regina Manifesto, the "founding document" of the federation, than is generally the case. The CCF, like labour parties before it, did have a "program," but such documents had rarely been very systematic in the past and parties were not really defined by them. Labourist parties, for instance, were much less identified with specific policies than they were as instruments of working-class representation in the halls of power. The Regina Manifesto would eventually take on considerable importance in the political climate of the 1950s, as it was mobilized by the left wing of the CCF as a bulwark against the drift to the right, when both socialist policies and class identification were downplayed.

Historian Michiel Horn has drawn attention to what he suggests is the anomalous language of the closing statement of the manifesto. Following the long and unusually detailed list of policies, the manifesto suddenly asserts: "No C.C.F. Government will rest content until it has eradicated capitalism." Horn suggests this final declaration "made the document sound rather more radical than it was."[21] However, that closing, much more than the manifesto as a whole, reflected the sentiments of the movement. This was, after all, why the CCF had been formed. What was new and unusual was the rest of the manifesto—a document that bore the hallmarks of technocratic planning. Written by members of the LSR, it anticipated the league's forthcoming 500-page *Social Planning for Canada* that was published a couple of years later—a book that made no mention of working-class self-organization and leadership. Indeed, class—the leitmotif of interwar socialism—is barely mentioned in the book.

Interestingly, and tellingly, there was very little debate at Regina about the content of the manifesto; in keeping with labourism in the past and events like the Winnipeg General Strike, the real focus of concern lay beyond specific political planks. In this case, it was with building a large and effective movement. It was axiomatic the CCF would be beholden to workers, farmers, and others victimized by capitalism. And, for labour members, the affiliated workers' organizations were uniquely capable of providing the CCF with the necessary direction. As well, the manifesto did not necessarily represent the sentiment of CCFers, since the Regina convention that adopted it was quite unrepresentative; western farmers could attend relatively easily and the LSR members could afford to go, but very few labour delegates could. In the depths of the Depression, they were unemployed and could not afford to leave their families and travel, or they had a job and could not abandon it. Notably, such debates that were had were not over the content of the planks of the manifesto, but over issues that socialists had long debated, such as the minor spats over violence and compensation for socialized property. And few joined the debate: better not to upset the still fragile federation. Woodsworth explicitly acknowledged the concessions labour socialists made at Regina in the interests of getting the CCF off the ground.[22]

The LSR and the Regina Manifesto have been characterized as "Fabian," and by extension, so has the CCF. Fabianism refers specifically to members of the British Fabian Society, a middle-class organization that proposed a particularly gradualist, and classless, form of "gas and water socialism," referring to public ownership of utilities. This does not describe the CCF of the 1930s at all. Nor do analogies to the British Labour Party. In part, this is simple reductionism. Political scientist Gad Horowitz put it most bluntly: the CCF was Fabian and Labourist because it was British— that is, rooted in British immigration.[23] The ethnic character of the CCF was quite British, but Horowitz's comment both underestimates the complexity of the British left and labour movement and fails to examine what British-Canadian socialists actually believed. As Norman Penner notes, "Most of the British socialists who came to Canada [before World War I] were in fact staunch opponents of laborism and fabianism."[24] Canadian socialist activists were far more likely to adhere to the British Independent Labour Party (British ILP), a socialist affiliate to the Labour Party dedicated, in the interwar years, to pushing the Labour Party to the left.

Indeed, this link to the old world persisted. Provincial weekly CCF newspapers regularly printed material from British ILP leaders such as Fenner Brockway and H. N. Brailsford. In the early 1930s, the British ILP gave up on the Labour Party and disaffiliated; its place within the larger party was taken by the Socialist League. Although they disagreed about whether it was worthwhile remaining in the Labour Party, both the British ILP and the Socialist League shared a feeling that capitalism was in a period of deep crisis and that the political labour movement needed a more radical strategy than the Labour Party offered. The collapse of the Ramsay MacDonald Labour government in Britain in 1931 demonstrated that the larger party was incapable of dealing with the Depression. More than that, it was inadequate in dealing with its consequences, including the rise of fascism and the threat of war. A socialist party in government had to be prepared to break with capitalism and have both the necessary mass support as well as the fortitude to use its power to begin the transition to socialism. CCFers in Canada watched these developments closely, reading books and articles by the impressive list of socialist intellectuals in both the British ILP and the Socialist League; regular educational forums reflected these interests. This, in some ways quite a vague program, appealed to a range of CCFers.

Perhaps most interesting, many central figures of the League for Social Reconstruction moved rapidly to the left and found themselves in the same political space, although at an interestingly elite level. Initially, those LSRers who were most active in orienting toward the new CCF were still closely tied to the Liberal Party and hoping to construct a left-Liberal coalition in the new federation. But several key league members, studying in Britain in the 1930s, came under the sway of the often-wealthy leadership of the Socialist League, including important intellectuals George Cadbury and Stafford Cripps. The latter came to Canada twice at the invitation of the Ontario CCF leadership, explaining to large crowds that "we in Great Britain have learned that it is futile for a workers' party to attempt to reform capitalism."[25] His connection with the CCF was deep; he helped fund the Ontario federation's printing operation, which was named Stafford Press in his honour. Solidifying the connection, Cripps acted as a mentor for soon-to-be national CCF secretary David Lewis, offering him a position in his law office.[26] *Canadian Forum*, which was closely associated with the LSR, came to reflect this orientation as the magazine closely followed British labour politics, including extended reviews of works sympathetic to communism, such as John Strachey's *Theory and Practice of Socialism* and R. Palme Dutt's *World Politics, 1918–1936*.[27]

Indeed, the simplistic notion that socialism was clearly bifurcated between a "revolutionary" communist movement and a "reformist," "social-democratic" CCF is clearly belied in the 1930s. The attitude of

CCFers to the communists was varied and complex. First, many CCFers chose their organization over that of the communists for reasons that had much less to do with the expressed "revolutionary" intent of the communists than the actual practice of the Canadian Communist Party. And the reasons could vary. Even though there was widespread support and even identification with the Soviet Union among non-communist socialists throughout this period, some socialists did not join the Communist Party in the early 1920s because they rejected some of the stringent conditions the Communist International stipulated for affiliation or they disagreed (as did the One Big Union in Canada) with their "united front" policy of working within the more conservative trade unions. By the early 1930s, many radicals disagreed with the refusal of the communists to work with other socialists and saw the communists' hyper-militancy as adventurist. More than a few quit or were expelled from the Communist Party in this period and joined the CCF.[28] Plus, there was a growing recognition by some of the increasingly authoritarian nature of the Stalinist leadership of the USSR and the international communist movement. Indeed, some CCFers occasionally declared themselves to be better representatives of communism than the communists: "Let us take Communism from the Communists, and use it intelligently," in the words of the British Columbia socialists on the eve of the formation of the CCF.[29]

Second, both the CCF and the Communists were fueled and informed by similar notions of social class. They both embodied the sense of working-class identity and mission apparent in the Winnipeg General Strike and other events after World War I. And they shared a Marxist understanding that labour both created value in capitalist society—the labour theory of value—and had the capacity to defeat capital and build a new social order. Even though communists and CCFers could be the most ardent adversaries, as they were in the early 1930s, there was always a grudging acknowledgement that they were both "working-class parties" that often supported the same campaigns. The labour and socialist parties that affiliated to the CCF felt it was, therefore, their working-class duty to defend the communists from repression at the hands of a capitalist government, regardless of what they felt about their behaviour.

Third, CCFers considered themselves to be "revolutionaries." What they meant by this was less the process of social change than its extent. They rejected "palliatives" and "reforms" to capitalism in favour of a root and branch transformation of the social system. To their mind, capitalism was unreformable and, while they were not opposed to legislation that would ameliorate conditions, it was far from their goal. In some cases, reform was potentially dangerous. Among the more interesting debates in the CCF was the reaction to measures such as President Franklin Roosevelt's New Deal legislation in the United States. While the CCF may have supported some specific measures, it was at best seen as an effort to save capitalism in crisis. At worst, it brought augmented powers to the capitalist state with unclear repercussions for working people.[30] The same was true of nationalizations. Without socialism, nationalizations simply led to "state capitalism," and the rise of powerful authoritarian capitalist states in Europe boded ill for democracy.[31] Not surprisingly, they preferred the word "socialization," which implied a more democratic means of controlling public property under socialism.

And finally, in middle of the 1930s, CCFers came to see themselves, with good reason, as considerably more radical than the communists; indeed, they accused the communists of betraying working-class principles and abandoning the struggle for socialism. In 1934 and 1935, the communist movement internationally—or more specifically, the leadership of the Soviet Union—came to realize the unique threat that fascism, and particularly Nazi Germany, posed not just to the workers' movement in general, but to the Soviet Union, the home of world socialism in their mind. The communists' solution was to attempt to form popular fronts—alliances of all potential opponents of fascism. To make this happen, they downplayed their radical politics. The popular front would have, as a goal, the defense of liberal democracy. Socialism was, at best, relegated to the back burner.[32]

This was an astounding about face. Previously, socialists across the board, communists and CCFers alike, had been united in the understanding that fascism was a product of the crisis of capitalism. It was, as one CCF wag commented, "capitalism gone nudist."[33] Capitalists lost the ability, or will, to make concessions to workers, as they felt the need to cut wages and reduce living standards to maintain their profits and, in the end, their businesses. As workers fought back, capitalists chafed at a liberal democracy that allowed independent unions and oppositional political parties; employers' response would be fascism. And wary of what had happened in Europe, CCFers were highly sensitive to potential parallel developments in Canada.

Communists were keen that the CCF, which they had denounced without reserve in the earlier part of the decade, join in the popular front movement. CCFers had long been divided over working with the communists and, although the CCF officially kept their distance from the communists, there were a range of practices. Given the activism of the communists, for instance in the unemployed movement, CCFers often joined in joint campaigns. As well, CCFers, and many others, including some church youth groups, participated in the hugely successful, communist-established Canadian Youth Congress.[34] Occasionally, too, they worked together in municipal electoral campaigns; in Regina, a joint communist-CCF movement came to dominate the city council briefly.[35] For the most part though, CCFers came to stake their own turf to the left of the communists as the decade wore on. This was clearest in the BC CCF, where a strong minority supported working in the popular front while others explicitly argued that this was a betrayal of socialism.[36] Similarly, David Lewis and some of the LSR-oriented leaders of the CCF criticized young CCFers active in the Canadian Youth Congress for their socialist purism; indeed, Lewis got himself named as a delegate in order the avert a break with the communists and the isolation of the CCFers.[37] Quite quickly, most young CCFers lost interest in the communist-dominated youth movement.

The 1930s was a challenging decade for socialists. The economic collapse, along with growing threats of fascism and war, both spurred CCFers to action and forced them to hone their understanding of what was happening around them. The course of this debate was a difficult one because the CCF was a complex organization. It was not a party of individual members but of affiliated organizations of several types. At the core, though, were the labour and socialist parties that often had deep roots in Canadian working-class communities. These organizations reflected the working-class identity that was so apparent in the aftermath of World War I in events such the Winnipeg General Strike. The members of these parties were convinced that workers held the key to social transformation. And in the shadow of the defeats of labour after the war, they honed their politics; the Great Depression demonstrated the bankruptcy of capitalism, and the threats of fascism and war demonstrated the dangers of capitalism in collapse. A term like "social democracy," with its contemporary connotations of Keynesian fiscal policies, mixed economies of public and private ownership, and social welfare, fails to describe their program or social vision.

"Social democracy" has come to assume a kind of natural evolution into the kind of party the CCF and New Democratic Party became by the 1960s and 1970s. In the 1930s, though, social democratic parties responded in different ways to the crises of the 1930s. Gerd-Rainer Horn demonstrates how even long-established European social democracy "underwent a serious identity crisis" and, in some brief instances, engaged in insurrectionary responses to repression. Perhaps even more portentously, many social democratic parties moved well to the left and worked closely with the communists in that brief moment (1934 and 1935) when the communists had drifted away from their early-1930s sectarianism and before their embrace of liberal democracy during the popular front.[38] Much was possible, and the trajectory of at least some social democratic parties was undetermined.

The character of the CCF was even more inchoate. In contrast to the well-established European parties, the CCF was born at a moment of international crisis and without an established institutional party structure and ideology to restrain it. Its future was particularly open to various potential developments. And, to the extent that it identified with European socialist currents, these were generally to left-wing factions on their way out of European socialist and labour parties. Most importantly, the CCF looked to the British Independent Labour Party (which had recently walked out of the British Labour Party) for political direction. The British ILP was a key member of the London Bureau, an organization of like-minded parties across Europe that defined itself as "revolutionary Marxist." Was it? Indeed, what was "social democracy" in the 1930s? Leon Trotsky noted, at the time, the crisis of traditional "reformist" social democracy and the rise—and in some cases, even the growing dominance—of what he called "centrist" currents: "those who hesitate between reformism and a revolutionary position."[39] He spoke specifically of the British ILP and the London Bureau in this regard, noting that "its centrism can go far in analysis, evaluation, criticism" of the social democratic movement from which they emerged, but had considerable difficulty in developing an alternative revolutionary strategy.[40]

This thoroughgoing critique of "reformism," along with an inability to formulate a revolutionary program, quite accurately describes the CCF in the 1930s. Both the labour core of the party and, by mid-decade, the LSR identified with the "revolutionary Marxism" of the London Bureau. This was reflected in weekly party newspapers across the country, although the CCF, in its efforts to attract wider middle-class and farmer support (although they had very little of the latter outside of Saskatchewan and Alberta), contained a range of viewpoints. Still, the CCF was committed, as socialists had been for decades, to "making socialists" through education, and the CCF did attempt to educate this heterogeneous membership in a kind of left-wing socialism that was critical of "reformism," including that, for instance, associated with the British Labour Party. Trotsky's broader point about centrism was that it was, over time, unsustainable; such hesitation could not be sustained indefinitely. The CCF of the 1930s should be seen, then, not as irredeemably "social democratic" or reformist, but as an organization searching for political solutions in keeping with socialist transformation and a working-class agenda. What its political trajectory would be was not at all clear in the depths of the Depression as crises swirled around it.[41] The CCF itself was fractious, particularly in its first three or four years of existence; it could easily have fractured along what members did tend to see as "class" lines. Certainly, the shape of what we think of the CCF and NDP tradition—social democracy—was not really cemented until the context in which it operated changed, as it did during World War II and the post-war boom and the Cold War. But that history cannot be read backwards onto the CCF of the 1930s.

CHAPTER 2

RELIGION AND THE RISE
OF THE CCF/NDP

————

John Brewin

James Naylor's *The Fate of Labour Socialism: The CCF and the Dream of a Working-Class Future* describes the crucial role of working-class Marxists in setting the goals, language, policies, aspirations, and character of the Co-operative Commonwealth Federation (CCF). Naylor argues that the increasing involvement of middle-class "intellectuals" and others in the party led to an undermining of the role of class within the CCF (and later, it would follow, within the New Democratic Party). They pushed "labour socialists" to the margins as outsiders in the party they founded, with the result that the party became something other than what it was intended to be.

I have no reason to challenge Naylor's account of the founding of the CCF as a working-class party committed to socialism, a "labour social-ist" party. I agree that the working-class founders were concerned that, in accepting the electoral need to broaden the party's base, the party would become dominated by those who did not share the party's working-class interest, analysis, or perspective. They worried with some good reason about the commitment of newcomers to their formulation of the party's objective. And, undoubtedly, there were many who joined the new party who did not see themselves as working class. These recruits may have, in fact, played prominent roles in shaping the party's character, policies, and strategy as it developed over time.

My position is, however, that the story was more complex; there was more to it than middle-class "intellectuals" taking over a labour socialist party of working people and pushing them aside. In this chapter, I offer the experience of my father, Andrew Brewin, an early middle-class recruit to the CCF, as an example of a more complicated and more positive reality. I will argue that for many like Andrew Brewin, in joining, supporting, and participating in the CCF, they were expressing a mainstream socialist religious conviction or attitude. Understanding this aspect of the formation of the CCF is important to an understanding of its character and appeal.

Brewin did fit clearly into Naylor's definition of a middle-class "intellectual." He was a young Toronto lawyer with solid establishment connections and had been educated at an English "public" school where he learned to write Greek poetry and play English rugby with the sons of the British aristocracy. Despite that, he joined the CCF in 1935 and became influential in CCF and NDP councils for over forty years, including seventeen as an NDP Member of Parliament from 1962 to 1979. Why he joined the party may tell us more about what he and others like him brought to the CCF. It will tell us something about how he and others conducted themselves as active participants in the party, what they shared with labour socialists, and why they were able to work together through the ensuing decades. This enquiry may add to our understanding of how and why the CCF, and later the NDP, had the effect it did in shaping twentieth- and twenty-first-century Canada.

The central thesis of this chapter is that it was Andrew Brewin's religious faith and culture that brought him to the CCF. He and others were able to help the fledgling party speak to a culture that, in the first half of the twentieth century, was overwhelmingly Christian in its identity. Each of the mainstream Christian denominations at the time had a well-formed political theology developed in reaction to the impact of the industrial revolution on the Western world. The Anglican version, known as Christian Socialism, was first articulated by an English cleric, Frederick Maurice, and others in the 1850s. By the inter-war years in the twentieth century, it was the dominant political theology among Anglican clergy and many others active in the Anglican Church in Britain, the United States, and Canada.

It was not a stretch for Brewin and others of his persuasion to join with labour socialists in a new political party. Naylor notes in his concluding chapter that the labour socialists who were central to launching the party in 1933 committed the party to replacing the capitalist system, based as that was on "the pursuit of profit and organized around wage labour," with "a co-operative society led by the working class." Christian Socialists had no difficulty in sharing this objective. They, too, supported a radical transformation of society from one based on greed and selfishness to one based on co-operative principles. That meant, in a democracy, by the weight of sheer numbers, working-class leadership.

Andrew Brewin was much more than a middle-class intellectual with roots in Canada and Britain; he was an active and serious Christian formed in the Anglican tradition. He joined the CCF to put his theology into practice. He brought into the party the culture and sensibilities of his religious orientation and opened a doorway into a national base of similarly committed Anglicans and other Christians.

The Social Gospel has been widely written about in both its Canadian and American iterations. Methodist, United Church, and Baptist clergy played well-recognized leadership roles in the CCF—J.S. Woodsworth, Tommy Douglas, and Stanley Knowles among the best known. The Anglican formulation of "Christian Socialism" was not significantly different from the Social Gospel in its articulation of a Christian political analysis or in its conclusions. Within the world of organized religion at the time there were strong currents of interest in breaking down barriers between denominations. This was especially true of those interested in the Social Gospel and Christian Socialism. Brewin's story carries the core elements of others who were drawn to the CCF for religious reasons, regardless of denomination and theological expression. The key point is that Christian socialists of whatever variety or label were able to work in harmony with labour socialists, sharing as they did the central objective of societal transformation.

When Andrew Brewin joined the CCF he was twenty-eight, already established as a lawyer with considerable experience in the Ontario courts, and well respected by his colleagues. Born in England, he moved with his English-Scottish-Canadian family to Ontario when he was three. He was educated in a private school in Ottawa and at the English "public" school, Radley College, outside Oxford in England. His father was an Anglican priest, at the time the Rector or minister in charge of a prominent church in Toronto, the Church of St. Simon-the-Apostle. His mother, Amea Fenerty Blair, was the daughter of Andrew Blair, a Cabinet minister in Sir Wilfrid Laurier's Liberal Government from 1895 to 1903 who had previously served as premier of New Brunswick. Brewin married Margaret ("Peggy") Biggar, a parishioner at St. Simon's and the daughter of a successful Scottish-Canadian business family with strong Liberal connections.

Why would Brewin have even contemplated joining the CCF? His circle in Toronto was very conservative. "Everyone wondered why in the world would Andy become a CCFer," remarked a friend. The CCF was an "aberration" in her view. "Outside the norm." His Liberal and Conservative friends, while they did not understand his political behaviour or agree with his ideas, nonetheless remained his friends throughout his life.

The answer to "why the CCF?" lies partly in the times. The Great Depression had reached its depths by 1935. The parish church in which Brewin was active as a young man, St. Simon's, served south Rosedale, one of the wealthiest neighbourhoods in Canada, and north Cabbagetown, one of the poorest. The Depression devastated the people and parishioners of Cabbagetown. The travesty of the Great War had ended less than twenty years earlier. More than fifty young men from this one church were killed in the war. Rumblings from Europe of old societies collapsing were felt in Toronto and throughout Canada. The Depression, the war, and the shifting societal norms sent tremors through Canadian society that reached even into south Rosedale.

Initially, Brewin's experience with the realities of the 1930s came through his experience at St. Simon's. The brutal impact of the Depression was felt by people he had come to know and love. What was happening to them had a profound effect on him.

Chief Justice McRuer came close to the mark when he wrote Peggy Brewin at the time of Brewin's death in 1982: "In my view, he would have been one of the leading counsel of Canada, had he devoted his talents in that direction. However, he chose a career which was dedicated to the service of others." Anglican Archbishop Ted Scott came even closer. He knew Brewin well in his later years, especially through their shared work on apartheid in South Africa. He also knew the St. Simon's story. When asked why Brewin was a socialist, he said it was because of St. Simon's. "At St. Simon's, Andrew became aware of the ghettoizing of society. People were locked into their situations, especially the young people, for reasons over which they had no control. It was through this experience that he became convinced of the need for structural societal change."

Brewin's small-p political life in Toronto began, therefore, in his twenties in the church where he was a member. The main unit of governance in the Anglican Church is the Diocese and its parliament or "Synod." He quickly became active at that level, later participating in the councils of the church in the wider world, including the Anglican Church of Canada's national or General Synod and as one of its representatives at the World Council of Churches. He presented a motion to the 1935 Toronto Synod on behalf of the Diocesan Council for Social Service on the sub-standard housing conditions of the poor and working class of Toronto housing. It was described in the Diocesan weekly newspaper as "perhaps the most outstanding pronouncement at the Synod." In an article in that paper around the same time, Brewin set out a Christian response to the social conditions caused by the crisis in capitalism.

The mood in the Anglican Church in Canada at the time was surprisingly radical, at least on paper. In 1915, a Synod committee argued that the "Christianizing of the social order and a more equal distribution of the proceeds of industry" was the task to which the church was called. In 1918, the Synod was told that the "attempt to run society as a business has failed." The Diocesan newspaper explained to its readers that individual philanthropy was insufficient to solve social problems. Social politics was needed to remove the causes of social evil, it was argued. The Church encouraged its adherents to pray: "To free our commercial, industrial and political life from the un-Christian ideals which so largely dominate it: we beseech Thee to hear us, good Lord." That same prayer more than 1,300 years earlier had asked: "From the perils of the Norsemen, Good Lord, deliver us." The sentiment was the same; only the identity of the threat had changed.

The Diocesan Council for Social Service led Diocesan efforts to review social and political issues and to prepare programs and positions in response. In 1931, the Synod adopted a resolution that emphasized "the vital need for such a change in the spirit and working of much of social, economic and industrial life, alike in production and distribution, as will bring it into greater conformity with the Mind and Teaching of our Lord and Saviour Jesus Christ." On May 23, 1935, Archbishop Derwyn Owen, Primate and Bishop of Toronto, issued a Lenten pastoral letter in which he said that people "are caught in the grip of a system which disregards any motive or result except gain, whether for the corporation or the individual . . . Economic justice is one of the foundations of righteousness on which the Kingdom of God must be built."

It was in that atmosphere that Brewin began to observe the early development of the CCF. He and his wife Peggy were intrigued with J. S. Woodsworth and with M. J. Coldwell, a Regina teacher, MP, and later the second leader of the CCF, after Woodsworth. J. S. Woodsworth had been an ordained Methodist minister, deeply influenced by the Social Gospel. Coldwell was an Anglican. Both spoke to Brewin's growing understanding of public issues in a way that resonated with his religious worldview.

That religion should move someone from the sphere of conservative or liberal politics, with all its inherent advantages, to life in a fledgling socialist party with few prospects would, in today's world, appear counter-intuitive—unless they were leaving their religion behind in reaction to its obvious follies. As noted, Brewin never did leave the church, though others who were drawn into socialist politics, such as Woodsworth, lost patience with the institutional conservatism of the church. Brewin continued to be a committed, active, practicing Anglican to the end of his life. Not only did he see his religion as consistent with his socialism, but he felt socialism was an expression of his faith and practice. In his view, each influenced and brought clarity to the other, although he never proselytized for his church among his political comrades.

Today, the public voice of the churches is predominantly conservative, far removed from the call for social change to a co-operative and egalitarian society that marked the churches of the 1930s. Religion is now widely identified with conservative or reactionary positions on social, economic, and environmental issues or with an intolerant dogmatism that is the source of war and violence. Part of this public perception is due to the high visibility in Canada of the aggressive right-wing politics of many religious institutions in the United States and beyond. As the more progressive forces within the Canadian churches decline in number and in public influence, public perception is matched with reality, even in Canada. That was not always so and is not entirely true even today. It is easy to forget in today's climate that a religious life can be congruent with radical social activism and socialist politics.

Brewin was a reader and lifelong learner. As his experience led him to see his society through the lens of the people he came to know at St. Simon's and the realities of their lives, he was reading R. H. Tawney's *Religion and the Rise of Capitalism* and George Bernard Shaw's *The Intelligent Woman's Guide to Socialism.* He discovered that, within the Church of England, the nineteenth-century work of Frederick Maurice and his successors had developed the theology they called Christian Socialism. They promulgated the understanding that Christianity was about the building of an earthly society in the present that reflected Christian principles, one that was based on co-operation and love of neighbour, paralleling the Social Gospel of the Methodists and others and the social theology of the Roman Catholic church.

Brewin said he was drawn into the CCF through the League for Social Reconstruction (LSR) and its Fabian-inspired approach to politics that focused on the development of detailed, practical, and well-thought-through policies to present to voters. To that extent his story reinforces Naylor's thesis. It does appear that the LSR provided an intellectually sustainable framework for someone of Brewin's background. Once he became committed, however, he was more interested in the practical side of politics. He threw himself into the administration of the party and eventually into election work. He was an assiduous canvasser, capable of knocking on doors hour after hour, day after day, leaving those much younger than himself in his wake. He liked meeting people and working at persuading them one vote at a time. He came to enjoy the social activities of the party: the Greenwood NDP Saturday night social club, for example, modelled on the Labour Clubs in Britain. He listened and learned. In the end, it was the shared vision that captured him and, undoubtedly, all those who came to their socialism from a religious perspective.

The Social Gospel, Christian Socialism, and Catholic social theology extracted from their tradition and from scripture the themes in which the meek and humble were honoured; the rich and haughty were denounced; the slaves were to be liberated and led across the wilderness to the promised land, the New Jerusalem; the faithful were to work for the establishment here on Earth of a kingdom of peace, justice, and equity. The myth of Jesus' birth had him being born in a manger because there was no room for him in the inn, in contrast with the luxurious birth stories of the Roman emperors. His disciples were working people—fishers, tax collectors, ordinary folk—not society's elites. Jesus was portrayed as a carpenter. After his execution, triggered by Jesus throwing the money changers out of the temple, his followers established a community in which everyone contributed all their personal resources and met their needs from the common wealth.

When Brewin ran for the leadership of the Ontario CCF in 1953, he told the delegates to the leadership convention that he took his political philosophy from the biblical Song of Mary, in which God is praised because "He put down the mighty from their seats and exalted the lowly; he filled the hungry with good things; and the rich he hath sent empty away."

Both labour socialists and Christian socialists believed in the democratic path to political power as the best way in Canada to bring about the new co-operative commonwealth. There may have been some differences in the fine print, but everyone seemed to agree on the need to strengthen democratic people's organizations, such as trade unions, farm organizations, and co-operatives. Public ownership or control of the means of production would result in democratic control. Where one came down on the extent of public ownership became a matter of intense debate as the party grew and the context changed. It was always a litmus test of the depth of one's socialism. The parliamentary electoral system was the vehicle for gaining power. It was expected that once the people learned about social-ism and the changes that were possible, the party would win power. All it would take was education and organization.

An in-depth analysis of the role of class in the formation and early days of the CCF is beyond the scope of this paper. Brewin's class history under the surface of his immediate background might make a small con- tribution to the discussion. In his own way, Brewin would have reflected the state of class in Toronto in the twentieth century. Beyond that, on his maternal side, his roots were in the Lowlands of Scotland, south of Edinburgh. His father's family on the paternal side can be traced back to Wigston Magna, a farming village south of Leicester in the Midlands of England. A social history of the village concludes that for 1,000 years, the descendants of Danish farmers, including a family of Brewins, operated the village on co-operative principles. That involved a regime of holding meetings, adopting by-laws, taking minutes, and moving motions, a great genetic preparation for participation in the CCF and the NDP centuries later. Brewin could not claim, nor did he, that he was of the working class or of a working-class background. However, he would say that he learned, in part through St. Simon's and even more significantly through his lifetime experience in the CCF and the NDP, to work comfortably and respectfully with colleagues of all backgrounds.

So what conclusions can we draw from this account that might be helpful in today's politics?

A moral underpinning for the stated objectives of the NDP and broader social movements continues to be important. Is there a shared morality or set of common values deep in today's culture that we can point to and around which a coalition can be built? In the search for this com- mon ground in a much less religious age, today's generation of political leaders are up against the challenge of framing a narrative that is deep and broad. To this end, they can find insight and encouragement in the words and actions of twentieth-century democratic socialists who joined together in founding and building the CCF.

CHAPTER 3

THE LABOUR–ACADEMIC "BRAIN TRUST" OF THE EARLY CCF, 1930–1950

Jennifer Hassum

Every election, a small group of thinkers in the NDP brain trust have a cookie recipe and show off the new cookie machine that will mass produce them. Of course, they lose the election every time. But, they've studied what went wrong in the last showing and promise us that this time they will pull different levers stronger or faster. This time they say they have a better baking system or temperature control. But in the end their cookie machines make the same bland, goddamn crumbly oatmeal cookies. When will they understand that no one wants to eat our oatmeal cookies.

— *Steelworker parable*

In celebrating eighty-five years of the founding of the CCF, we are also celebrating eighty-five years since campaign postmortems. Contemporary leftists are not just concerned about repeated electoral defeats; many are frustrated to see weak policy programs put forward by socialist or labour parties still drawn to the Third Way. Others situate the weak electoral left as part of a wider, and much more catastrophic, demobilization of traditional socialist institutions and spaces.[1] What is to be done? Among the solutions is the call for a "return to the roots" of left-wing thought. It is easy for the left to venerate the Regina Manifesto, the League for Social Reconstruction (LSR), and early platforms of the Co-operative Commonwealth Foundation (CCF). The imagined past is one of deep research and policy presented with a complete analysis of the conflict between people and capital. A Google, wiki, or library search for the authors of these documents would bring up the names of academic heavyweights associated with the LSR, such as Frank Underhill, Frank Scott, Graham Spry, Eugene Forsey, and Leonard Marsh, or intellectual leaders like David Lewis and James Shaver Woodsworth. Indeed, this is who Michiel Horn identified as the "brain trust" of the CCF and Canadian socialism in its heyday.[2]

So, all leftists need to do to rekindle Canadian socialism is find half a dozen brilliant academics to publish a manifesto and we will finally taste ideological and electoral victory? Hardly. The secret to success was not in a small group of university professors trusted with the levers of power, but rather a much wider nexus where academics and labour intellectuals worked together. The examples of Charlie Millard and Clarence Gillis demonstrate how labour activists contributed intellectually to the formation of the CCF, as well as how instrumental they each were in creating a labour structure and culture inside the party.

Writing labour socialists back into the history of CCF thought is not a new concept but an ongoing project. The focus on Millard and Gillis is to add to the recent work that is being done by scholars, including James Naylor and Christo Aivalis, as well as an entire field of labour historians looking at the Congress of Industrial Organizations (CIO) in the 1930s and 1940s, such as Craig Heron, Wendy Cuthbertson, Laurel Sefton McDowell, and Desmond Morton. Naylor's descriptions of dozens of labour socialist collaborations, various socialist parties, reading groups, women's groups, and socialist neighbourhood or community associations in his *The Fate of Labour Socialism* demonstrate an active and heterogeneous left alternative.[3] However, in the same way that we lose the "broader context of a social movement against capitalism"[4] in the weeds of historians examining the CCF, so, too, have we de-emphasized Millard and Gillis and, in particular, the important role labour activists played inside the party. British historians, when writing about Keir Hardie, the prototypical working-class political hero, write about his life and work in the trade union movement and the Labour Party in a complimentary fashion. Canadian historians, by contrast, have placed the work of Gillis, Millard, and other unionists within the labour movement alone. The academic articles that exist focus instead on Millard and Gillis' roles in their unions. Isolating labour academics from the story of the early CCF treats the establishment of a labour party in Canada as inevitable, rather than the very slow, difficult, tedious project it was.[5] For socialists at the time, the work of building a labour party and the work of building trade unions are not mutually exclusive projects. Further, the labour-academic nexus of the CCF is much wider than Millard or Gillis. In addition to these relatively well-known labour figures, more research is warranted into women's and immigrant communities who also contributed to the intellectual foundations of the CCF: people like LSR member, journalist, and social welfare researcher Margaret Gould, who spent time as a labour organizer, or Agnes MacPhail, whose service as the first woman MP is well-documented but relatively little is known about her relationship with labour. Equally interesting would be to review the private papers of the LSR academics and learn more about exactly what they thought of the less refined, working-class labourites with whom they shared space.

In exploring the labour intellectuals of the CCF, Charlie Millard provides an instructive example. Millard is remembered as the workplace organizer who led the CIO-Oshawa General Motors strike of 1937 that won one of the first industrial union recognitions in Canada.[6] Certainly, his role in taking on Mitchell Hepburn's "Sons of Mitches," an auxiliary police force, earned him national profile. Later, becoming the first national director of the United Steelworkers, Millard became the left's lead government antagonist when pressing for industrial union labour law reforms during World War II. By 1941, Canada's Communist Party adherents supported the war effort at all costs and critiqued activists who took job actions in war industries. Millard, meanwhile, rejected signing any "no strike" pledges, encouraging Canadian workers to strike if they felt they had exhausted all other means to gain union recognition. Millard was even briefly jailed for refusing to denounce strikes. For Millard, it was about democracy and bosses not respecting the decision of a majority of workers. "What is the sense of going to Europe to fight Hitlerism when we have Hitlerism right here in Canada?"[7] His actions clearly got under the skin of Prime Minister William Lyon Mackenzie King, who wrote in his diary: "Dictated a long letter to Millard of the Steel Workers' Organization. He has assumed the role of a Hitler, possessing all power, to create civil strife and holding his threat over the head of the Government."[8] Harsh words from the prime minister.

But how did Millard work with the star academics at the LSR? Quite well, in fact. *Canadian Forum* ran a profile on Millard that began,

> At first sight, he looked more like an automobile sales man than an automobile workers' organizer. Slight, neatly dressed, carefully groomed, spats, anything but the popular conception of an "agitator" . . . spoke quietly and evenly, with no flights of eloquence or signs of agitation.[9]

Millard's 1930s hipster look and calm, confident speaking masked his relative lack of education and his family's economic struggles.[10]

Millard returned from World War I as an overachiever. He was the youngest soldier promoted to Company Sargent Major, but he despised working at General Motors:

> We had a lot of mixture of people in General Motors; farmers' sons and peo-
> ple who were used to being on the farm. Well, they found a great difference.
> Instead of being their own boss or having their father or uncle as boss, they
> had General Motors bosses and nothing to say about their own destiny.[11]

Millard's Methodist worldview included the need for democracy at the workplace and for individuals to have a say over their own conditions. A committed democratic socialist, Millard even attempted to hitchhike out to the founding convention of the CCF in Regina.[12] In the end, Millard did not need to leave his city to be part of the CCF, but he was able to organize and build enough of a base of CCF members in Oshawa that speakers regularly visited. J. S. Woodsworth himself stayed at the Millard family home and the two men began corresponding regularly.[13] In Oshawa, Millard attended numerous public meetings and events, wrote countless letters, and he was thus able to recruit an unexpected number of both union and CCF memberships. It was a microcosm of learning how to carry the same message of democratic socialism at work and in politics.

As the first Canadian director of the Steelworkers Organizing Committee, Millard joined with Aaron Mosher to create the new Canadian Congress of Labour (CCL). The labour alternatives to the Trades and Labour Council (TLC) are often characterized by the structure of the labour organizations they represent——trade unions vs industrial unions——but the CCL was also distinct ideologically from the TLC when it came to electoral politics. The TLC vowed to never endorse a political party while the CCL endorsed the CCF in 1943.[14] Within the CCL's constitution, organizing in the legislative arena was given equal prominence to organizing workers.[15] The endorsement and constitution were not empty words. The key players were all committed CCFers: Mosher was president, the leading LSR member Eugene Forsey was the director of policy, and Millard was appointed to be the director of political action. In his capacity, Millard was an architect of the infrastructure for unions to affiliate with the CCF. The affiliation system gave the party monetary resources and volunteers but, more importantly, it created a structural link between the unions and the party, which made the CCF into a real labour party.

Millard saw union and electoral efforts as one movement for democratic socialism. The president of the CCF, John Mitchell, remembers the directive from Millard, "I recall vividly exactly what he said to us, he said 'it is the duty of a Socialist to stand ready to help and give leadership to the trade union movement.'"[16]

Millard expected the CCF and its members to assist not only in the electoral arena to push for pro-worker legislation, but also to be involved locally in labour activism. He helped draft a resolution at the 1936 national convention that called on all CCF members "to associate themselves actively with the organizations of their trade, industry and profession to do everything possible to assist and promote the interests of the workers in the inevitable conflicts which are bound to rise."[17] The Co-operative Commonwealth Youth Movement (CCYM) in Oshawa took action during the 1937 strike and lent assistance to Millard's Local 222 members. Millard's determination and resolve made him demanding but, as Forsey explains, it was founded on his "fundamental moral and ethical principles."[18]

While Charles Millard was able to blend with the middle-class academics like Forsey, Clarence Gillis was unable to muster the courage to inhabit middle-class social spaces. Gerry Harrop described Gillis as literally fleeing from making a speech in an academic setting,[19] despite being considered an "effective speaker."[20] Like Millard, Gillis came from a humble background. Born to Gaelic-speaking Scottish immigrants in Cape Breton, his father was a coal miner. Growing up, Gillis remembers his family being kicked out of their company home in the middle of winter, forced to sleep in tents and in church basements. Gillis finished elementary school and joined his father at the mine. While his formal education ended in his early teens, he was greatly influenced by his local president, the legendary red unionist J. B. McLaughlin, and he took night classes to further his education. Elected as a CCF Member of Parliament in 1940, Gillis was an early example of a genuine, proud, blue-collar worker in the House of Commons. He kept his mine gaslight in his Ottawa office and the last shovel he used in the mine at his Glace Bay office to remind him of his roots.

Gillis did not really need reminders of the working people from which he came and whom he represented, since most of his career he worked toward making their lives better. His weekly public radio addresses on Cape Breton radio demonstrated the depth of his thinking and the ease with which he could speak about economics to working people.

The free enterprise system produced the growth of monopolies on the one hand and poverty on the other. Two packinghouses control 86% of all the country's packing and processing business and, consequently, they control the prices, which the farmer shall receive for his products. One large firm and three smaller firms control the entire farm implement industry on the North American continent and are able to set the price that the farmer will pay, and that price is always consistently higher than the price he receives for his products. This system produced in this country a state of affairs in which we had a million people on relief previous to 1939, people who were ill-fed, ill-clad and ill-housed and, when war broke out, according to government figures, 46% of the men called for service were rejected because that depression had left physical and psychological scars which will never be erased from that generation.[21]

He furthered his ideas in *Letter from Home*, a thirty-page book that laid out the post-war Canada possible under democratic socialism.[22] It was sold as a compendium to Scott and Lewis' *Make This Your Canada*. Published by *Canadian Forum*, the book was edited and approved for print by the very LSR Rhodes scholar-types that Gillis so dreaded. Undoubtedly, Gillis made a substantial contribution to democratic socialist thought on Canada's east coast.

Equally important in Gillis' career was his role in affiliating union locals to the CCF. His union local, United Mine Workers (District 26), was the very first to affiliate with the CCF in 1938. While David Lewis describes the decision taken by District 26 as completely spontaneous,[23] happening without any previous contact with the CCF, Gillis describes the act of joining the CCF as carefully planned and considered:

> We realized that the next step was the most important one—to take political action to harness our economic and social development. All this development was based on legislation. Hostile governments could wipe it out overnight. To protect it we must have our own people make the laws. So we affiliated the trade union to the CCF, whose aims and objectives in the political field were similar to our own.[24]

While the affiliation of the United Mine Workers was a milestone, it did not mark the start of mass affiliations; that required organizing. During his time as a sitting MP, the Ontario CCF hired Gillis to recruit unions to affiliate. In just four months, Gillis organized thirty unions to officially join the CCF, representing 50,000 workers across the province.

Prospects for building a labour party looked weak in Calgary in 1932, considering the lone representative from the labour movement at

the founding meeting, Aaron Mosher, came from an incipient labour federation. But dedicated working-class leaders like Millard and Gillis, alongside committed democratic socialists, joined in building the CCF into a
labour party. Working in concert with academics, they contributed to the
democratic-socialist program of the party, set up structures and systems
to allow labour integration into the party and electoral political mandates
inside labour federations, and patiently organized workers to join unions
and unions to join their political party.

The legacy of the labour-academic nexus of the 1930s and 1940s is
mixed. The CCF/NDP has been elected to government in most provinces.
The federal CCF/NDP has been in official opposition and has regularly
used its political clout to force the adoption of policies that are good for
working Canadians. But the magic of the milieu in which elementary
school-educated workers shared intellectual space with scholars on a common project of democratic socialism is long gone. The labour movement
changed under the post-war compromise, while the social-political environment of the academy shifted toward anti-communism and neoliberalism. Today, the spaces for democratic-socialist academics or researchers
to engage in debate and public policy formation are few and far between,
while blue-collar thinkers are completely removed from the intelligentsia
and are even less present in meaningful electoral roles. Both academics and
workers have been displaced by a new professional class of partisan operatives who run the cookie machine but who have little to no experience in
being part of a social movement.

The party that Charlie Millard and Clarence Gillis helped build still
exists, but as we face a neoliberal present and a hellscape future in which
workers' rights are eroded, wages are diminished, and the rich hoard record
levels of wealth, we will need to renew and recreate the kinds of spaces
forged by the labour and academic left of the early socialist movement in
Canada. Spaces for organizers and thinkers to collaborate together on how
a programmatically socialist electoral campaign can win is how we will
win. It is vital that the NDP relearn the lessons of its past and renew the
ties between both its labour and intellectual branches. I am hopeful that
you and I can take this on as a project together.

CHAPTER 4

THE RHETORIC OF REGION

CLARENCE GILLIS, THE CCF, AND THE PROTECTION OF ATLANTIC CANADA

Corey Slumkoski

The history of the Co-operative Commonwealth Federation (CCF) in Atlantic Canada remains largely unwritten.[1] In many ways, this is not surprising. The CCF generally had limited success in the provinces of Prince Edward Island, New Brunswick, and Newfoundland and Labrador, at both the federal and provincial levels. At the provincial level, the CCF unsuccessfully contested a number of seats in PEI's elections between 1943 and 1958, and did not win a seat until 1974, by which time the party had been rechristened the New Democratic Party (NDP). Similar results were seen in New Brunswick, where it would not be until 1982 that an NDP member was elected to the legislature. The CCF managed to hold a seat in the Newfoundland legislature in the 1950s, but only because in 1955, Newfoundland MLA Sam Drover left the Liberals to sit for the CCF; in the 1956 Newfoundland provincial election, Drover failed to win re-election. It was not until 1985 that an NDP candidate was returned to the provincial legislature in St. John's. A similar lack of success was seen in federal elections. Only in 1982, when Fonse Faour was elected for Humber-St.George's-St.Barbe, did Newfoundland and Labrador see its first NDP Member of Parliament. In New Brunswick, CCF/NDP electoral success took even longer to achieve; in 1997, Yvon Godin and Angela Vautour were elected as that province's first NDP MPs for the ridings of Acadie-Bathurst and Beausejour-Petitcodiac respectively. As of this writing, no NDP candidate has ever won a federal seat in PEI. Only in Nova Scotia did Atlantic Canadian success come early to the CCF at both the provincial and federal levels, and even there, electoral victories and party membership were largely centred on Cape Breton.[2]

The first CCF politician elected in Atlantic Canada was Clarence "Clarie" Gillis, who won the 1940 federal election in the riding of Cape Breton South.[3] For seventeen years Gillis would serve as the only CCF MP from east of Ontario. On the surface, it might seem that being the sole Atlantic representative of a political party that was strongly rooted in the west would put Gillis at a disadvantage in parliamentary debate. His riding—which encompassed the coal mining town of Glace Bay— was, after all, economically depressed, and the issues faced by the residents would seem to be quite different than those of the constituents of Prairie CCF ridings. Yet, despite this seeming disadvantage, Gillis was hailed as a strong advocate for Atlantic Canada.[4] As Ian McKay notes, Gillis even went so far as to propose the formation of an Atlantic Canadian bloc in the House of Commons, where Atlantic Canadian MPs from the various parties would set aside their partisan loyalty to champion regional causes.[5] Although nothing came of this proposal—it was likely that any formation of an Atlantic Canadian bloc of MPs would have been curbed by the party whips, who were disinclined to subvert party interests to regional ones— Gillis had little to lose in making the suggestion. As the only CCF MP in the House, he was surely aware that the chance of all other Atlantic Canadian MPs setting aside party affiliation to support regional issues was highly unlikely, yet, in making the proposal, Gillis was able to cast himself as a spirited regional advocate, one unafraid of looking outside established political frameworks in an effort to best represent his constituents.

A closer examination of his political positions reveals, however, that Gillis' capacity—and, indeed, perhaps even his commitment—for being a defender of the region was more muted and was likely influenced by the political reality of the day. After Newfoundland's 1949 entry into Confederation, Ottawa increasingly conceived of the four easternmost provinces as one region, with the clearest example of this trend being Term 29 of Newfoundland's Terms of Union, which linked the new province's level of development and taxation to the Maritime, not the national, standard.[6] The Atlantic region's premiers took a similar approach to federal-provincial relations during the 1950s, a decade that saw the formation of the Atlantic Premiers Conferences and the Atlantic Provinces Economic Council in attempts to co-operate on issues of shared concern. Since Gillis' first commitment was to the community he called home and the men and women who voted him into office, it seems likely that such a savvy political player would recognize that in a political climate placing greater emphasis on the concept of "region," adopting a similar approach to advocate for his constituents might be fruitful. Thus, while he was quick to use the language of "region," his interests, viewed closely, were decidedly more local. Through an examination of three events important to Atlantic Canada—the fight to have a permanent fixed crossing from Cape Breton to Nova Scotia built over the Strait of Canso, the 1955 extension of unemployment insurance to self-employed seasonal workers in the fishery, and the oil and gas pipeline debates of the late-1950s—this chapter reveals that Gillis' advocacy for Atlantic Canada as a region was largely strategic; the CCF MP most strongly championed Atlantic Canada when what he perceived as the needs of the region aligned with those of his own constituency, or Cape Breton Island. In this manner, Gillis' advocacy appears to have been born less of a commitment to regional interests than a political tactic designed to best represent the voters who sent him to Ottawa. It has been said that "all politics is local": for Gillis and his use of regionalism as a bargaining tactic, this certainly appears to hold true, for he often used the rhetoric of region as a means of promoting causes that were of more localized importance.

Clarence Gillis' life and upbringing certainly leant weight to his reputation as a spirited regional advocate in the House. Born on October 3, 1895, in the Nova Scotia mainland town of Londonderry, Gillis found himself living in Cape Breton in 1904, as his father, J. H. Gillis, a Gaelic speaking coal miner, moved the family across the Strait of Canso to secure work in the coal fields. Not eager to toil in the mines, J. H. Gillis became an active member of the early labour movement in Nova Scotia and even helped to found a miners' union in the province, which led him to become acquainted with legendary Cape Breton labour leader J. B. McLaughlin. Indeed, J. H. Gillis played a prominent role in helping to get District 26 of the United Mine Workers of America (UMWA) recognized. In the heated climate of early twentieth-century labour politics, such actions were frowned upon by management, and J. H. Gillis was blacklisted. Barred from employment in the mines of Nova Scotia, the elder Gillis moved to the United States and found work in New England's mines from 1909 until 1923, when he was again able to return to the coal fields of Cape Breton. In 1926, at the age of thirty-one, Clarie Gillis joined his father in the Cape Breton mines.[7]

As a miner and active proponent of labour, it should not be surprising that Gillis was taken with the Co-operative Commonwealth Federation.

Indeed, it was Gillis himself who, at the 1937 meeting of District 26 of the UMWA, moved that the union support the CCF, a proposition that received unanimous support. Actions such as this, combined with a preponderance of working-class miners in the riding of Cape Breton South, led the national CCF to view this as a winnable seat. To that end, Gillis was nominated to carry the CCF torch in the 1940 federal election. During that contest, Gillis won a slim plurality over Liberal incumbent David Hartigan. For the next seventeen years, he would continue to represent the riding of Cape Breton South, winning four consecutive elections, often being the only CCF member from east of the Ontario border. It was not until 1957 that Gillis was defeated at the polls, when Conservative Donald MacInnis rode to victory on the tide of support for Conservative leader John Diefenbaker that swept the country that year. Although he would contest the 1958 federal election—again being defeated by MacInnis—Gillis' formal involvement with Canadian politics essentially ended in 1957, and he died shortly after in 1960.[8]

The discussions that led to Newfoundland's 1949 entrance into Canadian Confederation afforded Gillis the opportunity to advocate strongly on behalf of his Cape Breton constituents by using the rhetoric of region. For Gillis, the debate surrounding the pending union highlighted a number of issues important to Atlantic Canada—it illustrated the necessity of a fixed crossing connecting mainland Nova Scotia with Cape Breton Island across the Strait of Canso, it sowed the seeds of division between Cape Breton and Halifax over the issue of freight rates, and it revealed the apparent necessity of federal railway rate policy sympathetic to the Cape Breton coal industry. In this manner, the debate following the inclusion of Newfoundland in the family of Canadian provinces seemingly afforded Gillis the opportunity to represent the region by championing a crossing at Canso and by advocating for improved railway connections to Sydney, while also playing the role of staunch defender of Cape Breton's own interests with regard to freight rates. In this manner, Gillis was careful to put Cape Breton's concerns at the forefront.

A fixed link across the Canso Strait was something long-desired by Nova Scotians. As early as the 1880s, lobbying had begun for a bridge across the strait, but these calls went unheeded. During the 1930s, demands for a crossing were made again, but the Great Depression undercut the construction of a fixed link. The Second World War revitalized the nation's economy and, by 1943, the federal and provincial governments began considering desirable post-war reconstruction projects. In its 1944 survey of

Nova Scotia's post-war prospects, the MacGregor Dawson Commission on Provincial Development and Rehabilitation formally endorsed the idea of a crossing over the strait, a view reinforced in the House of Commons in 1948 by Conservative Cumberland MP Percy Black, who said "[t]here is one undertaking on which the 650,000 people of Nova Scotia speak with one voice, namely the construction of this bridge."[9]

Clarence Gillis was an early proponent of a fixed crossing across the Canso Strait. Indeed, historian Gerry Harrop contends that Gillis was the most spirited advocate of the crossing in the House of Commons.[10] As early as 1945, he had seized on the MacGregor Dawson Commission Report and was using it to pressure Minister of Transport Lionel Chevrier on the necessity of a bridge or causeway to connect the mainland to Cape Breton Island. Speaking in the House of Commons, Gillis made clear that it did not matter to the residents of Cape Breton Island if a bridge, causeway, or tunnel was built, so long as a permanent crossing of some sort was completed. However, in advocating for the crossing, Gillis' language blurred from championing the project as something that would benefit Cape Bretoners to being something of importance to all of Nova Scotia—and if the situation warranted, to all of the Maritimes—saying: "It is one thing on which the people of that section of the country [the Maritimes] are solidly united."[11] Later that year, Gillis again used conditions in the Maritime provinces as justification for the construction of the Canso Crossing. This time, though, he spoke of chronic Nova Scotian unemployment since the end of the war as being fodder for the building of a bridge or causeway. As Gillis stated in a radio address shortly before Newfoundland joined Canada:

> This project means a lot to Nova Scotia and particularly to the Island of Cape Breton. It will go a long way to relieving our unemployment problem. It will stimulate production of necessary materials in Nova Scotia and elsewhere. It means an expenditure of $13,500,000, the major portion of which will be spent in Nova Scotia.[12]

Gillis also used the need for a Canso Crossing to lend weight to other issues of importance to Cape Bretoners during the 1949 session of Parliament. For example, when the House debated the issue of whether or not the provisions of the *Maritime Freight Rates Act* (*MFRA*)—which gave a 20 percent preferential shipping rate to goods shipped from central Canada to the Maritimes—would be applied solely to goods shipped through the port at North Sydney, or if the lower rate would also apply to goods passing through Halifax, Gillis again brought the issue back to the need for a crossing at Canso. In some ways, the debate did not matter to Gillis, as he suggested that shippers would still prefer Halifax over Cape Breton because of the "outmoded railroad" to Sydney and the lack of a permanent link across the Strait of Canso.[13] In the end, the decision was made to apply the *MFRA* only to goods passing though North Sydney, thereby ensuring that the Halifax route to Newfoundland would cost more to shippers. This development undoubtedly pleased Gillis and his constituents and likely added greater incentive to get an agreement in place on the construction of a crossing at Canso.[14]

During the late 1940s and even into the early 1950s, Gillis successfully linked Newfoundland's entrance into Confederation to a number of issues he claimed were important to the Atlantic region—the need for a crossing at Canso, the replacement of the outmoded rail system that crossed Cape Breton Island, and the desirability of a freight rate policy favourable to the coal industry. Yet it seems quite clear that all three of the issues that Gillis linked to Newfoundland's entry were really local, or at best Cape Breton-wide, issues, and not the regional issues that Gillis sometimes held them up as in order to gain political support for the projects. In this manner, Gillis was content to use the language of regionalism to lend weight to issues that were, in truth, of narrower importance.

Another issue on which Gillis had the potential to use his reputation as a regional champion for Atlantic Canadians surrounded the 1955 revision of the *Unemployment Insurance Act*. This Act, in place since 1940, was undergoing a series of modifications, the most important of which to the Maritime Provinces was undoubtedly the extension of unemployment insurance benefits to fishermen.[15] To be sure, Gillis was not against this extension. Throughout his time in the House he steadfastly championed the extension of unemployment insurance to as many Canadians as possible. As he stated in the House of Commons on June 10, 1955, "I was pleased to see that the commission are continuing to accept the main principle of the Unemployment Insurance Act, and that is to expand it to take in more people."[16] To this end, Gillis was pleased to hear that unemployment benefits would soon be extended to fishermen. As he noted:

> ... two years ago anyone suggesting that fishermen would be included at all in the act would be considered crazy, but during the deliberations of this committee and after a continuing study by the commission it was decided and recommended by the committee that there was a group classified as fishermen

that might be brought under it, that is, about 6,000 wage earners that could be administered and handled under the act as it is today. That is a beginning.[17]

Yet, despite the fact that the extension of benefits to fishermen was a subject that clearly had regional implications, Gillis did not once speak about it in terms of the benefits that would accrue to the fishers of the Atlantic region. Instead, during the debate surrounding the amendment of the *Unemployment Insurance Act*, Gillis' primary concern remained coal miners, as the mine at Westville, Nova Scotia, had recently closed, leaving upwards of 400 miners and their families out of work. Furthermore, the periodic slow-downs and temporary mine closures that plagued the Cape Breton coal industry made unemployment insurance for miners a pressing concern and prompted Gillis to speak out against perceived threats to mineworkers, such as automation, which he saw as benefiting industry by increasing production while decreasing the number of employees. Gillis' concerns with automation did not end with its effect on mining—he also thought the process would hurt fishers, stating "The fishing industry is being mechanized today. The old type of fisherman is disappearing from the waters and is being replaced by trawlers."[18]

It is somewhat surprising that Gillis did not speak out more forcefully about this issue. After all, Cape Breton Island was not just home to the coal and steel industry from which Gillis drew so much support; it was also home to a modern fish-processing facility constructed less than a decade earlier at Louisburg. Indeed, it seems likely that the presence of this facility on Cape Breton Island would have been fresh in Gillis' mind, as the debate surrounding its construction was fraught with conflict over modern versus traditional fishing techniques, and with debate over who would most profit from the changes being wrought in the Cape Breton fishery— the small-scale local fishermen or large-scale corporate interests located in Halifax and New England. While Gillis was not directly involved in the negotiations over the fish plant, he was probably familiar with the issue— and with the evolving status of the Cape Breton fishery—given that his Glace Bay home was less than fifty kilometres from the new plant.[19]

So, why then was Gillis relatively silent on the matter, at least insofar as speaking for the region? It could be that he did not need to champion the issue. These revisions to the unemployment program attracted prominent support from the Liberal government of the day, and Minister of Fisheries James Sinclair was an active proponent for the extension of these benefits to fishermen. Indeed, much of the tenor of the debate is that this was a done deal, and it might be that by injecting the concerns of coal miners into a debate that was ostensibly about fishermen, Gillis was attempting to ride the coattails of a parliamentary decision that was all but made. It could also be that this was an issue being spearheaded by western MPs. Not only was Minister of Fisheries Sinclair from British Columbia, but much of the CCF's strength in the House came from that same province, and these western CCFers made their support for the program known. Finally, it is important to note that, although he did not frame his support in terms of the benefits that would accrue to the Maritimes, Gillis did support this initiative. It could be that he saw this as an issue that transcended region—that Gillis viewed this as an issue of national importance. Not only was it important for the Atlantic Canadian fishers of New Brunswick, Nova Scotia, Newfoundland, and Prince Edward Island, it was also a pressing concern for fishers across the country. Perhaps Gillis feared that if he were to try to reframe the debate in regional terms, it might weaken the cause. For whatever reason, though, it is surprising Gillis did not use this opportunity to speak on behalf of Atlantic Canada's fishers on the importance of extending to them unemployment insurance benefits.

Gillis also used the rhetoric of region in negotiations surrounding the oil and gas industry, in particular, the linking of Alberta's oil fields to central Canada via pipelines. Of concern to Gillis was the effect that this new source of heating fuel would have on the Maritime coal industry. As a former coal miner and union organizer, Gillis had long been an outspoken champion of the coal industry in the House. As early as 1945, he was speaking out against external threats to the industry, although in the 1940s his primary concern was the importing of cheap American coal to supply the central Canadian market. As Gillis made clear in a broadcast to his constituents on CJCB radio in Cape Breton, ". . . if we handed over the Ontario and Quebec markets to the American operators during the war years . . . [it would take years to] get back into the Quebec market and establish a market for Nova Scotia coal in Ontario."[20] In a March 25, 1950, radio address Gillis returned to a favourite issue—freight rates—to illustrate the difficulties that the Maritime coal industry was facing. For Gillis, freight rates were intricately connected to coal mining. In his view, one of the impediments to most fully realizing the potential of the Cape Breton coal industry was the cost of delivering coal to markets in central Canada at prices that allowed it to compete with American coal. In his radio speech, Gillis lamented the Liberal government's apparent disinterest in subventions for Maritime coal, stating that "if you attempt to make any reference to railways or freight rates you are immediately ruled out of order." In his mind, a government freight rate policy sympathetic to the needs of the coal industry would benefit not just the Maritimes but all the country, as it would "see to it that every last ton of Canadian Coal is mined and markettcd [*sic*] in the areas it is practical to do so."[21]

By 1954, the threat to the Nova Scotia coal mining industry had shifted north and west, from competing American coal to Albertan oil and gas. Of concern to Gillis was the threat raised by pipelines that, he feared, would bring prosperity only to the provinces from Quebec westward.[22] That year, the House debated granting permission to Niagara Gas Transmission to construct a natural gas pipeline from Alberta to southern Ontario. As Gillis saw it, the construction of this pipeline would decimate a Maritime coal industry already reeling from unfavourable tariffs with the United States and a seemingly disinterested Canadian government. Speaking in the House of Commons on March 12, 1954, Gillis reminded his colleagues of his earlier objections to a proposal to pipe natural gas from Alberta to Quebec. Although this earlier initiative, Gillis claimed, had the potential to fuel the homes of both Montreal and Quebec City, it would decimate the Nova Scotian coal industry, as these two cities were "the only economic market for maritime coal."[23] Such pipelines, Gillis argued, should not be viewed as projects of national importance since "certain sections [of the country] are going to be injured or thrown into complete economic chaos" as a result of them.[24]

In that same session, Gillis further attempted to dissociate the oil and gas industry from the coal industry, warning his fellow parliamentarians that they should not "be in too great a rush to close down the coal industry of Canada." Gillis used the opportunity to reinforce the conclusion of a report by the Minister of Mines and Technical Surveys that a closed coal mine was difficult to get running again. Mines should be maintained, Gillis concluded, because of the "disturbed and uncertain world" in which Canadians lived. The growing animosity between the United States and Russia meant an "uncertain future," which necessitated the continued operation of Canada's coal mines in case another global conflict erupted.[25]

The effect of oil and gas pipelines on the Maritime coal industry was still on Gillis' mind in 1956, when the government was debating the construction of the Trans-Canada Pipeline. As Gillis told Cape Bretoners in a CJCB radio address, ". . . if this line is never built it will be in the best interests of the Maritime Provinces." However, for Gillis, the Trans-Canada Pipeline project would not just adversely affect Atlantic Canada; it also would be of no benefit to British Columbia.[26] Gillis was quick to point out that development of the oil and gas industry in Alberta had essentially sounded the death knell of that province's coal industry, with the clear implication that the extension of pipelines transporting natural gas to central Canada would do the same for Maritime coal interests. Moreover, there was apparently still a market in Ontario for Nova Scotia coal, as Toronto's NorCanada Engineering Company was seeking someone to supply them with fifty tons of coal per day.[27] Despite Gillis' protestations, the Albertan oil began flowing through the Trans-Canada Pipeline to Ontario in October 1958.

It is in the debate over the construction of oil and gas pipelines that we most fully see Clarence Gillis linking local and regional issues. As Margaret Conrad has shown, during the 1950s the importance of the coal industry—and of coal miners—began to wane as "competition from new sources of energy [and] the increasing obsolescence of mining and milling operations" took a toll on the long-important Maritime industry.[28] Indeed, by 1957, the Dominion Coal and Steel Corporation, the Maritimes largest coal company, had been acquired by Montreal-based A. V. Roe, a company more concerned with securing government grants than with maintaining the Atlantic region's coal industry. In this climate, the threat of losing a share of the central Canadian energy market to oil and gas from the west was seen as a threat not just to the constituents of Cape Breton South, whom Gillis represented, but also to the entire Nova Scotian economy. And Gillis seems to have recognized the writing on the wall regarding the waning viability of the Maritime coal industry. In a June 1, 1954, radio address he called for the creation of a federal body to regulate all aspects of the energy sector, suggesting that "coal, natural gas, electricity and hydro electric should all be placed in the hands of a competent body with the necessary authority to determine the fuel requirements of the country."[29] Unfortunately for Gillis and for the Cape Breton coal industry, such a regulatory body was not implemented and, as the opening of the Trans-Canada Pipeline in 1958 vividly illustrates, by the late 1950s, satisfying the interests of the Alberta energy sector and of central Canadian consumers desirous of cheap gas and oil had eclipsed the need to maintain Nova Scotia's decaying coal industry.

In considering these three examples, one should not lose sight of the fact that, in advocating for Atlantic Canada more widely, Gillis was thinking largely of the interests of his Glace Bay constituents who had sent him to Parliament. Indeed, the fact that much of Gillis' regional advocacy was rooted in local concerns should not detract from the fact that he was still championing issues that had resonance in the Atlantic region. But, to what extent were his actions in defending the region representative of the position of the CCF? To be blunt, they often were not. In many instances, the stance Gillis took ran counter to that of the rest of the CCF. The oil and gas pipeline debates are a case in point. In these deliberations, the national CCF was willing to endorse the construction of the pipelines, knowing that supporting them might help to win some seats in important, vote-rich southern Ontario, while at the same time maintaining, and even courting, support in their western stronghold. Gillis was under no such political pressure. He knew that his Cape Breton South seat was largely secure, and that he was generally free to advocate for his constituents as he saw fit. In this political climate, Gillis' status as CCF outlier allowed him the flexibility to advocate a position that ran counter to that of the national CCF, safe in the knowledge that his position (and reputation) as an out-spoken regional champion would protect him from the party whip. Similarly, it seems likely that the national CCF recognized that their prospects in Atlantic Canada were generally poor. The region had a long history of supporting the Liberals or the Conservatives; since Gillis' riding was seen as the CCF's only reasonable opportunity for electoral success, the national CCF seemed willing to grant the Cape Breton South MP some leeway in being a regional spokesperson.[30]

Gillis' role as a regional advocate is somewhat reminiscent of the writing of feminist scholar bell hooks. In her writing on black feminists, hooks argues that their marginalized position was not necessarily a weakness, and that it instead freed them to act as they wished in furthering their cause.[31] Something similar can be said for Gillis as a regional advocate. On the surface, his status as a third-party politician from a depressed and peripheral part of Canada might seem a weakness; however, when examined more closely it seems that this apparently weakened position actually afforded Gillis an opportunity for personal success to which many of his other CCF colleagues could not always avail themselves—to act in the manner that best supported their constituents.

Does this apparent freedom of action mean that Gillis consistently used his position to speak for Atlantic Canada and Atlantic Canadians as a sort of third-party regional representative? Here the answer is less certain. To be sure, Gillis seemed to be held by his colleagues as an expert in issues related to the Maritime region. As David Lewis described him, "Gillis was universally respected as a sturdy champion of his people and as a labour spokesman."[32] Yet, for all his authority on regional issues, Gillis tended to view his primary responsibility as being to the people who had elected him—the working men and women of Cape Breton South. Throughout his tenure in parliament, Gillis was steadfast in his defense of the residents of Glace Bay, and he was quick to criticize colleagues who made policy suggestions that he suspected would be poorly received in his riding. Where Gillis transitioned from local advocate to regional advocate was in instances where the local and the regional overlapped. When this occurred, Gillis would strongly use the language of region, knowing that this would give his stance greater weight. In the end, however, it is difficult to draw any broader conclusion from these three case studies than the simple fact that Clarence Gillis used arguments premised on the notion of region in the House when he felt it would best further his cause, and most often that cause revolved around issues important to the residents of his Cape Breton South riding.

CHAPTER 5

THE LEFT AT HOME AND ABROAD

BROADENING THE DOMINANT
NARRATIVE OF CANADIAN HISTORY

Stephanie Bangarth

The optimism that certain progressive Canadians seemed to have felt with the election of Justin Trudeau and his Liberal government is already being undermined by the continuation of the arms deal to Saudi Arabia, questionable decisions around partisan fundraising, and other indications that the new direction of this new government is not so new at all. For Canadian scholars of and on the left, this comes as little surprise. This chapter will insert a left narrative into three episodes in Canadian history: human rights in 1940s and 1950s Canada; humanitarian aid and Biafra in the late 1960s; and Canada's approach to China in the 1970s. Each of these episodes carries a persistent historical association with Liberal or Progressive Conservative narratives; however, in all three cases, action by the Canadian state resulted from pressure by the Canadian left. This study, using the work of lawyer and CCF/NDP MP Andrew Brewin as the biographical focal lens, will contribute to an overall understanding of how important issues such as human rights, the social democratic movement, and campaigns for a just foreign policy are part of a larger national and transnational historical narrative. This chapter will also serve to insert the political left into foreign policy directives, which have also been largely neglected by scholars of Canada's place in the world.

Andrew Brewin was a pioneer in civil liberties and human rights movements in Canada, using his legal training to defend union members and minority groups and his Christian compassion as a member of the Anglican Church of Canada to comment on major issues of social justice. Brewin was also an architect of the social democratic movement in Canada. He was active in the Co-operative Commonwealth Federation (CCF) as its Ontario president from 1946 to 1949 and was a member of the Founding Committee of the NDP. Brewin was elected as a Member of Parliament for the CCF/NDP from 1962 to 1979 for the riding of Greenwood in Toronto and served nearly seventeen years in federal Parliament. In his political life, Brewin spoke out against racial injustice and discrimination in immigration policy. He was a passionate critic of Canada's foreign policy from the 1960s to the late 1970s. His concern for human rights continued throughout his career and he campaigned in the House of Commons, along with other parliamentarians such as David MacDonald (PC–Egmont, PEI) and Louis Duclos (Liberal–Montmorency, QC), to develop a foreign policy to deal with difficult situations in Pakistan, Venezuela, and Chile. He was a founding member of the Group of 78, a Canadian non-governmental organization (NGO) formed in 1970 that seeks to promote global priorities for peace and disarmament, equitable and sustainable development, and a strong and revitalized UN system. As Foreign Affairs and Defence critic for his entire political career, Brewin held a post that afforded him the opportunity to shape NDP policy with respect to a number of major issues in Canadian external relations throughout the 1960s and into the late 1970s.

Frank Scott once remarked that, "constitutionally speaking, the 1950s was predominantly the decade of human rights." He was referring to a spate of cases that would become famous for their articulation of a constitutional theory known as the "implied bill of rights."[1] Brewin was a strong advocate throughout his legal and political career for a bill of rights that would be entrenched in the Constitution, and he played a central role in the articulation of the "implied bill of rights" principle.[2] The Committee for a Bill of Rights (CBR), which followed closely on the heels of the Japanese-Canadian campaign and shared many committee members with the Co-operative Committee on Japanese Canadians (CCJC) (including Brewin), used the example of the Japanese-Canadian issue in connection with the wider issue of the passage of a Canadian bill of rights. In building upon the success of the campaign to end deportations of Canadians of Japanese ancestry following World War II, Canadian advocates began to forward the idea that, in light of events at home and abroad, it was necessary to demonstrate clearly to all Canadians the urgency of a "basic law which recognizes human personality and the right to freedom under the law of every Canadian irrespective of race."[3] The enshrining of a bill of rights in the Constitution was a popular idea among advocates in post-war Canada and even received serious attention in Parliament and in the Senate.

At Brewin's urging, the CBR was created in early 1947 as an adjunct of the Association for Civil Liberties specifically to lobby the federal government and to capitalize on growing attention being paid to such a proposal.[4] The campaign for a bill of rights would bring together both civil libertarians and egalitarians and would promote the protection of such rights as free speech and freedom of association, but also the right not to suffer discrimination on the basis of race, religion, or gender, reflecting the post-war discourse of human rights in Canada.

In 1948, the committee presented the minister of justice with a petition signed by 200 "respectable" members of the community from across the country calling for a bill of rights. The petition represented their official submission to the Special Joint Committee of the House of Commons and Senate on Human Rights and Fundamental Freedoms. For the drafting of the brief, the CBR turned to Brewin, who was by this time the president of the Ontario CCF.

Brewin's proposal was for an amendment to the *BNA Act* [1867] that would prohibit the federal and provincial governments from enacting legislation that would infringe upon certain civil rights, including freedom of religion, freedom of speech and religion, and the right to lawful assembly, among others. To contextualize the brief's purpose, Brewin provided an historical account of a variety of state-inflicted infringements on civil liberties from the pre-Depression era to the time of the drafting of the brief and noted that international developments in the realm of human rights merited their protection in Canada. The brief overwhelmingly reflected the emerging discourse of human rights, despite its completion ahead of the 1948 United Nations Declaration on Human Rights in December. Consider the following quote: "It has been officially recognized by the nations of the world that fascism which brought upon the world the most destructive war in history was rooted in contempt for human rights and that, conversely, the peace of the world must rest ultimately upon the universal respect of human rights and fundamental freedoms." He continued by noting that "we in Canada are in a position to give positive adherence to these fundamental international ideals," recognizing the usefulness of UN ideals in forwarding the Canadian agenda of the CBR.[5] Three years later, the committee would again pressure the Liberal government of Louis St. Laurent with a version of the brief even more rooted in international concepts of human rights. But despite the clear hypocrisy of having Canada as a signatory to the United Nations Declaration of Human Rights (UNDHR), the federal government refused to move on a constitutionally entrenched bill of rights. As Carmela Patrias has noted, the Liberals of the day were hesitant in supporting a national bill of rights for fear that state action on political rights would lead to state action on social rights and the welfare state.[6]

Diefenbaker's arrival to the prime minister's office in 1957 challenged him with the task of obtaining consent from provincial premiers such as Quebec's Maurice Duplessis to achieve a constitutionally entrenched rights guarantee. Without such co-operation, he fell back to the defense that a federal parliamentary statute, rather than a constitutional amendment, could provide adequate and effective protection of Canadians' rights. This argument was rejected by constitutional scholars such as Frank Scott, Bora Laskin, and Brewin, who correctly anticipated the limited effectiveness of Diefenbaker's bill of rights. It represented, as Lambertson has suggested, half a loaf, but it also represented the conclusion of a major struggle for the emerging human rights community in Canada.[7] As for Brewin, his activism would finally turn toward Parliament. Brewin, like other social democrats of his generation, entered politics with the aim of advancing his humanitarian activism at a national level. Within the party, he was an eloquent and unrelenting advocate of the party's high placement on the values of equality and the rule of law. He was also a proponent of engaging Canada within the world community in a principled manner.

The involvement of an NDP parliamentarian in the lengthy process of engaging China in the mid-twentieth century also situates the NDP in the articulation of Canadian foreign policy. Studies abound on the role of the two "traditional" political parties, the Liberals and the Progressive Conservatives, in the development of Canada's place in the world. Yet, it is clear that the NDP had something important to say about Canada's foreign policy directions and that many Canadians agreed with their viewpoints. While the recognition of the People's Republic of China (PRC) in 1970 was reflective of the changing norms ushered in by Pierre Trudeau's ascendancy to the leadership of the Liberal Party and the prime ministership of Canada in 1968, it was also part of the kind of arguments that Brewin and the NDP had maintained for some time and the pressure they brought to bear on those in government. Additionally, this case study, though rooted in Canada's past, also hints to the present, as China has become a significant world power since Brewin's first pronouncements on the importance of engagement. The recognition of the PRC was not solely an outcome of Trudeau's idealism. Over fifty years ago, Brewin and others argued for a way to engage China pragmatically and constructively with rational viewpoints and not confrontationally, which characterized much of US policy toward China until Richard Nixon's administration. Early in the twenty-first century, many world leaders have also come to the same conclusion; for example, Prime Minister Stephen Harper pursued a more pragmatic approach with China after his government's disastrous start upon coming to office in 2006. As Paul Evans has noted, the visit of the prime minister to China in December 2009 "closed the chapter on 'cool politics, warm economics' and reopened the engagement strategy of previous Canadian governments."[8]

For much of his political career, Brewin wrote and argued extensively for Canada's place in the new military order of the post-World War II period, a role that included peacekeeping.[9] Brewin was a Canadian nationalist in that he desired Canada to be an exemplar to the world, independent and sovereign, and not tied to any one particular nation, including and especially the United States, when it came to foreign policy. Unlike many in the left, and certainly in his own party, Brewin did not wholly approach the United States with scepticism.[10] While highly critical of American intentions in Vietnam, and aspects of American foreign policy in general, his advocacy for the PRC and its recognition and membership in the UN was not influenced by knee-jerk, anti-American sentiment. In many ways, Brewin's views were part of a healthy debate on China that engaged a variety of members of parliament from the 1950s to the 1970s. In fact, the absence of a consensus among the various political actors and certainly among the wider population of Canadians stands in glaring contrast to the unanimity of opinion that characterized American views in the same period.

The question of China's recognition was something that had preoccupied External Affairs and parliamentarians since the Communist succession in 1949. Cold War politics of containment, and principally Canada's evolving relationship with the United States, proved to be the major stressors in the development of a China policy for Canada. Many were quite concerned with how recognition of Beijing would affect Canada's ties with Chiang Kai-shek's Guomindang (Nationalist) government in Taiwan, which claimed to be the government of all China. For a time, Canada responded by floating the two-China policy initiated by a department of external affairs study authorized by Secretary of State for External Affairs Howard Green in 1961.[11] The Nationalists were quite unhappy with this policy, but as historians Norman Hillmer and J. L. Granatstein noted, if Canada could continue to recognize them as the government of China at the same time as it recognized Beijing, they might be prepared to "live with their anger."[12] Mao Zedong's government would have none of this, and neither would the opposition Progressive Conservative and New Democratic parties. Both before and during his time as a parliamentarian, Brewin spoke frequently about the need for bringing China into the world fold. In November 1966, in a lengthy statement in the House of Commons on this and other related subjects, Brewin stated his party's position on China. He indicated that the two-China policy flew in the face of facts and the views of both regimes—that of the Communists and the Nationalists—in question. Brewin often called the two-China policy a sham and spoke frequently about the counter-productiveness of the policy, in that it appeared to foster some kind of real prospect that by means of counter-revolution the Nationalist regime might regain control of mainland China. In part, Brewin was expressing his view that quiet diplomacy had had its place, and that, while Canada had contributed much in this regard to the world, the context and the conditions of the mid-1960s world required "a more open form of diplomacy, a diplomacy of frank, clear and open statements on the principles of some basic issues," which included the recognition of China.[13]

This was nothing new for Brewin. As early as July 1953, in a statement sent to some newspapers, he called Liberals complacent and self-satisfied about domestic and international issues.[14] As a committed pacifist, Brewin also rationalized his party's calls for the recognition of China from that vantage point, as well as from the vantage point of multilateralism, both of which Brewin did not view as mutually exclusive. Indeed, Brewin was quite concerned with the need for reconciliation between "one quarter of the world's population governed by the People's Republic of China and the rest of the world." He felt the role of his generation was to create functioning, worldwide institutions, such as the United Nations, to breach the gaps of power, wealth, and ideology that threatened the world in this period of the nuclear age.[15] In his view, it seemed as if Communist China was prepared to turn its back on its past in order to become a member of an organization dedicated to peace. Thus, dialogue rather than estrangement, support rather than scepticism, and multilateralism rather than unilateralism were central to his approach to China throughout his political career.

Brewin was quite sympathetic to China, in fact. In a speech in the House of Commons, Brewin called upon his historical knowledge to assert that China suffered from a long period of humiliation from the Western world. To most of his fellow parliamentarians, Brewin must have seemed unusual in his view that, by welcoming China into the world community, the more extreme forms of its revolution could be curtailed over time. In fact, he often used a comparison to Stalinist excesses in Russia to make the point of the problems to which isolation might lead. Brewin's notes also reveal his view that the world community was xenophobic in its historical and current perception and treatment of China.[16] Again, to some of his fellow parliamentarians he must have seemed a typical socialist, but, as a firm believer in the power of multilateralism and collective world institutions like the United Nations, his views on such issues would mark much of NDP foreign policy into the 1960s and 1970s. In his capacity as foreign affairs and defence critic for the NDP throughout his entire political career, this was especially the case. In so doing, however, Brewin's efforts placed the NDP at the heart of many debates about Canada's involvement in foreign policy and humanitarian crises.

The Nigeria-Biafra conflict that occurred fifty years ago marked Canada's first encounter with an African relief effort. While Prime Minister Pierre Trudeau rhetorically replied, "Where's Biafra?" when asked what role Canada would play in humanitarian relief efforts, groups of Canadians, including those from the Canadian International Development Agency and Canadian churches, combined their resources to form Canairelief to supply the breakaway nation with food via an airlift for a population that was starving. As a Christian socialist, Brewin was well aware of the responsibilities the churches bore in the colonial project in Africa and battled for a more responsible attitude toward post-independence Africa. Brewin, along with others inside and outside government circles, believed in the role of international bodies as vehicles of change and observation, and thereby worked to entrench multilateralism as a feature of Canadian foreign relations. In light of current affairs in Somalia, and perceived Western inaction in Yemen, the analysis of the failure of political activism for aid to Biafra provides an historical example worth studying. Biafra raised many issues that are still of importance today, including: the legitimacy of a "war of famine"; the meaning of genocide; and the limits placed by international law on a nation's sovereignty when it violates basic human rights. The Nigerian secessionist conflict is not generally well-known to Canadians today, and for good reason. Despite the fact that the Canadian public was, for some time, roused to ire over its government's indifferent response, the historical record is nearly silent on the whole affair. This is likely due to the regret that some activists feel today at how Biafran leaders, particularly General Ojukwu, the ersatz Biafran leader, manipulated Western guilt via a sophisticated public relations campaign.[17]

Canairelief was created through the financial support of Jewish leaders, the Roman Catholic Church, and the major Protestant church denominations (mainly the Anglican, Presbyterian, and United churches), along with a partnership with Oxfam. Canairelief made its first flight on January 23, 1969, and its final trip was on January 11, 1970. It completed 670 flights and delivered 11,000 tons of desperately needed food and medical supplies into the blockaded state of Biafra. All of this was done without official sanction from Parliament. Other countries, however, were sending aid directly, such as France, Portugal, and Israel. And so, activists, particularly Ted Johnson of the Presbyterian Church and his team, decided to go the political route at the time and arranged for two MPs—Progressive Conservative MP David MacDonald, a United Church minister, and Andrew Brewin, an NDP Anglican layman—to fly into Biafra on a Canairelief flight to embark on a fact-finding mission. Trudeau's biographer, John English, remarks that the trip "infuriated" Trudeau, who was convinced that support for separatist Biafra was risky.[18] While Brewin and MacDonald's fact-finding mission angered Trudeau, it also generated considerable public interest and even more considerable activity in the House of Commons. Their official report of their fact-finding mission, *Canada and the Biafran Tragedy*, was published as a book in 1970, recommending that Canada use its position to prod the United Nations to negotiate a ceasefire, participate in relief operations, push to have Nigerian civil rights violations under the UN charter enforced, and give money for humanitarian relief. They also wrote evocatively about the starvation they had witnessed.[19]

One of the main issues addressed in their report was the question of federalism and how the desire of the Nigerian federal government to preserve "One Nigeria," and the Biafran claim to self-determination, effectively shaped the attitudes of other nations toward the conflict, including Canada. Brewin and MacDonald carefully argued the speciousness of the comparison drawn between the secession of Biafra and the threat of secession in Quebec. Although government officials denied the effect of the spectre of Quebec separatism on Canada's policy, it seems clear this was the case from, among others, the Minister of External Affairs Mitchell Sharp's own statements on the Gabon-Quebec parallel in defending the government's position.[20] In February 1968, Gabon, under pressure from

France, invited Quebec and not the Government of Canada to attend a Francophone education conference. Despite protests from the federal government, Quebec attended the conference and received full state honours. Shortly thereafter, then-Prime Minister Lester Pearson broke off relations with Gabon, which achieved independence from France in 1960. But as Brewin and MacDonald note, the effect of the Quebec situation was likely to strengthen and rigidify a policy that would have been adopted regardless of separatist tensions.[21]

The Nigerian conflict continued to be present in House of Commons debates, due in large part to Brewin's constant efforts there and in the press throughout 1969. As of January 1969, Canadian churches and Oxfam organized relief flights to Biafra—Canairelief—and continued to press the government for both financial and diplomatic assistance in obtaining permission from both belligerents for direct relief flights into Biafra. But then, a major breakthrough occurred, which Brewin described as being "directly as a result of successful pressure on the government by these interested groups and by the public."[22] Finally, on January 9, 1970, the Trudeau government allocated funds for relief, including $1 million for Canairelief. On January 12, 1970, the Biafran resistance collapsed, rendering void the monies set aside for Canairelief.

In many ways, Brewin and MacDonald's recommendations in *Canada and the Biafran Tragedy* were clearly forward thinking, and certainly foreshadowed a trend of increasing internationalism in Canadian foreign policy. Indeed, the historical record indicates that what many Canadians argued for, including Brewin, MacDonald, and Johnson, was a preliminary form of R2P (responsibility to protect, a United Nations initiative established in 1995). R2P is a norm or set of principles based on the idea that sovereignty is not a privilege, but a responsibility. It focuses on preventing and halting four crimes: genocide, war crimes, crimes against humanity, and ethnic cleansing. While the ineffectiveness of the world community's response to the Rwandan genocide is frequently cited as the genesis of this principle, a close reading of the appeals to Trudeau and Sharp, and to other Western governments, reveals remarkably similar ideologies.[23] Successive governments could no longer avoid the shifting international circumstances brought about in a globalizing world. The Progressive Conservative government under Brian Mulroney would appreciate this, and throughout the 1980s forged closer relationships with Latin America and served as a world leader in its approach to South Africa.

These three, brief case studies all highlight ways in which the left contributed essential new directions in Canadian foreign policy and in the framework of our rights culture. Long before the Bill of Rights, and especially the *Charter*, CCFers in the late 1940s and early 1950s were highlighting the need for a constitutionally entrenched rights guarantee, something which is often attributed to Pierre Trudeau's Liberals in the 1970s. When Canada finally recognized China, Pierre Trudeau was lauded for his efforts. But the historical record indicates the left as the foundation of this now-prescient move. Lastly, R2P is largely credited to Lloyd Axworthy, a prominent Liberal Cabinet minister of the 1990s. R2P was, in fact, foundationally enunciated by Brewin and MacDonald in relation to the Biafran crisis.

So, what are the solutions? As Paul Dewar has asserted, we need a new left-wing narrative in global affairs.[24] Furthermore, I emphasize that historians of the left need to be more assertive in claiming our space in the articulation of the development of Canadian foreign policy, both then and now. The historical record has distorted the important contributions the left has made in this regard. The left itself shoulders some of the blame, for its stubborn reverence for party figures and a static history that is rooted in a specific place of the past, such as with the creation of universal health care or labour reforms. As M. J. Coldwell wrote, "I do not believe that merely exercising the right to vote, often without examining the issues or understanding what the various parties stand for, is fulfilling the functions of . . . good citizenship . . ."[25] Certainly, to facilitate such an understanding requires the combined efforts of left historians to continue to create an awareness of the role of the NDP/CCF in the making of Canadian history and also of the NDP itself to embrace and support such a sustained critique.

CHAPTER 6

FABIANISM AND THE PROGRESSIVE LEFT IN BRITISH COLUMBIA

THE "NEW PARTY" IN HISTORICAL PERSPECTIVE

Robert McDonald

In *The Fate of Labour Socialism: The Co-operative Commonwealth Federation and the Dream of a Working-Class Future*, James Naylor argues that "the 'received' version of the CCF" fails to correctly identify how radical the CCF was at its inception. Heralding "a qualitatively different society from capitalism," the CCF at its inception was a political party based on distinctly revolutionary ideas quite different from the social reform ideas that came to define it during and after the Second World War. The CCF embraced Marxism and rejected liberal individualism. Emphasizing the centrality of "class" to an understanding of "labour socialism," Naylor concludes that the traditional narrative of the CCF "presents a skewed picture of the CCF in the 1930s and early 1940s" by "dramatically exaggerating the role of the middle-class leadership and liberal ideas at the expense of much of the party's activist core."[1]

The socialist intellectuals of the Fabian-influenced League for Social Reconstruction (LSR) provided the most obvious source of middle-class ideas and influence in the CCF. Fabianism emerged in London in the 1880s and, led by the movement's two most dominant members, Beatrice and Sidney Webb, articulated a distinctive version of socialism that "ignored revolutionary politics and was sceptical about the working-classes' potential to effect change: for the Fabians, socialism would instead be realized through experts and bureaucrats."[2] In 1932, academics Frank Scott of Montreal and Frank Underhill of Toronto founded the League for Social Reconstruction as a Canadian version of Britain's Fabian

Society. Envisioned as a research group of experts who would carry out social research and suggest proposals to inform public policy, the non-partisan but left-leaning league combined "a Christian sense of morality with a high modernist faith in the rational and scientific possibilities of social planning." It generated ideas that "played a significant role in defining the Canadian intellectual landscape of the 1930s and 1940s."[3]

This chapter returns to the subject of middle-class influences in CCF/NDP history by exploring first the concerted effort of two 1960s Fabian-influenced progressives in British Columbia (BC), Thomas Berger and Walter Young, to transform the class identity of the CCF at the point of transition to its successor party, the NDP. The CCF in BC, in the 1950s still essentially a working-class party, had always been ideologically to the left of the national organization. Tension between moderates and radicals—or, as liberal journalist Bruce Hutchison called them, "the gradualists and the sea-green incorruptible Socialists"—had been a persistent and distinguishing feature of provincial CCF politics, and would remain so in the sixties.[4] It then compares the political philosophy of these two 1960s reformers to the policy influence of two other Fabians, George Weir and Harry Cassidy, who had similarly advanced a modern, statist reform agenda for BC thirty years earlier. The key point is that Weir and Cassidy were tied to the Liberal Party and served respectively as a Cabinet minister in, and an advisor to, the provincial Liberal government of Thomas Dufferin Pattullo, elected in November 1933. The continuity of Fabian socialist influence in the thinking of these four influential progressives poses the question of how we should understand the relationship between ideas and partisanship on the left in BC during the formative years of CCF/NDP history.

The late 1950s movement to create a "progressive" party of the left by uniting Canadian labour with the CCF was national in scope. The branch of labour consisting mostly of newer industrial unions (the Canadian Congress of Labour) had endorsed the CCF as "the political arm of labour" in 1943, but opposition to political action by craft unions and the continuing tension between communist and non-communist unions had limited further consideration of a broader and effective political coalition. However, when the various branches of the trade union movement consolidated in 1956, forming the Canadian Labour Congress (CLC) at the national level and the British Columbia Federation of Labour (BCFL) at the provincial, the stumbling block formerly posed by divergent attitudes toward political action was diminished. When the CLC, at its April 1958 convention, moved to establish a new alliance of the political left in Canada with the

CCF, the CCF, devastated at the national level by its electoral collapse in the massive Diefenbaker Conservative victory in March, was receptive. In July, the national CCF joined the CLC to establish a joint committee, the National Committee for the New Party, which, through seminars, forums, and conferences, spawned about 300 "new party clubs" claiming 8,500 members across Canada.[5] In August 1961, the movement culminated in the formation of the national NDP, and, in October in BC, the provincial.

The New Democratic Party's first years as a provincial political party were marked by persistent tension that was at once both personal and philosophical, centring initially on a struggle for influence between two party officials, Tom Berger, the first provincial NDP president, and Robert Strachan, the legislative leader. Born in Victoria, British Columbia, in 1933 to a family of modest means, Berger finished law school at UBC in 1956 and quickly gained a reputation for outstanding work in the expanding field of labour law, where he specialized in court injunctions and the workings of the Workmen's Compensation Board.[6] A reform-minded progressive who sought to create a "just and equitable society," he had earlier been a Liberal but became caught up in the "new party" movement.[7] Berger's connections to the labour movement and his belief that the goal of creating a new party out of the old CCF depended on harnessing the progressive influence of organized labour led him to join the CCF in 1960 and to become the provincial NDP's first president, at the age of 28, in October 1961. Eight years of intense political engagement followed, including the party presidency, a year in Parliament from 1962–63, election to the provincial legislature in 1966, and active pursuit of the provincial party leadership that failed in June 1967, but led to a narrow victory in April 1969. It was his labour law work that propelled him into politics, and trade union encouragement that lay behind his quest for the leadership.[8]

A working-class Scot who spoke with what one writer called a "rich, porridgey Glaswegian" accent, Robert Strachan (1913–1981) had migrated as a teenager from his native Scotland to Nova Scotia as part of a farm labour immigration scheme. In 1931, he left the Maritimes for the west coast, where he found work first as a labourer in the copper-smelting town of Anyox, and then in Powell River as a carpenter, eventually heading the Brotherhood of Carpenters and Joiners of America in BC. First elected as an MLA for the working-class stronghold of Cowichan-Newcastle in 1952, he succeeded the ineffectual Arnold Webster as CCF leader in 1956 and led the provincial party during the CCF/NDP transition years, until Tom Berger replaced him in April 1969. Strachan was a CCFer who emphasized the rights of ordinary people and believed that the state should play an active role in the economy through public ownership of monopolies. British in origin and a skilled artisan by trade and outlook, he exemplified the self-consciously working-class culture of the old CCF, drawing on the traditions of an older modernity characterized by localism, face-to-face relationships, small-scale production, and a politics nourished by nineteenth-century radicalism, both liberal and socialist. He was not a Marxist, but he was a "socialist," a label he embraced with pride.[9] One NDP caucus member called him the "last of the classic socialists."[10]

A key source of Fabian influence in the NDP was Walter Young, whose book, *The Anatomy of a Party*, is a seminal text on the history of the CCF. Positing CCF's transition from a social movement to a political party, *The Anatomy of a Party* laid the foundation for what Alan Whitehorn describes as by far "the most frequent, best researched, and most enduring theme in the literature on the CCF/NDP: that of the 'protest movement becalmed'."[11] Less well-known is Young's influence in shaping the ideological direction of the "new party" in British Columbia. Serving first as an adviser for the 1963 election and then for several years as chair of the party's Policy Research Committee, Young was crucially important to the Berger group's agenda to reconceptualize the socialist CCF as the social democratic NDP.[12]

Raised in Victoria, in 1962 Young had accepted an appointment in the political science department at the University of British Columbia while working on his dissertation from the University of Toronto. Like Berger, a former Liberal who had converted to the CCF as part of the "new party" movement, Young had joined the movement in Ontario and, after coming west, remained committed to shaping the newly formed NDP in the tradition of the League for Social Reconstruction.[13] In November 1963, Young participated in the creation of the Exchange for Political Ideas in Canada (EPIC), an Ontario-based research group to promote the intellectual development of the democratic left in Canada.[14] At its founding, EPIC brought together over 200 individuals, about half of whom were New Democrats, while many others were Liberals. The organization soon collapsed, but Young's interest in it suggests how he envisioned the NDP: a party of "liberally minded" individuals, not "socialists."[15] Success would come only if the new party could reach out and gain the support of middle-class Canadians, many of whom were currently Liberal Party supporters. The often acerbic Young showed little tolerance for what he called "narrow-minded[,] shortsighted Puritanical socialists" and even spoke in one letter of keeping out of the reconstituted Fabian Society "all those damn dreary CCF'ers" whose "ideological stench" he feared would "drive away newcomers."[16] Tom Berger embodied Young's idea of a leader for the new party, and in the words of Dr. Ray Parkinson—victorious with Berger in the dual riding of Vancouver-Burrard in the 1966 election—Young "guided Tom" through his unfolding political career.[17]

The political ideas of both Young and Berger fall within the intellectual tradition of Fabian socialist thought that had informed the development of "new liberalism" in the British Columbia Liberal Party of the 1930s and 1940s and was one of the influences that shaped the formation of the CCF. Like Young, Berger was a progressive intellectual in the Fabian tradition who believed in the ability of planners, economists, psychologists, businessmen, and other types of professionally trained experts, including labour leaders, to organize prosperity and facilitate a socially just society.[18] The new party should look to "quality people," Berger and his supporters argued, professionals trained in the sciences and social sciences, for advice on social and economic planning.[19] We should look to trade unions for their social function, as "instruments of social engineering."[20] Once Berger had gained a seat in the legislature and begun campaigning for the leadership, he emphasized the talking point that more ought to be done "to bring the trade union people . . . and to bring people from the universities and from the professions into our party."[21] While his supporters viewed Bob Strachan as "a perennial loser whose yeoman style was unsuited to the swinging Kennedy sixties," as "not the right man to draw into the party enough university faculty and students, or professional men," Strachan resisted Berger's emphasis on educated elites and argued instead that no party could be "a truly democratic socialist party" unless it had within its ranks and among its elected members "a substantial number who earn(ed) their daily bread in the mines, mills, and farms of the country."[22]

The effort to present a "new look" to social democracy in the September 1963 provincial election did not prove effective; NDP support dropped five percentage points (from 32.7 percent to 27.8 percent, with the loss of two seats) from that of the CCF in 1960, while Social Credit (Socreds), the populist conservative government first elected in 1952, grew by 2 percent, netting one additional member. Explaining that the new party "did not have sufficient time" for its program to catch on with the electorate, Tom Berger, as campaign committee chair, also noted insightfully that NDP votes lost to the Socreds "appear to have been largely working class."[23] Electoral defeat in no way diminished the Berger group's agenda to make over the party and replace the leader, however. Press reporters talked openly about "back stage plots," some involving labour leaders, to resolve the party's "leadership crisis" by unseating Strachan.[24]

Perhaps nothing symbolized more the differences in outlook of CCFers and "new party" New Democrats than the question of state ownership. Throughout the 1960s, Strachan and the caucus majority continued to focus on the need to take over BC Telephone. Popular support within the party for continued adherence to the principles of the Regina Manifesto appeared within weeks of the 1963 election when, as Desmond Morton tells us, "a Trotskyite 'Socialist Caucus'" briefly controlled the provincial NDP convention and "persuaded delegates to endorse a sweeping programme of nationalization."[25] A May 1964 statement from the Strachan-led caucus of MLAs called for public ownership of telephone, natural gas, and other utilities, policies very much in the tradition of CCF platforms of the 1940s and 1950s. But the anti-Strachan executive no longer accepted this emphasis on public ownership, and the NDP's 1966 election platform, which reflected the Berger group's views, did not include policy statements that embodied two of the most important socialist concepts: economic planning and public ownership. Rather, with emphasis on education and the goal of decentralizing the delivery of health care, the document reflected Berger's view that public ownership was "beside-the-point" for a modern social democratic party. Money was better spent providing schools, financing universities, improving hospitals, or "solving the problems of air and water pollution . . ." than nationalizing the telephone or forest corporations; there is "more, much, much more to socialism than public ownership."[26] Interestingly, in the lead-up to the 1963 election, Berger had advised the NDP to drop its demand for a takeover of BC Telephone, a position he changed once he was openly in search of the leadership.

A more enduring source of division between the Strachan and Berger camps was the question of organized labour's role in politics, important because an alliance with labour was the most compelling argument for creating a new party, and because continued differences on this question significantly shaped the history of Dave Barrett's NDP government in the 1970s. While Bob Strachan was a product of the "old labour" craft union movement, the university-educated Tom Berger fit easily into the post-war system of labour relations in which businesses "conceded unions a measure of legitimacy and citizen rights, while unions accepted managerial prerogatives and labour's place within a capitalist social order."[27] The new system of "industrial legality" was increasingly bureaucratic and generated a demand for legal specialists such as Berger, who had emerged as the BC Federation of Labour's legal counsel and the province's leading labour lawyer. Ray Haynes, secretary-treasurer of the BCFL, enthusiastically supported both the "new party" movement and, later, the leadership candidacy of Tom Berger. BC's largest industrial union, the IWA (International Workers' Association), also endorsed the "new party" idea and "was a driving force behind many of the NDP's policy planks (in the 1960s)," with the rank and file providing "more support for the NDP than any other trade union in British Columbia."[28]

Bob Strachan represented a different opinion, one more sceptical of the party's connection with labour. Trade unions and the CCF had never been close in BC, partly due to Marxist influence in the movement's early years.[29] As former MLA Grace MacInnis noted in 1958, "We have in British Columbia CCF people who have been nurtured in the idea that unions are very bad for a socialist party—something like an unhealthy, alien growth."[30] Two Kootenay politicians, MP Bert Herridge and MLA Leo Nimsick, feared that the new alliance would not continue to fight for the socialist ideals of the Regina Manifesto and opposed the "new party" movement; the radical leftist and former MLA Dorothy Steeves fretted about losing the party's connection to its socialist past.[31] Strachan, sceptical of big organizations and elites, drew on the tradition of former Crowsnest Pass coal miner Tom Uphill and other left populists when concluding that neither labour nor management "should run the country . . . The government should run the country"; the NDP should not elect a leader who makes the political party, through its connections to the labour movement, a "tied house."[32] When stepping down from the party's leadership several years later, he asserted bluntly that he had come to believe the trade union movement "was part of the establishment," its "grass roots quality" having been "bargained away for so many cents an hour" by labour movement "insiders."[33]

In the September 1966 provincial election, Tom Berger moved from the back rooms to the legislative front bench by winning a seat in the dual-member riding of Vancouver-Burrard. Almost immediately, talk of a leadership challenge began to build, backed by a team of Berger supporters that included Walter Young; 'Pat' O'Neal and Ray Haynes, secretary-treasurers of the BC Federation of Labour from 1958–66 and 1966–73 respectively; and four caucus members, including Frank Calder, Canada's first Indigenous MLA.[34] As articulated by Ernie Hall in the

Surrey Democrat, what some perceived as Strachan's poor public image was a problem, this in a decade when the Kennedy mystique was enhancing the role of image and charismatic appeal as important sources of political capital.[35] Hall was most impressed, however, by Berger's status in academic circles and his potential "to attract better quality candidates." That "better" meant "university-trained" struck Bob Strachan as blatant snobbery, which he resented.[36] In early May, five UBC professors publicly endorsed Berger's claim to the leadership, the latter seeing in this gesture recognition of the "much greater role in society" now being played by the academic community.[37]

The challenge was "disastrously pre-mature and poorly organized," with the June 3 vote of 277–178 leaving a diminished Strachan still in charge after receiving support from slightly more than 60 percent of the votes cast.[38] Characterized by journalist John Mika as a battle between "nostalgic CCFers" and the "Young Turks," the election appears to have separated the "ordinary grass roots" of the party from its "intellectuals, and organizers, some of its youth and several important segments of labor."[39] Many party veterans and a majority of the caucus deeply resented the challenge, believing, as did Dave Barrett, the former social worker first elected in 1960 in the Coquitlam-area riding of Dewdney, that "it represented untrammeled ambition in someone who lacked experience."[40] "Weary and wounded," Strachan gave notice in late 1968 that he would step down, leading to another vote in April 1969 that Berger won narrowly (by a vote of 411–375) over Barrett.[41] Supported by only four of the party's sixteen caucus members, the winning candidate built his majority from a political base that rested squarely on support from Ray Haynes and the BCFL.[42] The majority of the 110 labour delegates supported Berger, the numbers augmented by a surge of new affiliations with the NDP in the month prior to the convention.[43]

Sensing an opportunity to dispose of the NDP before its new leader could establish his authority, Premier Bennett dissolved the legislature on July 21 and called a provincial election for August 27, a summer date that offered Socreds the further advantage of absent university students. While the government had lost five by-elections in the previous year, three of them to up-and-coming New Democrats, boom conditions continued in British Columbia. Population growth at 3 percent was double the Canadian rate, while unemployment was at a three-year low of less than 5 percent of the labour force.[44] The robust economy provided an excellent backdrop for Bennett's usual pre-election routine, including new bills such as a

Human Rights Act and a splurge of new spending. So, too, did a summer of extensive labour unrest, which Premier Bennett exploited with the slogan: "Take home pay with Bennett or strike pay with Berger." The NDP leader later conceded that "our union affiliation did hurt us."[45]

Despite heightened expectations for the NDP, when the ballots were counted, Social Credit had taken thirty-eight seats, up five from 1966, and the NDP twelve, down four. The Liberal Party dropped one, to five. Tom Berger was one of the casualties. The 1969 platform reflected the Berger group's attempt since the early 1960s to define the NDP as a social democratic party. Socialist principles were "downplayed, ignored and almost contradicted," with no mention of economic planning and little commitment to the concept of a mixed economy, other than the take-over of BC Telephone and the promise of public auto insurance. Decentralization of health services and concern about social welfare funding continued to be emphasized, but there were also new emphases on pollution control and human rights that foreshadowed greater attention to social movement politics.[46] The NDP campaign itself focused on Berger's credentials as a lawyer, but the emphasis proved ineffective. The leader had not had time to familiarize himself with the hinterland regions of the province, and his tendency to overwhelm people, in the fashion of a lawyer presenting a case with "facts, logic, and repetition," did little to broaden electoral support.[47] There was, then, some truth to Bennett's charge that Tom Berger was a "city-slicker lawyer," though none to the premier's predictable screed that the Leader of the Opposition was an agent of "Marxist Socialism," or that Berger's leadership "marked a distinct turn to the left for the NDP."[48]

A longer view of BC provincial politics turns up a second cluster of two middle-class progressives who, like Berger and Young, had been influenced by the insights of Fabian socialism to believe that the "trained intelligence" of a "meritocratic public service" led by "quality people" could play an important role in shaping a "progressive" society. Yet, what is interesting about this second group is that one member, Dr. George Weir, had been recruited from the University of British Columbia by Pattullo to seek a seat for the provincial Liberals in the 1933 election and, once elected, to take on the social services portfolio as provincial secretary; and the other, Dr. Harry Cassidy, an assistant professor of social science at the University of Toronto, was hired by Weir to head BC's provincial planning office. The parallels between Weir and Cassidy from the 1930s and Berger and Young from the 1960s are uncanny.

Pattullo assigned Weir the task of modernizing his government's education and health services.[49] Described at his death in 1949 as "an advanced thinker," Weir throughout his career had embraced "new liberal" ideas emphasizing an activist state and a scientific response to social and economic problems.[50] Education reform was his obsession and, in a 1924 survey of provincial education co-directed with educator J. H. Putnam of Ottawa, he had forcefully promoted the educational philosophy of "progressivism," which emphasized child-centred learning, vocationalism, and enhanced testing and measurement. His *Survey of Nursing Education in Canada*, published in 1932, urged the adoption of scientific testing, "one of the foundation stones of progressive education," as well as the professionalization of nursing in place of traditional in-service hospital training.[51]

Convinced that society must encourage "more state intervention if people are to get the necessities of life," Weir made government-supported hospital and medical services his priority.[52] His enthusiasm for modernizing social services fit easily with Pattullo's commitment to organize a system of state health insurance, established as Liberal Party policy in 1932, and together the two men bear political responsibility for perhaps the Pattullo government's most significant achievement: the reorganization of health and welfare services. As historian Megan Davies has found, under their direction, British Columbia restructured and regularized hospital finances; rationalized community medicine; created specialized medical divisions to deal with venereal disease, tuberculosis, and vital statistics; and established a provincial laboratory system. Nowhere else in Canada, Davies argues, do public health reforms appear to have been "implemented on the systematic and wide-reaching scale that took place in one short decade in British Columbia."[53]

A key part of the thinking of new Liberals like Pattullo and Weir was the need to recruit into the provincial civil service professionally trained personnel. This was especially so at the administrative level where, in Weir's words, "a few highly trained men of outstanding ability and long experience" were required to "give real intellectual leadership" to government in areas such as health policy.[54] To this end, in June 1934, Weir recruited one of the University of Toronto's brightest young stars, Dr. Harry Cassidy, to head a provincial planning office.[55] Cassidy, like Weir, had been strongly influenced by the Fabian belief that a "trained intelligence" in the form of a "meritocratic public service" could play a central part in implementing government policy. He was one of the Toronto and Montreal members of the Fabian-oriented League for Social Reconstruction who, in 1933, contributed to a first draft of the CCF's philosophical principles, later rewritten by Underhill as the Regina Manifesto. Unbeknownst to Pattullo, Cassidy had also been a member of Toronto's St. Paul CCF Club until fall 1933.[56]

Cassidy represented an important change in thinking about government, a change that connected him to a North American-wide movement of middle-class reform. Like Weir, he was a social scientist who believed that empirical research would generate facts necessary to engineer a socially just society. In the early 1930s, he published important surveys on unemployment and relief in Ontario and labour conditions in Canada's men's clothing industry, and he wrote two of the chapters of *Social Planning for Canada*, published in 1935, with like-minded intellectuals to advance the LSR's reform agenda.[57] His social science and political activist connections extended to virtually every reform-minded thinker in the country, from League for Social Reconstruction members, such as Canadian historian Frank Underhill and Montreal lawyer Frank Scott, to the sociologist Leonard Marsh and the Social Science Research Project at McGill, to the Rockefeller Foundation that played a huge role in funding and promoting social science research during the interwar period in both the United States and Canada and that was "critical to public health expansion in B.C."[58] Reflecting his connections to a network of American "progressives," Cassidy labelled the Pattullo government's reforms "our local New Deal."[59] Cassidy stands as one of the important founders of the welfare state in Canada, including British Columbia, though his role in BC is little known.[60]

Yet, what also stands out about Cassidy, as it does for the Fabian-inspired leaders of the provincial NDP thirty years later, is how much he self-identified as middle-class. As told by historian Keith Walden, Harry and his wife Bea (née Beatrice Pearce) had "viewed the world from a middle-class perspective and hoped to build a better society by imposing middle class values on it."[61] To this end, after returning from the war, Cassidy, the son of a Fraser Valley dairy farmer, had set about constructing for himself "a middle-class professional identity" and, through "the alchemy of higher education," the persona of an "educated, cultured man." The "brand of socialism" that he embraced was, not surprisingly, that of "a mild Christian variety, aimed at alleviating the excesses of capitalism, not overthrowing the system."[62]

What, then, are we to make of the persistence of Fabian socialist influence on progressive politics across the formative period of CCF/NDP history in BC? First, the Strachan-Berger division underlines the extent to which the CCF in British Columbia continued into the sixties to be a plebeian party that remained culturally tied to its working-class roots. Strachan envisioned the NDP, in the tradition of the CCF, as a party of working people, while for the Berger group its future was to be found in an expanding middle class of skilled technicians, unionized workers, and professionals. Class differences were revealed in contrasting notions of rhetorical style, with Berger and Young stressing reasoned debate rather than, as Desmond Morton phrased it, "walloping the enemies of the common people."[63] Clearly Berger was challenging the cultural influences that had come to shape BC's rambunctious politics, a style that Strachan's bombastic speeches exemplified. Strachan represented a CCF that, while committed to a mixed rather than fully socialized economy, dwelt on economic issues and emphasized policies of state ownership. Thus, for example, Strachan's policy focus as NDP leader remained the nationalization of the telephone company, to the frustration of the Berger group. In addition, the CCF as Strachan envisioned it was a party of small producers, working people, and local communities, shaped by a populist critique of big capital but not a rejection of capitalism *per se*.

The Strachan tradition continued under the leadership of Dave Barrett, a university-educated social worker who became party leader in 1969 and premier in August 1972. Like Strachan, Barrett stood strongly against the influence of the big unions and from the outset as leader argued that "trade unionists should affiliate with the party as individuals—just like anyone else—and not as unions."[64] The NDP was "a broadly-based people's party rather than . . . a labour party," he insisted when reflecting back on his political career: it "is not a labour party" and "never has been a labour party."[65] In addition, Barrett's "mercurial, emotional, populist style," very much in the Strachan tradition rather than that of the Fabian-influenced "new party" progressives, was "trusted more by the old guard socialists" than was the intellectual demeanor of the "calmly rational" Berger.[66] In BC, the divisive politics of the late 1960s and early 1970s, rooted in substantially different conceptions of what the New Democratic party was to be, left "lingering animosities" and mutual distrust that one observer characterized as "almost a thing of legend" among New Democrats.[67]

Second, all four of the intellectuals examined here drew from a common reservoir of Fabian socialist ideas. Berger and Young espoused an interventionist form of "advanced" or "new" liberalism characterized by an activist state directed by middle-class professionals. Similarly, Cassidy's modernizing agenda had been shaped by the ideas of both Fabian socialists and "new (or statist) liberals," leading him to play what Michiel Horn describes as an "indefatigable role," along with other key LSR members such as Frank Underhill and Frank Scott, in promoting Canada's social reconstruction.[68] Yet, in British Columbia, where socialism had deep historical roots and where the resurgent CCF embraced a working-class and Marxist form of socialism, Harry Cassidy's decision to work with George Weir to advance LSR initiatives through the Duff Pattullo-directed Liberal government was for Cassidy an ideologically consistent act of political agency. In BC during the Great Depression, then, the unique strength of the left channeled the influence of Fabianism around rather than through the provincial CCF. The Fabian approach to social modernization re-emerged again in the 1960s as an important source of policy direction, this time in the NDP. For historians of the progressive left, the point is that an understanding of the provincial CCF's Marxist orientation in the 1930s should not obscure our understanding of the longer trajectory of progressive ideas that owed much to the influence of middle-class Fabians.[69]

CHAPTER 7

WAFFLING IN WINNIPEG AND LONDON

CANADA'S NEW LEFT AND THE NDP, 1965–75

David Blocker

The Waffle movement, which formed around the "Manifesto for an Independent and Socialist Canada" and challenged the leadership of the New Democratic Party (NDP) from 1969 to 1972, represents a dynamic convergence of many of the social movements that comprised the New Left in Canada. The Waffle argued that the NDP should promote socialist measures to combat American economic domination and ensure Canadian independence. NDP and trade union leaders, reluctant to adopt such a radical approach, expelled the Waffle from the Ontario NDP in 1972. By the mid-1970s, the national movement had lost momentum and, as a political force, faded into irrelevancy.

The history of the Waffle, however, is not only one of intra-party conflict, nor is the group's impact limited to the resurgent Canadian nationalism of the 1970s. Instead, the Waffle's struggle within the NDP both developed out of the existing work of New Left activists and inspired Wafflers to engage in local, extra-parliamentary struggles. This chapter examines the grassroots of the Waffle movement in two cities, London, Ontario, and Winnipeg, Manitoba, demonstrating that Waffle activists, in addition to working within the NDP to advocate for socialism and Canadian independence, engaged in extra-parliamentary social movements. These movements included second-wave feminism, anti-war protests, aid for draft resisters, and support for striking workers, as well as participating in municipal politics. This chapter, thus, extends our understanding of Canada's New Left during the "long sixties," demonstrating that Canadian New Left activists sought to achieve profound and transformative social and political change through both mainstream partisan politics and extra-parliamentary social movements.

The Waffle movement in the NDP emerged from supporters of the Waffle Manifesto at the 1969 federal NDP convention in Winnipeg. The manifesto, written by a group of young academics and party activists, including James Laxer, Mel Watkins, and Gerald Caplan, reflected the rising tide of Canadian nationalism, the exhilarating potential of youthful New Left social movements, and the disenchantment with the NDP expressed by the authors and many other leftists in the late 1960s. The Waffle challenged the established NDP leadership on a range of policy issues, most prominently public ownership, Quebec's right to self-determination, and gender parity within party structures, as well as mounting unsuccessful campaigns for the Saskatchewan and federal party leaderships. Accusing Wafflers of acting as "a party within a party," the Ontario NDP forced the Waffle to leave in the summer of 1972, and the Waffle in Saskatchewan left the NDP of its own accord the following year.[1]

The Waffle's struggles with the NDP and the labour movement took place primarily among the leadership of those respective groups. Former Waffler Dan Heap subsequently criticized the Waffle's "elitist tendency" and argued the group focused too much on "convention battles over policy statements."[2] However, local Waffle groups emerged in cities across Canada in response to the Waffle Manifesto's strident call for public ownership as a means of ensuring Canadian independence, and, to this point, little historical attention has been paid to the grassroots of the Waffle movement and the nature of their interaction with the local NDP.[3] The Waffle groups that emerged in Winnipeg and London can be considered typical of the movement. Each developed largely independently of the Waffle's national leadership, included over 100 people drawn from other elements of the New Left, and never managed to win control of the local NDP riding associations.

Over the winter holidays in 1969–70, an initial gathering of "about thirty" people established a Waffle group in Winnipeg following the manifesto's well-publicized defeat at the federal NDP convention just a few months before.[4] In many ways, Winnipeg was an ideal city for the Waffle to organize support. Winnipeg's status as the "gateway to the west" declined as the city grew and transformed in the post-war decades. In becoming a major urban centre for the surrounding hinterland, metropolitan Winnipeg increasingly dominated the province's economy, especially in finance, insurance, trade, services, construction, transportation, communications, and other utilities, and nearly two-thirds of the province's employment was in the city and its periphery.[5] Although the city of Winnipeg itself experienced a slight population decline in the 1960s, the rapid expansion of the surrounding suburban communities meant that metropolitan Winnipeg's population increased by over 30,000 to 540,000 in the five years prior to 1971.[6] Skyrocketing demand for post-secondary education led to the creation of the University of Winnipeg, newly separate from the University of Manitoba, in 1967.[7] The city historically attracted a diverse population, and in 1974 only 42.5 percent of the city's population identified their place of origin as the British Isles.[8] Although working-class north Winnipeg had a well-deserved reputation for radicalism, electing both CCF/NDP and communist representatives at municipal, provincial, and federal levels, south Winnipeg was equally conservative.[9] The city's municipal politics had been dominated by a pro-business, anti-socialist coalition since 1919, but the Manitoba NDP's provincial election victory in 1969 depended on strong urban support, and seventeen of the party's twenty-eight MLAs came from Winnipeg.

Although initially focused on the New Democratic Youth (NDY), Winnipeg Wafflers prepared position papers on economic development in Manitoba and on labour issues, hoping to influence the Manitoba provincial NDP convention in the autumn of 1970. Throughout 1970, a group met regularly in the Dimension Bookshop run by Cy Gonick, the NDP MLA for the Winnipeg riding of Crescentwood, for discussions about topics including foreign ownership, the Americanization of universities, and independent Canadian unions.[10] The Winnipeg-born Gonick had attended university in the United States but returned to Canada to teach in the early 1960s, founding the socialist magazine *Canadian Dimension* in 1963. Gonick joined the NDP and sought election with the encouragement of a group of his students and, to his own surprise, was elected by a narrow margin in June 1969. Gonick sat as a backbencher in NDP Premier Ed Schreyer's government, and, as a spokesperson for the Waffle in Manitoba, often criticized the government's policies from the left, arguing that American corporations exploited Manitoba as a "resource colony."[11]

Although the Waffle had an organized presence at the Manitoba NDP convention in November 1970, it was not able to win a majority of delegates to any of its positions, although the provincial party did override Premier Schreyer's objections by endorsing the federal caucus's position, supported by the Waffle, opposing the use of the War Measures Act.[12]

That fall, two young Wafflers, Arthur Schafer and Michael Mendelson, began hosting regular political education meetings, and the Manitoba Waffle elected a steering committee, chaired by Sheila Kuziak. However, because it struggled to attract members from outside Winnipeg, the Manitoba Waffle shifted its focus from the NDY to preparations for the federal NDP leadership convention planned for April 1971.[13] The Winnipeg Waffle group managed, by its own account, to elect "a number of delegates largely representing the New Democratic Youth and the federal constituency of Winnipeg South" to the federal NDP leadership convention in support of Waffle candidate James Laxer.[14]

In the summer of 1971 the group restructured, began publishing a newsletter for the Manitoba Waffle, and started to organize for Winnipeg's municipal elections, scheduled for October 1971. The group exhibited greater influence at the November 1971 Manitoba NDP convention, distributing pamphlets and winning support for several of its policy resolutions.[15] Despite this limited success, the Waffle did not engender widespread support among the convention's delegates. Gonick estimated that 125 of the 555 delegates were sympathetic to the Waffle, and Waffler Una Decter lost to incumbent party president Lawrence Bell in a 290 to 146 vote.[16] The Waffle held several educational meetings in the spring of 1972, but these were the "last real activities" of the Waffle in Winnipeg, as Gonick, personally exhausted by fighting losing battles in the NDP caucus and without significant Waffle support, decided not to run for re-election.[17] The Waffle in Manitoba had failed, not only to exert substantial influence on the provincial NDP, but also to extend its support much beyond Winnipeg. Indeed, all but seventeen of the 182 names on the Manitoba Waffle's mailing list in late 1971 were from Winnipeg.

Like the Waffle in Winnipeg, the Waffle in London drew a large portion of its members from the university, although, unlike Winnipeg, it also had a base in the labour movement, specifically in the large United Autoworkers (UAW) Local 27. London, in the late 1960s and early 1970s, was, in many ways, true to its image as a conservative, white, Anglo-Saxon Protestant town. The city of 200,000 was home to insurance and trust companies and to John Robarts, Conservative premier of Ontario from 1961 to 1971. However, there were also signs of change. The city had grown rapidly through a decade of suburban expansion and industrial growth. The University of Western Ontario (UWO) also expanded, adding eight new academic buildings and three student residences through the 1960s, while Fanshawe College of Applied Arts and Technology opened in

1967.[18] Immigration changed the face of London in this period, as diverse communities expanded across the city.[19] Furthermore, London fostered a dynamic art scene in the 1960s, and nationally renowned artists worked, taught, and met in a vibrant creative atmosphere.[20] Although the two traditional parties had long dominated London's politics, this too began to change in the 1960s. In 1969, Anglican archdeacon and NDP candidate Kenneth Bolton was elected in a by-election in Middlesex South, a riding containing part of London, and Jane Bigelow became the city's first female and first NDP mayor in 1972.[21]

The key figures in the London Waffle were Mary and Al Campbell. Mary Campbell, who worked at the UWO library, was active in a variety of social justice groups, including the Committee to End Canada's Complicity in Viet Nam, the Voice of Women, and the Women's Auxiliary for Auto Workers. She was also involved in early attempts to unionize staff at the university.[22] Hilary Bates Neary, who worked with Mary Campbell, describes her as "an organizer . . . She knew exactly why she held certain political attitudes and beliefs. I'm not saying she was a rabid proselytizer, but she never lost an opportunity to remind people why things were the way they were and how they could change."[23] She and Margaret Simpson, a social work professor at Fanshawe College, remember Mary Campbell welcoming and helping American draft evaders in addition to her other activism. Both Mary Campbell and her husband Al, a former president of UAW Local 27, were active in the NDP riding association and supported Waffle positions, with limited success, at local party meetings. In addition to Mary Campbell, the London Waffle mailing list featured the names of professors and graduate students at UWO, alongside Al Campbell's co-workers at the Eaton Automotive plant, and members of London's burgeoning arts community. Among several London artists involved with the Waffle, Greg Curnoe is the most well-known.[24] In 1968, Curnoe had gained national notoriety for his 110-foot mural at Montreal's Dorval airport, which was taken down after only four days for its "anti-American" content.[25] In 1972, the group's mailing list included 128 names, although this is likely not truly indicative of the group's support in London, as a number of New Democrats included on the list ran for party offices in opposition to the Waffle or denied any involvement in the Waffle.[26] Another London Waffler, Paddy Musson, a professor at Fanshawe College, suggests, "Mary Campbell would see all of those people as people she could talk into supporting something she was interested in."[27]

The London Waffle's primary activity outside the NDP was support for workers, demonstrated by opposing the closure of the American-owned Eaton Automotive factory and traveling to Brantford in support of striking workers at a Texpack plant. In the summer of 1972, the London Waffle helped to organize the Ontario Waffle's conference in Delaware, where, after contentious debate, the group split, and the majority decided to leave the NDP to form the Movement for an Independent Socialist Canada (MISC). Mary Campbell was one of three MISC candidates in the 1974 federal election, but she achieved only a fraction of the NDP's vote in the riding of Middlesex-Lambton-London.[28]

Like the Waffle in London, the Winnipeg Waffle directed its efforts at local issues, taking an active interest in the 1971 municipal election in Winnipeg. Despite many of the manifesto's original authors' familiarity with the successful community-organizing efforts in north Kingston that, supported by the local NDP, resulted in the election of a New Left activist to council, the leadership of the Ontario Waffle showed little organized interest in municipal politics.[29] However, Wafflers outside of Ontario undertook several municipal election campaigns. The creation of the "unicity" in 1971, and the first municipal elections for the newly amalgamated metropolis of Winnipeg in the fall of that year, engendered much local public debate, including among members of the Winnipeg Waffle. Furthermore, the NDP had decided to run an organized slate of candidates on a unified municipal party platform. The Winnipeg Waffle, concerned that "unless the left within the party draws up a concrete set of proposals for the NDP's policy convention, there can be little doubt that the party will run on a platform indistinguishable from the platform of real estate groups," organized an Urban Policy Conference in June 1971.[30] At the conference, the Winnipeg Waffle developed policies on housing, taxation, transportation, and citizen involvement in the Unicity, planning to support the nominations of Waffle sympathizers and left-wingers for NDP candidacies in the upcoming municipal election.[31] At the NDP's Municipal Policy Convention in August 1971, the Winnipeg Waffle was, in its own description, "relatively successful in winning support for its policies."[32] Indeed, the NDP's municipal platform strongly reflected the Waffle's policy goals and included proposals for public ownership of the Greater Winnipeg Gas Company, the creation of a Winnipeg public housing corporation, a mass-transit system, and a more progressive taxation system.

Although Waffle sympathizer and incumbent Metro councillor Andrew Robertson lost to fellow councillor Art Coulter for the party's election chairman by a vote of 125 to 90, Robertson was elected to a three-man leadership committee for the municipal NDP organization, and the Waffle successfully passed a resolution binding NDP councillors to the party's policy platform.[33] Nevertheless, only three of the Waffle-supported candidates won nomination as NDP candidates, and none were elected in the October general election.[34] In fact, the NDP elected only seven councillors, while the right-wing Independent Citizens' Election Committee (ICEC) won thirty-seven seats; however, one Waffle-supported candidate and four other New Democrats achieved success in elections to the school board, creating a left-wing majority on Winnipeg's board.[35]

The London Waffle's primary extra-parliamentary activity was to support local left-wing labour causes. Al Campbell, as president of the large UAW Local 27, was the long-time editor of the local's newsletter.[36] Campbell was a former member and candidate for the Communist Party (CP) who, although he had left the CP in 1956, was still regarded as a leftist within the UAW by the union leadership.[37] However, in 1971 the Eaton Automotive plant in London, which had been the base of the left wing of UAW Local 27, closed, and Campbell had no choice but to leave the UAW.[38] The Waffle responded by organizing a meeting in London in the spring of 1971 to decry plant closures by American-owned companies. Alongside the activists of the Militant Co-Op group, London Wafflers picketed the Eaton Automotive plant but were unable to inspire any further action, such as an occupation, by the workers.[39] In September 1971, London Waffle supporters became involved in the Texpack strike in Brantford. The strike involved a small, independent Canadian union representing a primarily female workforce fighting a large American-based multinational corporation.[40] While wages and benefits were at the forefront of the strike, the leaders of the Canadian Textile and Chemical Union (CTCU) saw the phasing out of manufacturing operations in Brantford as fundamental. The CTCU claimed the American Hospital Supply Corporation was using the Texpack plant to repackage and sterilize surplus US army bandages and label them "Made in Canada," suggesting that the company planned to turn the Texpack plant from a thriving manufacturing operation into little more than a warehouse.[41] The tensions of the strike were exacerbated by the company's hiring of replacement workers and then seeking, and being granted, an injunction limiting picket lines at the plant. The protection given to replacement workers by the Brantford police was another source of frustration for the striking workers. While the local labour movement was sympathetic to the strike, the leaders of the CTCU, Kent Rowley and

Madeleine Parent, had been expelled from the mainstream labour move-ment in the communist purges of the 1950s, and, during the strike, the Textile Workers Union of America, affiliated with the Canadian Labour Congress, raided the CTCU's Collingwood local and attempted to sign up replacement workers.[42]

The Texpack strike encapsulated a number of significant issues for the Waffle, including Canadian economic underdevelopment, foreign ownership, exploitation of female workers, and the influence of conser-vative international unions. London Waffler and UWO professor Craig Simpson recalls:

> The issue involved the strikebreakers, who were coming up in their buses, and he [Rowley] broke the containment of the police and ran off in front and tried to position himself—like the man in Tiananmen Square with the tank—and the lead bus had to stop. And he was whacked a couple of times by the cops and hauled out of the way. And that infuriated many of us, and the cops formed a cordon protecting the area for the buses to go into plant.[43]

As the crowd of demonstrators surged forward, the police ordered them to disperse, as the court injunction limited the number of pickets at the plant to seven. Several Wafflers became involved in heated arguments with the police, including Craig Simpson, who had to be restrained by his friends. Waffler Henry Roper, another UWO professor, was arrested along with thirteen others, including Al Campbell and London UAW member James Napier.[44] Although the strike was not resolved until October, the Waffle's participation in the Texpack demonstration drew attention to the company's use of replacement workers and the Waffle's criticisms of for-eign ownership.

As in the broader Waffle, the London and Winnipeg Waffle groups attracted activists in the burgeoning women's liberation movement, includ-ing those involved in the creation of a Women's Resource Centre, Abor-tion Action Committees, and consciousness-raising groups. Women's lib-erationists in the Waffle were among the organizers of the 1970 Abortion Caravan, which travelled across the country to protest against the contin-ued criminalization of many abortions and the difficulty in accessing legal abortions in many parts of the country, and Wafflers welcomed the caravan as it arrived in each city.[45] The Abortion Caravan held a press conference at the University of Winnipeg, where a travelling member of the Vancouver Women's Caucus promoted their abortion information service, explaining, "within five years women will come to women's liberation groups instead of psychiatrists . . . they will realize they're not mentally ill in seeking an abortion."[46] Winnipeg Wafflers and women's liberationists were also active in the Abortion Action Committee of Winnipeg. They responded to Manitoba NDP Cabinet minister Joe Borowski's high-profile opposition to abortion by supporting the health clinics criticized by Borowski for referring women to resources for legal, out-of-province abortions and by demanding that Borowski and other anti-abortion MLAs be driven out of the NDP.[47] Some of the most contentious convention debates between the Waffle and the party and union leadership took place over the women's liberationists' demand for increased guaranteed women's representation on party bodies, such as executive and council. After the NDP federal council refused to seat five female delegates elected by a women's committee at the party's convention, Carol Fogel, a thirty-six-year-old Waffle sympathizer and executive assistant to Manitoba Cabinet minister Philip Petursson, suggested that the youth and activist backgrounds of the women contributed to the party's refusal to seat them at the council in Toronto, commenting, "I think if we had elected four nice middle-aged women, they wouldn't have protested."[48]

Indeed, women's liberationists such as Jackie Larkin, Varda Burstyn, Krista Maeots, and Kelly Crichton took on high-profile roles in the Waffle. Female Wafflers in Winnipeg recall the effect of seeing other women taking on leadership roles in the group, and one anonymous Waffler commented, "The activity of other women in the Waffle in speaking had an impact developing my confidence, overcoming feelings of shyness and intimidation."[49] Two Waffle-backed candidates in the 1971 municipal elections, Carol Fogel for council and Gloria Mendelson for school board trustee, were encouraged by their experience in the women's liberation movement to become political candidates. As one female Winnipeg Waffler explains, "The women's liberation movement says go, do, fight, it gives an impetus and a motivation to activity."[50]

However, the relationship between women's liberationists and the Waffle was sometimes strained. One woman in the Winnipeg Waffle explained:

> During Waffle educations there was a kind of intellectual one-upmanship. I often had strong arguments with the men about this. The whole consciousness raising experience and democratic thing, the sense of the quality of experience and environment, isn't part of male culture, and therefore you can't bring that into political life.[51]

Another Winnipeg Waffle woman suggested that the "women's liberation movement has forced men in the Waffle to look at themselves to see if they are male chauvinists."[52] Male Wafflers asked about the effect of the women's liberation movement described their appreciation of the necessity of changes in both their personal relationships and conduct and their political structures and priorities.[53] Yet not all female Wafflers were convinced of the immediacy or extent of their male counterparts' conversions.

Similarly, the experience of women's liberationists in the London Waffle led the women to deepen their commitment to feminist activism. Paddy Musson remembers being asked to leave the Delaware conference after a confrontation with a Waffle leader. She recalls:

> He came in and made this broad statement in terms of this issue, and as an energized university student who was interested in social change, I thought his analysis had serious flaws in it. I dared to tell him and I was told to be quiet and I told him that I owned this meeting as much as he did and that the whole principle of the Waffle was to move away from the domination of the party centre control and . . . here he was practising the same techniques that had been practised by the party centrally and that was the point at which I left.[54]

Neither Paddy Musson nor Margaret Simpson remembers the Waffle as a feminist movement. Margaret Simpson recalls feeling like "an onlooker" at the Delaware conference, and neither she nor Musson saw signs of either feminist concerns or female leadership. Simpson remembers, "I feel I was just some young kid trailing along on the coattails of the professors who understood about socialism, the political movement, and the CCF."[55] Her main commitment, however, was to feminism. In comparing the fun and excitement of her involvement with feminist groups and actions in the 1970s to the Waffle experience, Paddy Musson recalls, "The Waffle was not fun. Those were not fun men . . . they were earnest, all of them."[56] Thus, the Waffle not only attracted women's liberationists, but the experience of women within the Waffle in both London and Winnipeg strengthened their commitment to feminism and inspired them to greater political involvement.

The story of the Waffle's conflict with the NDP and union leadership as a result of the group's efforts to reshape the NDP into a socialist and nationalist party has achieved a certain notoriety.[57] However, the experience of grassroots activists involved in the Waffle and NDP at a local level has received little attention. In fact, the story of the Waffle at the grassroots, as seen in Winnipeg and London, contributes significantly to the conventional narrative of intra-party conflict. Indeed, the story of the Waffle in Winnipeg and London indicates that activists in a variety of New Left social movements were attracted to traditional electoral politics as a result of the Waffle's efforts to shift the NDP to the left, even as party members, influenced by the Waffle, worked toward an independent and socialist Canada through extra-parliamentary, non-electoral means.

CHAPTER 8

NEW LEFTISTS, "PARTY-LINERS," AND MUNICIPAL POLITICS IN TORONTO

Peter Graham

The Toronto municipal election of December 1, 1969, saw the beginning of a radical turn to the left with the election of two young New Left-influenced alderpersons in Ward 7. Both John Sewell and Karl Jaffary helped pioneer a new kind of grassroots politics, which emphasized participatory democracy and clashed with the ideas of many veteran NDPers. The city's social democratic mayor, William Dennison, claimed their views smacked of communism. As the 1970s progressed, left-wing community organizations mobilized to elect more radical candidates. Their efforts helped redefine muncipal left-wing politics by fusing it with a distinct New Left urban vision. A study of radical community organizations, focusing on the Ward Six Community Organization, the Movement for Municipal Reform, and selected individuals like Jack Layton, reveals the surprising influence of New Left ideas on both city politics and social democracy. But by the end of the decade, its importance declined, as activists were forced to choose between competing movement and party priorities.

New Leftism is frequently associated with student movements, but it actually set the pace for left-wing activism across the city. In sharp contrast to the centralized, bureaucracy-laden governments of communists and social democrats, New Leftists envisioned a decentralized society, operated largely by self-managed communities.[1] Residents would design and control their neighbourhoods, tenants would manage their apartment buildings, parents, students, and teachers would operate schools, and so on. Pedestrians and small-scale developments were favoured over automobiles,

expressways, and other megaprojects formerly hailed as ideologically neu-
tral symbols of a modern city. The socialist future would be postmodern.

The local movement's first victories came amidst an upsurge in
municipally focused social movement activity. Prior to their victory, Jaffary and Sewell had taken an active role in mobilizing working-class residents against "neighbourhood destroying" urban renewal projects. And the
tenant movement, which only began to take off in the late 1960s, would
also play an outsized role. Black power, feminism, gay and lesbian liberation, and other social movements became more influential later on. Though
this chapter focuses on council politics, the New Left's greatest electoral
influence was at the public school board level, where many trustees could
unreservedly be called New Leftists. Most left-wing alderpersons, on the
other hand, could be more accurately described as having been influenced
by New Left ideas.

A broadly similar New Leftism urbanism could be found in many
European and North American cities. Paris' famous May 1968 uprising,
for example, spawned campaigns to halt new expressways and stop urban
renewal projects, which would not have looked out of place in Toronto.
Closer to home, the Montreal Citizens' Movement and Vancouver's Coalition of Progressive Electors reflected many of the trends seen in left-wing
Toronto politics during the 1970s.[2]

Left-wing community organizing itself was hardly a distinct New
Left phenomenon. Communists and social democrats had been doing it
for decades. Members of the Co-operative Commonwealth Federation
(the NDP's predecessor) founded residents' associations and had been
leaders in struggles against urban renewal through the 1950s. These organizing campaigns enhanced the party's grassroots credibility and helped
the Ontario NDP win seats in Toronto's east-end during the early 1960s.[3]
But the NDPers who had sat on council prior to the 1969 election were a
rather sorry lot. Each of them had decades of experience in municipal politics, but they lacked the ambitious policy proposals and big ideas that had
once animated the city's social democratic alderpersons. And some of their
socially conservative views placed them at odds with younger leftists. Most
of them foreswore the possiblility of bringing social change to city hall by
joining a Progressive Conservative-dominated body whose sole purpose
was to secure the re-election of city hall incumbants.

John Sewell was an exemplar of what he called the "new politics."
Like many of his youthful peers, he had started moving to the left because
of the war in Vietnam. His disagreements with the status quo multiplied

after joining the Toronto Union Community Project, a New Left-influenced group dedicated to helping residents fight against urban renewal. Project members believed that residents had to be directly and democratically involved with all decision-making, from organizing opposition activity to planning the neighbourhoods of tomorrow. As Sewell recalled: "In my mind it was the process that was all important." When asked to consider running for the NDP, he refused, because he thought the party was too focused on elections and out of touch with the ward's grassroots. The main role of an alderperson, as he saw it, was to serve as a community organizer and help solve issues prioritized by residents themselves.[4]

Karl Jaffary was also a passionate opponent of the war in Vietnam and had led one of the ward's most influential residents' associations. The first year that the NDP ran official party candidates in a Toronto municipal election was 1969, and Jaffary was one of those candidates. The party's most prominent policy promise was to amalgamate the cities that made up Metro Toronto. Yet its election platform also contained proposals more germaine to the emerging New Left moment in urban politics. It opposed all downtown expressways, supported collective bargaining rights for tenants, promised an independent citizens review board for the police, and included free public transit as a long-term goal. Though it envisioned a system of ward councils, the proposed bodies lacked the kind of grassroots decision-making powers coveted by New Leftists and were likely a sop to those afraid that amalgamation would weaken local democracy. But the platform's call for school and community education councils, and promises of student and teacher "self-determination," offered real power instead of mere participation.[5]

All of those promises were overshadowed by the attention lavished on the mayoral race, where NDP member William Dennison successfully sought re-election. Dennison had won his first term promising economic constraint and low taxes and was now supported by all the city's major newspapers and property developers. Refusing to run as an official party candidate, he was "out-lefted" by both his main rivals, who were members of the Liberal and Progressive Conservative parties. Dennison claimed that members of the NDP's left-wing Waffle caucus had joined one of the rival campaigns hoping to defeat him.[6]

After their election, both Ward 7 alderpersons tried to bring direct and decentralized democracy to their constituents. They established a ward council in early 1970 so that residents could hear from their elected representatives and tell them how to vote on key issues. These meetings initially attracted a hundred residents on average, but the council later disbanded after attendence shrunk to a handful of constituents. An attempt to revive it some months later floundered amidst similarly disappointing turnouts. In lieu of this council, Jaffary and Sewell did their best to consult with local community organizations before voting on issues at city hall, a practice that clearly annoyed some of their fellow alderpersons. In supporting this neighbourhood-focused democracy, Sewell was occasionaly subjected to accusations that he was a dangerous, American-style New Leftist. Jaffary, who tended to more cautious rhetoric, claimed that popular democratic bodies like ward councils had been pioneered by the Co-operative Commonwealth Federation and were thus a Canadian tradition.[7]

Jaffary and Sewell frequently worked as a tag-team during city council sessions. Both were intent on busting up what they considered to be a cozy club unduly influenced by corporate lobbyists. To this end, they sought to polarize debate and politicize issues before council, sometimes using guerilla theatre to emphasis that the real decisions were being made in back rooms with lobbyists or to lampoon conservative councillors.[8] Their style and politics exacerbated existing differences with NDPers seen to support the status quo. In two particularly heated moments, Dennison claimed that Jaffary had hit him (film evidence showed otherwise) and Horace Brown struck Sewell in the face, knocking off his glasses. Relations were less fraught with Reid Scott, a career NDP politican who had served as an MP and MPP before being elected to council in 1969, but he tended to be seen as a member of council's "old guard." Archie Chisholm, the third novice NDP alderman, tended to take Scott's lead, but was also prone to agree with Jaffary. The duo had stronger working relationships with a handful of Liberals and Progressive Conservatives who self-identified as "reformers."

With the 1972 election approaching, none of the NDP councillors wanted to run under the party label. They were arguably making a pragmatic decision, recognizing that formally independent incumbents stood better chances of re-election. But while Scott wanted to end the NDP's special relationship with organized labour, seeing it as a barrier to attracting business owners and professionals, Jaffary sought to increase the party's ties to social movements. He co-chaired a federal NDP committee on social movements with Waffle spokesperson James Laxer, which urged the party to form ties with community-based organizations like tenants' associations. Locally, Jaffary thought that a broad coalition was needed, encompassing the NDP, unions, and community organizations. He was inspired by the Front d'action politique (FRAP), a radical municipal party in Montreal, and hoped something similar could be built in Toronto. He was on the same page as many local New Leftists, who embraced FRAP's grassroots activism and support for community control as a model. Some of the most radical proposals advanced by Toronto New Left urban activists during this decade first appeared in FRAP's 1970 platform.[9]

But there was still no FRAP-style party in 1972, when the next municipal elections occurred. Some activists hoped a loose network called Community Organizing in 1972 could fill this role and bring "people power" to city hall. But there was a discernable split between socialist and social democratic candidates campaigning in low- and middle-income wards and liberal-leaning candidates running in more prosperous areas, who thought their couterparts were "too radical." In the end, the low-profile network did little beyond distributing donations to the reform-oriented candidates it had endorsed. Many of them won election, including NDP members Michael Goldrick, Dan Heap, and Dorothy Thomas. All three shared Jaffary's New Left-tinged politics rather than the business-like social democracy embraced by Brown and Scott.[10]

The election of Thomas proved particularly important for pushing feminist issues like wage equity, affirmative action, and daycare onto council's agenda. She voiced her preference to be called a councillor rather than an alderman, won the right not to be referred to as "Mrs." during council meetings, and worked with the Rape Crisis Centre to campaign for a police unit dedicated to investigating sexual assaults. In putting forth a motion for sexist literature to be banned from municipal waiting rooms, she cited passages from a public health leaflet that dwelt on the importance of lipstick (because "Boys like girls to look like girls") and encouraged traditional conceptions of womanhood ("the most important career of all: being a wife and mother"). Yet Scott staunchly opposed her motion and defended the leaflet, placing feminism among the growing number of issues which divided "old guard" New Democrats from New Left-leaning party members.[11]

Heap was close in age to the more conservative NDPers on council, but was a staunch socialist, unionist, and peace activist who accepted many of the new mores in left-wing politics. In fact, his rare brand of religious radicalism made him somewhat avante garde, from his embrace of pacifism in the 1950s to the multi-family commune he lived in as of the mid-1960s. As an Anglican "worker-priest," his dedication to working among the people for social justice was both a religious and political commitment. He had been a factory worker for almost two decades when he won election in downtown's Ward 6, beating two incumbant alderpersons, including Brown.[12]

The ward's urban activists had previously tried to make links between community organizations and draw in more residents by establishing the Ward Six Citizen Council, but that venture ultimately failed. With Heap's victory, the concept was immediately revived and the Ward Six Council was established to foster collaboration between local community groups and increase their leverage over local politicians. This new council was delegate-based and largely consisted of representatives from the ward's parent, resident, and tenant associations. Members of nationality-based organizations were also allowed to serve as delegates in order to encourage outreach to non-English-speaking residents. Delegates discussed a range of neighbourhood-specific and city-wide issues and tried to co-ordinate some of their activities. They investigated the effects of lead pollution from a local refinery, advocated for rent controls, and fought against a large apartment complex proposed for Chinatown, which some Chinese activists saw as part of a broader pattern of racial discrimination and gentrification ("white painting" was the phrase used in the 1970s). But the council was plagued by questions about its ueesefulness and representativeness.[13]

By early 1974, it was replaced by a much stronger group called the Ward Six Community Organization (W6CO). As a more unitary organization, it issued a platform, highlighting its demands. Roughly half of them would not have been out of place in an old left-wing election leaflet. But calls for "local control over local issues," the elimination of cars from the downtown core, and "community control of schools" were part of a New Left urban agenda.[14]

There continued to be calls for a city- or metro-wide organization that would bring left-wing urban activists and politicians together. In early 1974, W6CO's Joan Dorion wrote a proposal for a Toronto-wide organization of community, tenant, labour, and education activists. It could be a movement, or a party, but had to be "horizontal" and "non-elitist." The proposed aims of the organization were rather vague—"A more humane city"; "People able to control their own lives/environment"; "Decentralization, stopping urban sprawl, etc."—but evoked the New Left's emphasis on community and self-determination.[15]

But there were only scattered attempts to realize the broad aims of this proposal until after the 1974 municipal elections, which largely reproduced 1972's results. The left's only seat pick up was by Allan Sparrow, an active member of the North Jarvis Community Association and W6CO.

After witnessing police violence at a 1970 anti-war demonstration, Sparrow had become very critical of law enforcement, and as an alderman would become reknown for defending civil liberties and criticizing the police department.[16]

Within days of the election, a gathering of 150 urban activists and councillors agreed to move ahead with forming a municipal coalition or party. A proposal written by Sewell outlined possible roles for alderpersons and suggested a new organization could be "a means of helping left groups to organize and express their power." A subsequent meeting decided on an interim steering committee composed of two representatives from each ward, with additional seats given to delegates from the Confederation of Resident and Ratepayer Associations, the Federation of Metro Tenants, and the labour council. The committee drafted a series of competing proposals and called a June conference, where delegates voted to form a metro-wide federation.[17]

The Movement for Municipal Reform, better known as ReforMetro, was formally founded in November. It largely mirrored W6CO in terms of its policies, which included decentralization, localized democracy, and community-controlled services. Its inaugural convention succeeeded in attracting a smatterring of activists from the boroughs surrounding Toronto, including a couple of North York councillors. All of Toronto's New Left-tinged alderpersons eventually became members. Scott, the only NDPer on council not to join, later scolded his colleagues for their "extreme position on the Left" and made a point of endorsing Metro Chairman Paul Godfrey, the bête noire of the city's left-wing reformers.[18]

By 1976, ReforMetro had active organizations in East York, North York, Scarborough, and about half of Toronto's wards. Its most high-profile campaign that year was against a transit fare increase, which gathered 15,000 petition signatures and drew 500 protesters to rallies at city hall and Queen's Park. In the lead up to December's municipal elections, ReforMetro candidates continued to see themselves as servants of a larger social movement. In a joint campaign leaflet, Heap and Sparrow presented themselves as modest community organizers:

> Well-meaning aldermen cannot do much against the entrenched power of big business. The million working people of Metro have the power to stand up to big business, but only by organizing. We offer ourselves to help in that organizing.[19]

The only wrinkle in the run-up to the polls was Thomas' resignation from city hall's reform caucus over a seemingly minor disagreement. In skewering her former colleagues—"The working-class people in my ward say they're glad I left the Reform Caucus. They say, 'We're glad you split from that bunch of crazies'"—she added credence to a critique advanced by conservative opponents of ReforMetro, who argued that its alderpersons were elitist, extreme, and polarizing.[20] But Thomas also announced that she would not seek re-election and ReforMetro made modest gains on election day.

Yet, criticisms within the NDP of ReforMetro began to proliferate. At first, the most vocal critics were members of two Trotskyist organizations active in the party. Both opposed New Left ideas like community control and saw ReforMetro as a "trap" preventing workers from voting for a workers' party. They campaigned for the NDP to run a full slate of municipal candidates, even if it meant supporting individuals who were more conservative than those backed by left-wing community organizations. In 1977, they played a pivotal role in a narrow vote rejecting participation in ReforMetro at an NDP regional conference, but were still unable to convince the party to run its own candidates. Heap confessed that he liked the idea of a party slate, but told the conference that it had to be a long-term goal because the NDP was still unable to mount an effective municipal campaign and needed closer ties to community-based social movements. Sparrow, rather less diplomatically, told conference delegates that the NDP had no base, would be unable to provide a real alternative, and that the idea of a party slate was "bullshit."[21]

Opposition to ReforMetro also became acute in Ward 4. In 1976, an NDP association there became the only one in Toronto to run its own municipal candidate. As with the Trotskyists, organized resistance to ReforMetro came largely from leftists who saw the party as indispensible for any meaningful social changes. The association's nominee, Joe Pantalone, hewed closer to traditional left policies than Lee Zaslofsky, who was ReforMetro's candidate in the ward. Though both men were party members, trying to push the NDP to the left, Pantalone promised he would never caucus with other left-wingers on council unless they agreed to run on an NDP slate in future elections. Both candidates lost, but Pantalone picked up more votes than Zaslofsky.[22]

By late 1977, these leftists were joined by more centrist party members. Key labour council figures, who allegedly saw ReforMetro as a bunch of middle-class homeowners concerned about neighbourhoods and not workers, took the initiative. They got most local NDP MPPs onboard and the party's Metro Toronto Area Council onside. Supporters of ReforMetro saw the move as part of "the same old conflict between activists and party-liners," which had resulted in the expulsion of the left-wing Waffle caucus from the NDP. In early 1978, the NDP council voted to establish ward-based party organizations and compete in municipal elections. This had immediate reverberations in Ward 6, when Heap and two trustees announced they would now run as NDP candidates and sever their relationship with W6CO.[23]

In justifying his decision to switch slates, Heap argued that an NDP campaign would be guided by a "socialist tradition" that would link local issues to "deeper and wider" ones. He questioned the organizational competency of his erstwhile compatriots, insisted the NDP would ensure better accountability from its elected candidates, and accused ReforMetro of acting like it had a monopoly on running left-wing candidates in municipal elections. Heap wanted to run a completely separate campaign from W6CO, but the ward's NDP members vetoed that idea. When Sparrow later won more votes, Heap complained (with some justification) that W6CO had minimized Heap's name in its campaign literature, fuelling further acrimony. As the NDP solidified its presence on the municipal scene, more ReforMetro candidates defected to run as NDPers, including most New Left school board trustees. Despite an NDP ultimatum that any candidate receiving their nomination from a community organization would not be endorsed by the party and could expect a party competitor, ReforMetro continued to run candidates in 1980.[24]

After Sparrow announced he would not seek re-election, W6CO hosted a particularly vigorous nomination battle. The contest pitted Ryerson professor Jack Layton against George Hislop, a gay activist whose politics were considered excessively liberal, even by some of his own supporters. While Hislop disagreed with some of W6CO's platform planks, opposed the group's long-term goals of an auto-free downtown and the eventual abolition of private property, and would not commit to supporting the organization's candidate if he lost, Layton's only quible was that the platform's targets for subsidized housing units were too modest. But Sparrow had gained the reverence of many activists because of his unrelenting fight for police reform and his strong support for gay liberation, and made it widely known that he wanted a gay activist to succeed him.[25]

W6CO trustee Joan Dorion, on the other hand, told members she would have great difficulty working with Hislop. She criticized him for not

being a member of the NDP and highlighted his questionable commitment to W6CO. She lauded Layton's dedication to the organization and
urged members to vote for "a socialist who is committed to [the] decentralization of political structures." Others argued, on seemingly pragmatic
grounds, that Hislop had a strong support base, while Layton was a root-
less academic, or that the ward's Chinese and Portuguese residents would
not support a gay candidate. In the end, Hislop won, 199 votes to 161.[26]

Hislop's nomination win, and the later election of an openly lesbian
COPE candidate in Vancouver, were partly due to the New Left's relatively intersectional ideology. While the NDP had adopted some gay- and
lesbian-friendly policies at its conventions, members of the public were
more apt to have heard local MP Andrew Brewin denounce homosexuality as a "sickness," or BC Premier David Barrett congratulate China for
having "cured" it. Lots of social democrats probably shared federal leader
Ed Broadbent's concern that getting involved in the issue would hurt the
party's electoral chances. Though Heap did not share Brewin's bigotry, he
could not understand why activists would specifically seek out gay or lesbian candidates. Discussions at city hall rarely touched upon sexual orientation, he observed, and gay and lesbian struggles did not seem to fit into
his "old left" socialist program: "I don't see gay rights issues related to the
general concerns of the working class . . ."[27]

The 1980 election proved to be a huge dissappointment for the left.
In a campaign beset by a reactionary homophobic tone, Sewell failed to
win re-election as mayor, Hislop lost to Progressive Conservtive member Gordon Chong by over 2,000 votes, and some left-wing trustees were
defeated. All of these losing candidates had supported gay liberation to
some degree, and in the election's aftermath, many NDPers appeared to
agree with Sewell's campaign manager that "1980 was a bit too early in the
twentieth century for that issue."[28]

ReforMetro, W6CO, and other electorally oriented community
organizations whithered in the aftermanth of the vote. Yet aspects of their
activist, New Left ideology could be found within the municipal NDP
through the work of former ReforMetro activists such as Jack Layton.

When writing about the New Left in the early 1970s, Layton had
tended to hew to more traditional socialist perspectives. He praised the
New Left for resurrecting radical egalitarian ideas, but believed it had
accepted liberal notions of individualism and failed to adequately link
inequality to private property. He also emphasized that participatory
democracy was more important in workplaces than in community settings.

A new ideology would be needed, he speculated, to bridge a disjuncture between "traditional workers' ideologies" and what he called "the new sensibility" and "the new culture."[29]

In joining the Waffle, Layton found something approaching the kind of synthesis between old left and New Left ideas that he thought was necessary, and he remained a member until its dissolution in the mid-1970s. Meanwhile, he had developed a keen interest in municipal politics. He had campaigned for FRAP in Montreal's 1970 election and enrolled in Michael Goldrick's urban studies class shortly after arriving in Toronto (his class paper was on "The Community Power Debate"). When Goldrick decided to run for council in late 1972, Layton signed on as his campaign manager. From his home in North York, he founded and supported a number of the borough's community organizations and campaigns. And when ReforMetro was struck, Layton joined it and eventually headed its North York chapter. Mimicking developments in Toronto, the area's NDP associations decided to form a borough-wide organization to combat the chapter's influence: "agreed that North York NDP should be set up to present alternative to reform Metro . . ."[30]

At the turn of the decade, Layton decided to move downtown. As a Ryerson professor and budding progressive politician, Ward 6 was both convenient and strategic. He immediately joined W6CO, which continued to demand ambitious programs, like free twenty-four-hour daycare and transit, and support New Left ideas. Issues like racism and minority representation had increased in importance and W6CO's statements against prejudice became more encompassing: "Discrimination on the basis of race, creed, ethnic group, national origin, socio-economic class, sexual orientation, physical and mental disability and against striking workers must be ended." Potential candidates were now formally expected to "take initiatives and speak out on behalf of minority groups and against racism, sexism and homophobia."[31]

Despite growing opinion in favour of running a full slate of candidates under the NDP's banner, Layton continued to be uncomfortable with the idea. He feared the party would be too focused on electoral activity, to the detriment of grassroots community campaigns that were more effective agents of social change. He disagreed with activists who insisted the NDP would ensure better accountability, arguing that the party machine would stick by its alderpersons no matter how they voted at city council,[32] and continued to endorse W6CO's view of elected representatives:

Aldermen should be required to function as delegates. They should be account-able—directly accountable—to their communities through the community committee which would direct that representative as to what he or she should do on council.[33]

He still advocated for tenant participation in apartment construc-tion and management, and supported community control as a means to shift the balance of power to the poor and working class.[34] Though small, socialist-directed projects were falling out of fashion, Layton insisted they could serve an important ideological function by helping people imagine living otherwise:

> I think the move into the area of support for non profit and cooperative and community development corporations, that kind of thing is a very small step but perhaps significant because by supporting that kind of venture, I think you start to convince people that maybe there are alternative ways of going about producing the goods that we need in order to live in a city other than giant multinational corporations and in a sense even though it may have a limited impact on the actual employment problem itself, it might get people thinking about some new options for the organization of economic activity.[35]

When election season returned in 1982, Layton decided to become Ward 6's NDP candidate. His 1,000-vote victory over Chong was hailed as a stunning upset by the *Toronto Star* and Layton subsequently recalled: "We were given no chance to win." But the result was hardly surprising, considering the groundwork laid by the area's community organizations and the ward's recent history of electing radical left-wing politicians. In the immediate aftermath of Layton's victory, his campaign manager rightly suggested that Chong's earlier win "has to be seen, if not as a fluke, at least as an anomaly in the history of Ward Six politics."[36]

Some NDP councillors happily turned their backs on the recent past. "A lot of the dreams we used to have about getting people together to make their own decisions just weren't workable," lamented one. But Layton tried to inject some New Left spirit, if not ideas, into the party's mainstream.[37] Though disctinctive New Left urban demands became rarer as the decade progressed, even as late as the mid-1980s, a document drafted partly by Layton, and adopted by the Metro NDP, reprised some New Left themes:

> Imagine a city which provides a home for all its citizens, which sees itself as an agent of social change; that is trying to end patriarchy and racism. A city that actively and patiently works to end exploitation and inequality in the city

and beyond . . . Imagine a city of activist neighbourhoods, tenant and resident councils, with many decisions being made locally through local health and neighbourhood councils . . . Imagine a system of free public transit which is completely accessible to all . . .[38]

New Left ideas had decisively shaped municipal left-wing discourse and organizing throughout most of the 1970s. With the help of a network of organizers, neighbourhood associations, community newspapers, and other activist bodies, alderpersons were elected who tried to implement some of those ideas. But, as a ReforMetro alderperson once noted, "You can't have socialism in one city."[39] Especially, she might have added, without a majority on city council.

New Left influence began to ebb in the mid-1970s, coinciding with a marked decrease in social movement activity. As inflation skyrocketed and unemployment increased, interest in New Left ideas about decentralization and democracy substantively declined. The rise of neo-conservatism and related "backlashes" also took a toll, as activists increasingly moved to defensive struggles. There was much less space for forward-looking blueprints or ambitious new public services.

The New Left-influenced alderpersons of the 1970s won a series of minor changes—and a few large ones—that made Toronto a better and more democratic place to live. Even for many of the battles they lost, like those over gentrification, it is hard to fault their analysis or tactics. That the movements lost and the party won is hardly surprising, yet there is a certain bewilderment to be had in that it was the reputably disorganized New Left that helped muncipal New Democrats expand their support base, renovate their ideology, and gain a renewed sense of purpose.

CHAPTER 9

TOMMY DOUGLAS, DAVID LEWIS, ED BROADBENT, AND DEMOCRATIC SOCIALISM IN THE NEW DEMOCRATIC PARTY, 1968–1984

Christo Aivalis

For as long as the CCF/NDP has existed, so too have debates around its historical trajectory. These debates have been intensified by economic crisis, back-to-back leadership contests, and a new constitutional preamble that removed commitments to social ownership, production for use as opposed to profit, and the abolition of poverty.[1] In general, scholars of the CCF/NDP might be divided into two camps: those feeling the party has kept true to its social-democratic/democratic socialist roots[2] and those seeing a departure from them.[3] These questions have deep historical and contemporary value, because the NDP—perhaps more than any Canadian party—puts great emphasis upon its legacy as a harbinger of social and economic progress.

This chapter explores this debate via an intellectual analysis of three men that each led the NDP during the Pierre Trudeau era: Scottish immigrant, Baptist minister, and Saskatchewan premier Tommy Douglas; Jewish immigrant, party architect, and labour lawyer David Lewis; and Ph.D.-holding son of an Oshawa autoworker Ed Broadbent. I argue that, while the contemporary NDP has not wholesale abandoned these leaders' legacies, there remains a stark difference between today's party and the NDP during the 1968–84 period, which comes after post-war capitalism's "golden age," but before the full-blown advent of neoliberalism in the mid-1980s. During these years, inflation, unemployment, commodity fluctuations, and slowing growth had re-intensified class conflict within a crisis of capitalism that revealed Keynesian liberalism's failure to solve capitalism's core tensions. Across this timespan, Douglas, Lewis, and Broadbent—both inside and outside their respective leadership tenures—put forward an anti-capitalist alternative, emphasizing wide-reaching democracy, comprehensive economic planning, and a more encompassing conception of equality.

Douglas, Lewis, and Broadbent held that economic planning and social ownership were essential to a productive, free, and just society, as well as a means by which to address energy insecurity, corporate power, and foreign dominance. Their approach differed from economic nationalists like Walter Gordon, or from the contemporary Trudeau government, which favoured Canadian private-sector empowerment over democratization. For Douglas, the merits of a planned economy were historically validated during World War Two, which proved the viability of "a planned economy dedicated to meeting human needs and responding to human wants." Emphatically, he suggested that if planning could defeat Nazi totalitarianism, it could best poverty and other social ailments.[4] The war proved Canada could marshal heretofore unimaginable resources, that innovation flowed from publicly owned entities, and that only a planned economy could give Canadians both "full employment and economic growth with a fair measure of price stability." Subsidizing and leaving the solutions to the private sector, conversely, was a hazardous choice because capitalist motivations predicated on profit maximization rarely produced democratic outcomes:

> The public provides much of this investment capital but the decision as to where and for what purpose it will be invested lies with the corporations. Left to the market forces, priorities for investment will undoubtedly be based on profitability which may not . . . be in accordance with national priorities . . . What is needed is a national instrument capable of influencing investment timing and priorities in the public interest.[5]

Related to this was Douglas' concern—popularized by political economists Mel Watkins and Kari Levitt—that without autonomy from the ardently capitalist United States, Canada could not build a planned economy. Douglas thus consistently emphasized the need for an independent Canada, but also the fact that corporations were too powerful, that capitalism facilitated this power, and that many corporations existed beyond the scope of Canadian sovereignty:[6]

> The fact is that the market forces are no longer "free" . . . The investment decisions and the priorities they establish are no longer within the public domain

but are made in the boardrooms of the giant corporations, many of them located outside Canada.[7]

To be sure, Douglas supported the Trudeau Liberals' Canada Development Corporation (CDC), which would ostensibly foster Canadian entrepreneurship and industrial priorities, though he suggested that if the CDC was to be more than a glorified mutual fund, it would have to include strong public imperatives over the direction of capital and be deeply integrated into a planned economy: "To go along with this, of course, would be government steps to encourage the re-designing and rationalizing of Canadian industry. We would work for a properly *planned* economy."[8]

This planning might not always entail ownership, but it would consistently assert democratic priorities and the production of necessities regardless of profitability. Still, it would require in many cases the "selective public ownership of the 'commanding heights' of the economy."[9] The solution, when dealing with strategic sectors like energy, was to control "the heights" via the state, supplemented with the participation of small business and co-operatives. This would allow the state to set prices, direct industry, and foster Canadian-based research and engineering.[10] Ultimately, ownership, direction, and control of industry was for Douglas the lynchpin to a better and more co-operative Canada and was the central endeavour of a democratic socialism built for the 1970s. But more than tinkering, this for Douglas was about seeking "a new motivation for our society" that put social needs before profit and aimed to convince Canadians that "they have the power to achieve anything that is physically and financially possible by democratically seizing the levels of power."[11]

David Lewis also criticized multinationals for using their publicly subsidized profits to perpetuate Canada's subordination. Why, he asked repeatedly, should Canadians prop up capitalists when they could socially own the fruits of their investment? As it stood, Lewis explained, the "free market" did little more than empower multinationals "so omnipotent that they can threaten the sovereignty and independence of entire nations." With this in mind, Lewis rejected the idea that Canada was a genuine democracy; rather it was being run less by citizens than by "the unelected and almost utterly unresponsive cluster of corporate decision makers."[12]

Related was how capitalists benefited from an economy planned in their interests. This for Lewis made the mythology of free-enterprise capitalism—the idea that "private planning is efficient and necessary while public planning is inefficient and bureaucratic"—"perhaps the most outrageous fib of all." And why was this fib so important? Because capital resented "any intrusion into their God-given domain of decision-making."[13] This observation was articulated within Lewis' broader campaign against the "corporate welfare bums": those corporations who —more than individuals on social assistance—benefited from the subsidies and tax manipulations that epitomized the "free enterprise merry-go-round."[14] Corporations were therefore given the immense power to essentially plan the economy in their interests, all while staunchly opposing socially orientated state planning. The result was a perverse system in which "the public invests, but the top executive class decides." The only alternative was "massive public investment to redress the balance," replacing the profit motive as the organizer of social and economic priorities.[15] The fetishization of markets and profit was simply incompatible with a democratic socialist conception of the economy, and the public control and ownership of key sectors, as a starting point, needed to be the rule rather than the exception.[16] Although public ownership for Lewis was not a panacea, he was driven by an opposition to "corporate power and an economy run basically for profit rather than for values that the people can live by and benefit from."[17]

Ed Broadbent came to these issues from the most adamant position. From his early days as an MP, he asked, in paraphrasing Lenin, "what is to be done"[18] about the economic *status quo*. Plainly, the answer was the end of capitalism:

> A privately owned economy is inherently exploitative and inherently unjust. We must develop a program whose eventual purpose is, in the words of the Regina Manifesto, to eradicate capitalism.[19]

Planning was superior because it shifted society from a competitive to a co-operative orientation:

> It is by providing more goods and services through public expenditure that we can begin to make inroads on the development of truly co-operative and free citizens. Only by freeing a man from the necessity to compete for everything he needs will society enable him to be free to give and be what he can.[20]

In essence, Broadbent held that the concepts of liberty and equality required a supersession of private competition by co-operative planning. This was based on his belief that democratic socialism was a foundationally different ideology than liberalism. Because, while liberals championed "the right to acquire property in 'means of production'," socialists rejected the "view that society should allow the means of production to be owned and controlled by a few."[21]

Out of this came his shared conviction with Douglas and Lewis that "so-called market forces—which are never free—have not and cannot solve Canada's economic difficulties."[22] This perception shined throughout his review of economist John Kenneth Galbraith's *Economics and the Public Purpose*,[23] which argued that modern markets did not reflect the classical theories of liberal capitalism and called for increased state intervention on behalf of the public good. Broadbent saw the potential of Galbraith's observations but suggested that the centre-left economist never carried his observation of capitalism's flaws to its rightful socialist solution:

> The only solution to getting adequate housing, a fair distribution of income, the production of necessities ahead of the frivolous, environmental control and custody of our non-renewable resources is to democratize corporate power ... The transition from "planning" capitalism to democratic socialism is essential if we are to live in a state of equity, decency, and creativity.[24]

But Broadbent was always insistent that socialist planning need not entail a "cumbersome, inefficient, stultifying centralized bureaucracy" that excluded workers, managers, entrepreneurs, and communities. He envisioned a program, for instance, where firms would deposit a portion of their profits, only to be used with state approval to reinforce democratic priorities, to address unemployment, mitigate automation's effects, and lower regional inequities.[25] Basically, Broadbent was proposing significant public oversight of most major firms and ownership of others. And, like his predecessors, none was a higher priority for him than the energy sector. In 1981, he announced his desire to nationalize Imperial Oil Canada and incorporate it with Petro-Canada to form the largest oil company in Canada.[26] This was his socialist alternative to Trudeau's National Energy Program (NEP), which, while increasing public control and ownership, primarily aimed to empower private Canadian firms.[27]

Two reports co-authored by Broadbent outline this effort. The first, with Alberta NDP leader Grant Notley, declared that democratization, and not merely Canadianization, was the key to Canada and Alberta's energy future: "Energy related revenues should be used primarily to enhance long term energy self-sufficiency, through conservation, alternative energy development, and greater public ownership within the context of a national industrial strategy." This would be accompanied by the social ownership of energy via "a Cooperative Energy Company," as well as equity compensation in exchange for tax breaks and subsidies.[28]

Similarly, Broadbent and federal NDP energy critic Ian Waddell explained that there was little difference between how Canadian and foreign energy companies subverted the public will and extracted undue state subsidies. So, rather than buoy Canadian capitalists via the NEP's Petroleum Incentives Program, the government should empower public enterprise: "If the taxpayers are to put up 93% of the costs for a private Canadian company to find oil or gas, why not put up the extra 7% and do it ourselves through a crown company so Canadians as a whole can reap all the benefits of their investment?" In addition to countering profit motives, a muscular Petro-Canada would "end the government's susceptibility to blackmail . . . If the private sector withholds development, crown corporations can step in and do the job."[29] Ultimately, Broadbent in this era was a consistent believer that public ownership, control, and planning was essential to build a prosperous, democratic, and vibrant economy.

When the three leaders extolled the virtues of planning and social ownership, they connected it to economic democracy, which went beyond state ownership to encourage increased worker representation, both through traditional trade unionism and worker management. Douglas, for his part, suggested that while labour and the CCF/NDP had done much to forge a humane Canada, social programs alone did not give ordinary Canadians a say in the direction of their daily lives. Democratizing the economy thus entailed "a new motivation for our society" that superseded both capitalism and communism. Douglas would say as much in 1969, when, after deeming Canada a "manipulated society," he declared

> . . . we must have more democracy—not less. But surely democracy means more than voting periodically for representatives to the law-making bodies of our land. People want a voice in the decision-making process as it affects their daily lives. Canadians of this generation want to be involved in making the decisions that affect their destiny.[30]

This was in line with his address to the 1969 NDP Convention, where he suggested that, while the CCF/NDP had "pioneered the welfare state," the party needed to turn its "attention to the second phase of socialist philosophy, which is to achieve the democratization of the economy." After outlining how Galbraith and John Porter showed the extent to which the powerful already controlled a planned system, he defined the need for, and value of, economic democracy:

The Canadian people shall have a voice in determining their economic destiny and be allowed to participate in building a humane and soul-satisfying society. True freedom means more than the absence of restraint. It means the freedom to . . . join with our fellow men in building a world free from the curse of war, fear, disease, and poverty.[31]

Douglas was not wedded to any exact form of economic democracy, instead choosing examples from many countries, including Yugoslavia. He supported the inclusion of workers on corporate boards, but, to avoid tokenization, also demanded that this representation be both meaningful and responsive to the will of rank-and-file workers. While Douglas did not see the need to immediately impose such a scheme throughout the economy, he did suggest it be applied to all Crown corporations, so it could be studied.[32]

More comprehensive was his 1970 proclamation that the "*sine qua non* of a free society was the right of workers to band themselves together for the purposes of bargaining collectively," and that a democratic socialist society would champion this, even as liberal-democratic and totalitarian regimes quashed worker dissent. But this was only the start: required was a new conception of industrial democracy, because automation was proceeding at a new pace and style. Economic democracy for Douglas was a recognition of industrial progress as a collective endeavour. The achievement of that progress—and the value derived from those achievements—should no longer be doled out as per the inegalitarian conventions of nineteenth-century property rights:

Scientific and industrial progress are not due to the efforts of employers alone . . . All have contributed to advances and all should have a voice in making the decisions that affect their interests . . . Workers already have the right to decide who shall govern them; they should equally have a voice in determining their economic destiny . . . But it is more than that; surely genuine democracy should enable us to participate in the decision-making process in every field of human endeavour.[33]

For his part, Lewis, as a labour lawyer, saw the root of most industrial conflict in capital's failure to recognize the worker's democratic rights in the workplace. Often, such struggles were the core causes of industrial strife, below the surface debates around pay and benefits:

The corporation resents any provision in a collective agreement which limits its right to . . . rearrange its work force as profitability demands. The struggle . . . is about participatory democracy: the right of the worker to have some effective voice in the decisions that affect his [*sic*] life . . . A few cents an hour may be the immediate cause of a strike, but underneath there is usually also bitterness, anger, and resentment that has built up because of neglect to give the needs of the employees the same attention as the profits of the corporation.[34]

Ultimately, Lewis wanted to address this by altering property rights, suggesting that the spectre of automation made necessary the recognition of the worker's right to employment: "I believe the time has come to extend our concept of property rights to recognize the rights of workers to their jobs."[35] The reason this had yet to happen, Lewis suggested, was that, while Canada's legal system was predicated on upholding property rights, it had not "developed the concepts of rights for large segments of the community who do not have, or have little property in the normal sense." This made it even clearer that the solution was not just organizing and bargaining, but also challenging the underpinnings of liberal property relations.[36]

Of the three men, none was more interested in economic democracy than Broadbent. He was convinced that worker empowerment was the only path toward a genuine democracy. To achieve it, he suggested that socialists had to differentiate themselves from liberals, because, whereas liberals held that elections and nineteenth-century liberties encapsulated democracy, socialists believed that "democracy requires that the average citizen should possess direct or indirect control over all those decisions which have a serious effect on his day to day life." As Douglas observed, capitalism offered no such freedom, meaning that it was the mission of democratic socialists to aid democracy in the transcendence of its current liberal limitations. And as Broadbent would say, this transition was imperative because liberal progressivism had done relatively little to eliminate "the great inequalities in power and wealth which exist and must exist in any capitalist society, even those converted into welfare states." It was thus vital for the NDP to replace an economy

controlled by a private few, with one controlled by the public many. It is only in such an economy that we can achieve our long-run moral purpose, which is a whole society—and not just its political institutions—which is both democratically administered and makes possible the opportunity of pursuing happiness equally available to all.[37]

In 1972, Broadbent would reiterate that "Canada is a parliamentary democracy, but an industrial autocracy" where "economic, autocratic power is assumed to be a 'natural' right." Solutions would come through planning and social ownership, but also empowering citizens in their daily lives:

"There is no democracy in society, with or without a publicly owned economy, whose members have simply the right either to advise or to oppose or protect." The principle here was that "effective power" entailed more than reacting to the dictates of management. So, while bread-and-butter bargaining would always have a place, the "ultimate objective" was breaking "traditional authoritarian control of profits, investments, pricing, discipline, and product innovation."[38] Only the triumph of industrial democracy over autocracy would suffice:

> This is not a Utopian ideal. It is not pie in the sky. Autocracy is no longer a practical form of government in industry, and will not be tolerated by the new generation of workers. The revolt against traditional forms of authority that we have witnessed on the campuses has had its counter-part in the nation's offices and factories . . . They demand a more humanized, more democratic environment in the workplace and insist that enterprises operate in a manner consistent with the welfare of the community as a whole. Politicians and governments should encourage this revolutionary change.[39]

Essentially, Broadbent here spoke of socialism as a two-front battle, whereby labour challenged "the so-called rights of ownership or management," and the NDP sought legislation undermining those "owning the economic system." The result would be a "socialist citizenship" that eradicated the "so-called prerogatives of management . . . that makes our present economic institutions inherently unequal and inherently undemocratic." This effort to delegitimize liberal property constructs could start, in Broadbent's view, by automatically unionizing all moderately sized workplaces:

> Just as a native . . . is not required to decide whether or not to become a citizen of a country so too in a place of work, men should not be required to show cause for the formation of a union . . . Unions should exist where working people exist, just as citizens exist where nations exist.

Eventually, this would lead to "the passing of a law which will remove all rights of control from those who own companies or who own shares in companies."[40] At base, Broadbent's industrial democracy was rooted in an endeavour toward a socialist society: "We must face all issues of work squarely . . . remaining firmly committed to the building of that fuller kind of democracy which alone can make it possible for the lives of all Canadians to be both just and exciting."[41]

All of this was enmeshed in the commitment to make Canada an egalitarian society. And for these three men, equality could not be compartmentalized from how, and in whose interests, the economy functioned. This conviction led them beyond a better distribution of capitalism's spoils. For while none supported a totalizing equality, each held firm that substantive inequalities of condition were inexcusable.

In 1969, Douglas operated from the principle that poverty was utterly avoidable, and that society could provide everyone with a decent living standard beyond contingent social security.[42] This was an issue fueling the intellectual and emotional fires of a "world in revolt." In this, Douglas stood with the young people, whose "long hair and miniskirts" did not invalidate their "revolt against our way of life," nor their protest "against a society that has failed to meet man's deepest needs and impedes the realization of man's finest aspirations." Simply, he saw the youth exposing the hypocrisies of equality in a capitalist society:

> We speak glibly about equality of opportunity but how much . . . is there between children educated in some of our well-to-do suburban schools and those . . . in our slums and in some of the depressed rural areas . . . On the television screen we show young people a glittering world of promise and then we slam the door in their faces because we have no meaningful role for them . . . To be young and poor is sad; but to be young and hopeless is a tragedy.

Likewise, Douglas would chastise the farcical concept of equality before the law, which he felt was non-existent, given that wealth could buy justice. Here, he declared that, before society demanded law and order, it had to "first insist upon 'law and justice'." And as a Christian, Douglas felt these inequities were socially sinful, indicative of how we privileged competition over co-operation. The solution thus went beyond social spending into an assertion of values:

> The value system we have established and the scramble for the almighty dollar have set man against his fellow . . . This is the inevitable consequence of accepting the concept that life is a battleground where "the race is to the swift and the battle to the strong." The crying need of our time is for a sense of social responsibility that recognizes the principle that we are "our brother's keeper" and, as St. Paul said, "we that are strong ought to bear the burdens of the weak."[43]

Clearly, Douglas' Christianity was a social one, and he marshalled it into a "desire to elevate mankind to new plateaus of social behaviour and spiritual enrichment." In his mind, the need for the spirit and reality of socialism was clear, because when it came to poverty and inequality, "the world will either find a socialist solution or no solution at all."[44]

David Lewis' concern for poverty came from his legal background as well as family ties to the Jewish Labour Bund. Expanding the scope and meaning of equality was central to his socialism. In a 1969 document, titled "I am a Socialist," he articulated his ideal form of equality:

> I want to see a society in which there is not only full equality of opportunities but also equality of condition for all people. Modern technological advance makes increasingly possible a standard of living from which material suffering, economic want, and the operation of insecurity can disappear. I want to break the prison walls built by economic pressures and insecurity so that the human spirit may be free.[45]

In 1979, Lewis stated that, while total equality was unnecessary, the notion that one could justify a $300,000 salary was absurd, suggesting a potential cap of $36,000. In 2017 dollars, Lewis was decrying the injustice of a $1.1 million salary, countering with a cap of about $120,000. Intriguingly, Lewis' proposal was less about tax collection and more about fostering a new social attitude: "You can't get much money by taking their income from them, but you can introduce an entirely new attitude in the society of Canada by taking that away."[46]

Another avenue through which Lewis critiqued the limitations of liberal equality was via Trudeau's "Just Society," which he attacked as being impossible without socialism. Above all, Lewis was angered by Trudeau's assertion that poverty was less an issue of inequality than wealth generation. In countering, he opined that Canada had no reason for poverty, outside of the fact that vested interests benefited from its preservation. Fundamentally, then, Lewis felt any just society needed both lower inequality and a different suite of values:

> A society can never be just or good when its system of values places material success . . . at the top of human achievement . . . We do not believe a society can ever be just or good when fancy office buildings take priority over homes; when . . . the Indian [*sic*], the Eskimo [*sic*], the Métis and the poor generally must wait long years before they are given the opportunity to join the mainstream of life; when the social system places competition and conflict ahead of human cooperation.[47]

Lewis would similarly note that Canada's legal system, while ostensibly egalitarian, was anything but. Whatever the lofty rhetoric, the law in the contemporary context was "one of the major instruments by which those enjoying privilege and power maintain their position."[48] The problem was both that legal equality was as untenable as equality of opportunity under capitalism, and that, as Lewis noted above, the legal system failed to imbue property rights with an egalitarian vision. Fixing this required seeing social benefits less as charity and more as a fundamental right:

> We have provided these benefits because we have recognized that poverty and degradation are not caused by the people themselves ... but are caused by social forces beyond the control of the individual. Society as a whole is responsible for conditions of poverty ... and society has an obligation to provide the victims of our collective failure with the physical, social, and psychological means to lift themselves out of their degradation. This is the basis for social security and the benefits should be recognized as a new form of property rights.[49]

As noted above, Broadbent perceived seismic differences between liberals and socialists. While the liberal was "basically selfish" in accepting the notion that vast wealth can justly co-exist with poverty, the socialist vision

> of justice is expressed in the traditional maxim: "from each according to his abilities; to each according to his needs."[50] A socialist does not believe that those with more ability *should* get greater material rewards (if anything they should get fewer rewards. Why ought a man be doubly blessed?).[51]

Additionally, Broadbent provided a metaphor to differentiate liberal and socialist equality. Liberalism was a race, for which there is theoretically an equal starting point, but in which inequities are practically endemic and accepted. Some will win, some will lose, but the result will be ostensibly just. Conversely, the socialist struggle was a co-operative mountain climb where the hikers were tethered to one another. In this metaphor, Broadbent believed that "it is the climbing together that really counts," and not any sort of victory or competition versus a fellow climber.[52]

Building on this was his abovementioned rejection of the idea that the "welfare state and socialism are synonymous," and his conviction that socialists had to differentiate themselves from liberals by rising above the welfare state.[53] In this, Broadbent perceived the revolutionary potential of a comprehensive Guaranteed Annual Income (GAI), calling it "the single most effective and efficient means of attacking ... both material and spiritual poverty in this country." But rather than treat a GAI as either charity or contingency, Broadbent demanded it be elevated to "a right of citizenship."[54] This could be related to his 1983 desire to see a "Charter of economic rights," including the right to a job, decent income, and social services. As it was for Lewis, making social assistance a basic human right was, along with workplace democracy and social ownership, essential in building a socialist citizenship.[55]

On the necessity of planning, the importance of democratic control, and the drive toward comprehensive equality, Douglas, Lewis, and Broadbent were anti-capitalists in how they viewed problems, and democratic socialists in how they envisioned solutions. This demonstrates at least some discordance with a twenty-first-century NDP that adheres to a market-centric approach that equates socialism with social welfare. Those wanting to simultaneously champion a capitalist NDP, and yet still claim these leaders' legacies as their own, should take pause, because Douglas, Lewis, and Broadbent's vision went beyond medicare and Mouseland; it aimed to transform society from the bedrock outward. As Douglas said in 1983 about those who eschewed said vision:

> If I could press a button tonight and bring a million people into this party, and knew . . . they didn't understand the kind of society we're trying to build, I wouldn't press the button because we don't want those kind of people.[56]

Around the same time, Broadbent was seeing the tide turn against the left. The rise of market fundamentalism, disdain for the poor, and anti-unionism was coming like a crashing wave. But he still demanded that the party retain its "socialist faith":

> We believe in equality not because it's popular. We believe in liberty not because it's a winner. We believe in social ownership not because of the polls. We believe in these because they are right, we must never forget it.[57]

But those who deny the NDP's radical potential should also take pause, because only in the recent past did its leaders advocate for a very different society. Within the NDP still exists this flame, and it can be re-ignited, surely more than in any other English Canadian party. And if Broadbent was correct that forging socialism was a two-front battle in and out of Parliament, the NDP will need to be both challenged and supported by the left. This is especially because the things that most distressed the three leaders—poverty amidst plenty, the disempowerment of workers, the growth of private property's power over the state, and the disenchantment of the young and marginalized—have not only persisted but have, in some cases, worsened.

We need novel solutions to twenty-first century capitalism, but the intellectual underpinnings may rest in Canada's democratic socialist tradition: the declaration that democracy goes beyond the ballot into our workplaces and communities; the conviction that human rights must include economic needs; the understanding that innovation is a social venture; and the commitment to an economy based on co-operation over competition. Compromise on the finer points is inevitable—Lewis would deem this the price of relevance—but if the NDP wishes to proudly wear its own history, policies endeavouring toward a democratic socialist Canada must be central. As Broadbent said in homage to CCF founder J. S. Woodsworth, only by building on the shoulders of left giants could the modern movement remain loyal to its legacy. The same applies to us today.[58]

CHAPTER 10

CHALLENGE FROM WITHIN

THE NDP AND SOCIAL MOVEMENTS

Roberta Lexier

In spring 2017, thirty activists from across Canada launched an organization called Courage: A Coalition of the Independent Left. The stated goal was "to create a national, member-based organization that would provide a democratic organizing platform for people on the socialist, feminist, anti-colonial left."[1] The principles, or "Basis of Unity," for the group are: building community and capacity, democratic economic control, inclusive society, working with the environment, international solidarity, decolonization and self-determination, and inclusive and asymmetrical federalism.[2] Although some of the participants were sceptical of electoral politics, viewing them as a "dead-end of neoliberal[ism],"[3] there was a growing belief in a "twofold approach: engaging with electoral politics from the left while also building social movement power beyond the ballot box for the long term."[4] According to one organizer, "movement people think that . . . spending as little time as possible with electoral politics is the way to go . . . and the people in political parties see winning elections . . . is one of the main ways to get things done. And they're both right in some ways . . . We need to find some strategic unity and see all those things as things that need to happen."[5] While the organization claims to be unaffiliated with the New Democratic Party (NDP), there is no doubt that the party is the main focus of attention. As Dru Oja Jay argues, "as a group we are not invested in the NDP but we see it as a tactical relationship . . . based on what we see as our common values."[6] The overarching goal is to find "strategic unity" between social movements and the NDP in order to realize the true potential of grassroots activism and achieve a truly transformative politics.[7]

Courage is just the most recent attempt by left-wing social movement actors in Canada to engage with electoral politics and, specifically, the NDP. According to Walter Young, the Co-operative Commonwealth Federation (CCF), the predecessor to the NDP, began as a coalition of activists who no longer believed that extra-parliamentary engagement alone could effectively transform the world; a political party, they insisted, could better effect substantive change than social movements outside the system.[8] And, yet, whenever social movements gain ascendancy in the wider society, tensions emerge between activists and the NDP. In the sixties, when a significant proportion of the youth population engaged in social movement activities, a group of individuals, known as the Waffle, sought to work within the NDP to transform it into a "radical agent" of social change.[9] In the late 1990s, when thousands of people marched in the streets in support of the Global Justice Movement, activists created the New Politics Initiative to work with the NDP to create a "new progressive party which better unites the electoral and non-electoral constituencies on Canada's Left."[10] And, in 2016, following the rise of the Occupy Movement and powerful Indigenous and environmental movements, individuals worked within their local riding associations to push the NDP to debate the Leap Manifesto as a way to "embrace the urgent need for transformation."[11] In each instance, the NDP resisted efforts to integrate more fully with social movements; the party's embrace of electoralism, though central to its history, nevertheless limits its ability to work with activists who employ different tactics and approaches and have distinctive issues and goals.

The sixties, in both myth and memory, is viewed as a period of conflict and change. A number of social movements developed around the world, including the civil rights, decolonization, anti-war, feminist, countercultural, environmental, and gay and lesbian movements; they confronted existing values and structures at every level of society. In Canada, too, this is remembered as a particularly turbulent period, characterized by emerging nationalist movements, growing demands for racial and gender equality, a rejection of many cultural values and norms, and opposition to the war in Vietnam.[12] The movements were largely youth driven: "This," explained one participant, "is a generational movement, it's a Canadian movement, it's a movement that has a very large number of students in it."[13] The students often espoused confrontational tactics, such as civil disobedience, protest, strikes, and occupations. They also grounded their analyses in the New Left and a particular understanding of democracy, which included social and economic equality, self-determination, and participatory democracy.[14]

While many were sceptical of electoral politics and viewed the NDP as a "very conservative party,"[15] some came to believe that they "should work through" the party, in part because it "reached a lot of trade unionists in Canada [and] some of the general population that the New Left students could never reach by themselves."[16] As one activist argued, "I was highly motivated to be in a political party that was contesting for power." However, the goal was to "make that contestation on the basis of stuff that [they] thought needed to happen in order to make that power real."[17] Thus, while the NDP was increasingly viewed as an important vehicle for social change, to accomplish the goals of social movement actors, it would need to be "a truly socialist party and a party which was both parliamentary and extra-parliamentary and tied into people's movements."[18]

With this goal in mind, and to stimulate dialogue within the NDP, in 1969 a group of activists drafted a document titled "For an Independent Socialist Canada." The document, which was referred to as a manifesto, decried American economic dominance and acknowledged the "existence of two nations within Canada, each with its own language, culture and aspiration." The authors insisted that Canada could be independent and united if it rejected its connections with the American capitalist "empire" and instead adopted a socialist model of political-economic organization; nationalism and socialism, for these individuals, were inextricably linked.[19] Over the next several years, participants also embraced many of the concerns raised by the nascent Women's Liberation Movement and sought to transform gender roles in Canadian politics and society. Moreover, they demanded the NDP adopt participatory democracy and work to ensure extensive participation from grassroots activists. Ultimately, the objective of this group, which became known as the Waffle, was to connect to the ideas and practices of social movements to "transform the NDP into the radical agent which would spearhead the struggle for an independent socialist Canada."[20]

The NDP, however, proved resistant to these demands. The Waffle Manifesto was officially debated at the 1969 national convention in Winnipeg; the established leaders of the party, including David Lewis, presented an alternative document, dubbed by opponents as the "Marshmallow Resolution" because of its supposed softness and lack of substance.[21]

While the paper acknowledged many of the concerns raised by the Waffle, especially the importance of democratic socialism and economic nationalism, its drafters scorned the calls for a more substantive embrace of socialism, the recognition of "two nations," and greater participatory democracy within the party.[22] Ultimately, delegates adopted this resolution and rejected, though by a relatively slim margin, the Waffle Manifesto.[23] However, the Waffle continued to organize, holding meetings and events, adding new members and supporters, submitting resolutions to provincial and national conventions, and launching a leadership challenge;[24] these efforts attracted significant media attention but failed, despite consistent support of approximately 40 percent of members, to make inroads within the party.[25]

By 1972, the NDP establishment lost patience with the Waffle and made the drastic decision to purge the group from the party. The official justification was that the Waffle was acting as a "party within a party" by creating a separate structure and maintaining its own membership lists.[26] Yet, there were also other, implicit or explicit, reasons for the purge. While there certainly existed differences of opinion over policy positions,[27] it was ultimately the orientation of the sixties activists that did not sit well with the party establishment. As Stephen Lewis, Ontario NDP leader and son of federal NDP leader David Lewis, later recalled:

> It isn't so much that the party didn't warm to the intentions because, in fact, the intentions weren't that much further than where the party was going. It's that the party recoiled from the bitterness with which the manifesto was being conveyed. It recoiled from the anger and from the nastiness of the critique and the personal attacks and the defiance of everything that we thought we were building.[28]

The Waffle embodied the style and strategies of social movements and the individuals were, according to their opponents, "difficult, destructive, and self-righteous."[29] The NDP leadership complained about the "sneering, contemptuous attitude" the nationalist Waffle showed toward the leadership of the still-internationalist labour movement.[30] As well, the hierarchical structure of the NDP, with a leader as primary spokesperson, conflicted with the anti-authoritarian orientation of the Waffle, especially when it came to the media. Stephen Lewis worried that the Waffle's positions were "given the imprimatur, the prestige of a separate faction—and with that authority there arises in the public mind inevitable confusion about what our policy really is, and where the devil we're going. And that is ultimately self-defeating."[31] It was self-defeating because these conflicts, the NDP establishment believed, threatened the electoral possibilities for a party seeking a breakthrough in the early 1970s. While Lewis insisted he was "more worried about what it was doing to the party, rather than what it was doing to our electoral prospects," he also acknowledged that he "wasn't a fool about it"; he "knew it wasn't helping [their] electoral prospects."[32] In the end, the decision was taken to purge the Waffle from the Ontario wing of the NDP and, in effect, though not officially, from the rest of the party. The Waffle, and its expulsion from the party, created long-lasting animosities and further exacerbated tensions between the NDP and social movements in Canada.

Decades later, the Global Justice Movement, or anti-globalization movement, mobilized activists around the world. Gaining attention and momentum in the 1990s, it included:

> a diverse constellation of organizations, groups, and networks, working with varying degrees of cooperation on a broad range of issues—from the indebtedness of the world's poorest countries, the inequities of the global trade in goods and services, international peace and environmental degradation, to the human rights of workers and immigrants, especially in less economically developed countries. These issues are linked by an emerging consensus amongst activists that their root cause is the neoliberal agenda, or "Washington consensus," that dominates global economic arrangements.[33]

Along with these issues, activists promoted greater participatory and deliberative democracy; they advocated for consensus decision-making and majority rule. As such, they developed "an organizational culture that stressed diversity rather than homogeneity; subjectivity, rather than obedience to organizational demands; transparency, even at the cost of effectiveness; open confrontations oriented to consensus building over efficient decision making; and 'ideological contamination' rather than dogmatism."[34] The movement, which achieved notoriety with the 1999 Battle for Seattle protests and demonstrations at the meetings of major economic and political organizations around the world, also known as "summit hopping," was seen as an "opportunity for the Left."[35] "The myth of youth apathy," argued one participant, "is being knocked down by thousands of new activists fighting for an end to the attack on the poor, the erosion of democracy and the destruction of our environment."[36]

However, similar to sixties activists, participants in the Global Justice Movement had "little interest in electoral politics."[37] The NDP had "experienced serious electoral setbacks,"[38] and was, according to some, drifting to the right and embracing "Third Way" politics that characterized the British Labour Party and other social democratic parties.[39] Moreover, it appeared to some that "politicians seem to have little interest in the activists and their communities."[40] As Murray Dobbin argued, social movements and political parties:

> should have been working together—at least informally—yet they existed as two solitudes. The NDP establishment detested social movements (and distrusted the labour movement) as naïve and uncontrollable troublemakers because when the NDP was in power they persisted in criticizing the NDP government and making things uncomfortable for the ministers . . . Social movement organizations saw the NDP almost as an alien entity—closed to any dialogue about policy or politics and weak and meek when it came to taking risks and pushing the policy envelope.[41]

And, yet, when the NDP began a renewal process in 2001 in response to its "three consecutive poor showings in federal elections,"[42] some activists argued that "links between social movements and political parties are mutually beneficial."[43] A group of young activists, representing a large number of organizations,[44] joined with more seasoned political players and NDP MPs Svend Robinson and Libby Davies to propose a collaboration between social movements and the NDP. They called their effort the New Politics Initiative (NPI). "It was," according to Judy Rebick, "the last try in Canada to bring together social movements and a political party. We were still hopeful that a political party could be the instrument of change."[45]

The group initially proposed the formation of a new left-wing party that would be more activist and democratic than the NDP and connected directly with the energy and personnel in social movements. "Our first idea," explained Rebick, "was to start a new party that would incorporate sectors of the NDP, the Green Party, and anti-globalization activists. It would be more radical than the NDP, more grassroots, more bottom up."[46] However, with the renewal process underway, NPI members decided to first take their proposals to the NDP federal convention in Winnipeg in November 2001; they proposed a resolution calling on the NDP to "initiate and undertake wide-ranging discussions over the next 12 months with labour and social movements with the objective of the federal NDP leading the process of building a bold, visionary, activist, progressive new federal political party focussed [*sic*] on the core values of democracy, sustainability, equality and solidarity."[47]

This resolution resulted from a grassroots campaign that began with a "discussion paper," not a "manifesto,"[48] which was leaked, some claim in order to discredit the movement,[49] to the *Globe and Mail*.[50] This statement included proposals for the adoption of more progressive policies and practices, including: electoral reform; rejection of corporate trade deals; and the expansion of participatory democracy in communities, workplaces, and political parties.[51] "Our goal," the authors explained, "is not to split the left, but to unite it. We want to expand the NDP's tent to encompass the passionate campaigners whose ongoing grassroots work is vital to our shared hope of building a better, fairer world, but who no longer see today's NDP as a reliable or inspiring force for progressive social and economic change."[52] The goal, then, was to link the energy of social movements with the NDP in order to achieve real electoral success and transform the world through both parliamentary and extra-parliamentary activism.[53] As NPI supporter Libby Davies explained, "it's not only what you stand for, it's how you do the politics."[54]

In response to the discussion paper, at least twenty-nine riding associations and affiliated organizations submitted resolutions to the NDP Federal Council calling for a new party, and the party's Resolution Committee agreed to put it on the agenda of the national convention.[55] The NPI held pre-convention meetings and rallies and attempted to mobilize support, but the resolution received only 37 percent support from delegates.[56] The world had changed between the release of the discussion paper and the federal convention; by fall 2001, the party was increasingly focused on the ramifications of 9/11 and the resulting debates over anti-terrorism legislation, and not on the increasingly defensive social movements.[57] Moreover, the party establishment, including the leadership and some of the powerful labour unions, rejected the supposedly radical shift in tactics promoted by the NPI.[58] Although the NPI continued to organize for two more years, the 2002 campaign to replace leader Alexa McDonough "paralyzed the NPI leadership and prevented the project from defining its own agenda."[59] In the end, many believed that Jack Layton, who was ultimately elected leader, would work to "build party linkages to social movements" and thus fulfill the demands of the NPI.[60]

As with the Waffle, there was a number of reasons for the rejection of the NPI. There was, for instance, confusion over whether the organization was seeking changes to party policy or simply to internal processes. While most NPI participants argued that the primary goal was to create a truly democratic, grassroots political party,[61] in a speech at the convention, supporter Svend Robinson overtly rejected Third Way politics and decried the move of the NDP to the "mushy middle." This led NPI opponent Bill Blaikie to speak out against the "self-righteous left," which failed to appreciate the work he and others had done within Parliament to promote a progressive agenda.[62] There was also confusion over the implementation of NPI policies; if they were adopted, how would the NDP, a very structured and hierarchical organization, actually become more democratic and better connect with social movements?[63]

Yet, similar to the Waffle, the main objections were in response to the social movement orientation of the NPI. Although supporters always tried to maintain a positive and encouraging tone, largely in response to ongoing critiques of Waffle members,[64] the NDP establishment appeared threatened by NPI participants and their proposals.[65] This, some believed, demonstrated that the NDP was afraid of its own members and the power they might yield if given the power to fully participate.[66] The NPI, Davies said, was viewed as a battle of the "members against the machine."[67] In a related vein, activists were painted as "outsiders," who were not committed to the party. At the convention, remembered Davies, "Bill [Blaikie] took to the floor and basically changed the discourse in the debate from, you know, this is an idea of a new way forward for the NDP ... to this is about loyalty to the party."[68] It did not help that the establishment was suspicious of some of the individuals involved in the NPI; Buzz Hargrove, president of the Canadian Auto Workers, had recently endorsed strategic voting and was seen as a traitor to the NDP; Judy Rebick had been in and out of the party since the 1970s and was painted as a fair-weather member; and Svend Robinson was a dedicated but confrontational party member.[69] As well, many activists joined the party to support the NPI and were seen as interlopers who would not contribute to long-term organizing or the hard work of electoral politics.[70] Blaikie and others were frustrated with social movements; activists, it was argued, were too willing to support Liberals in elections, too reluctant to give credit to the NDP, too focused on single issues, too ignorant of party functions and structures, and too dismissive of the importance of elections.[71] Opponents insisted that the NPI would condemn the party to the margins and prevent electoral success,[72] while supporters argued that connections with social movement actors would actually improve electoral possibilities.[73] Although, as some argued, activism had momentum and social movements could link their enormous energy to the NDP,[74] this did not coalesce with the electoral agenda of the party.

More recently, in the wake of the 2008 financial crisis and growing concerns about racial and economic inequality, climate change, and Indigenous rights, social movements again gained momentum. From the Occupy Movement and Arab Spring to Black Lives Matter and Standing Rock, extra-parliamentary activists are challenging existing political, economic, social, and cultural realities around the world. These social movements frequently emphasize intersectionality and attempt to build alliances across issues, classes, cultures, languages, and more. This, Avi Lewis argued, is the "special sauce" that has contributed to "surprise social movement victories."[75] For many, climate change is the overarching issue that will connect different groups together around a common goal, "the survival of humanity."[76] Moreover, these activists, like their predecessors in the sixties and the late 1990s, have largely abandoned electoral politics as a way to achieve their goals. "We live in an historic moment," explained Naomi Klein. "One that demands audacity, ambition, courage and since, unfortunately, many of our leaders are too busy watching the polls to grasp either the urgency or the incredible potential of this transformation, leadership is coming from outside electoral politics."[77] For activists, there was nothing inspiring about the NDP; many felt demoralized by the positions taken by the party in recent elections.[78] Instead, they argue that there is a "new political awakening that is happening whether the NDP likes it or not."[79]

It is within this larger context that a cross-sectoral meeting of social movement activists in Canada was called in 2015. The group, involving representatives from Indigenous rights, social justice, food, environmental, faith-based, and labour movements, used consensus to draft the Leap Manifesto. The document emphasized "respect for Indigenous rights, internationalism, human rights, diversity, and environmental stewardship" and a "Canada based on caring for the earth and one another." Its authors argued that "a rapid transition to renewable energy could be the occasion for an equally rapid redistribution of wealth and justice for Indigenous and other marginalized communities" and called on "all those seeking political office to seize this opportunity and embrace the urgent need for transformation."[80] According to one participant, the NDP was never part of the conversation.[81] Instead, the manifesto was released during the 2015 election campaign in an effort to encourage all parties and politicians to embrace a more radical approach to saving communities and the planet.[82] In this way, Leap differed from the Waffle and the NPI, which specifically targeted the NDP.

However, the media, which thrives on stories of conflict and confrontation, framed the Leap Manifesto as a challenge specifically to the NDP.

According to one story in the conservative *National Post*:

> The manifesto is essentially a shortlist of everything NDP leader Tom Mulcair has been carefully avoiding in his bid to convince voters that social democrats aren't nearly as scary as the Conservatives say they are ... [It] is essentially the left wing equivalent of a bunch of ex-Conservatives getting together to sign an open letter vowing to bring back the death penalty, reinstate prayer in public schools and extend "conscience rights" to all public bureaucrats.[83]

Not surprisingly, the NDP leadership distanced themselves from the Leap Manifesto and the demands it presented.[84] While Leap spokesperson Avi Lewis understood why people in the NDP might have felt it was "unfair to [release the manifesto] during an election campaign," he and others were impatient with the electoral system and wanted to push all parties to redefine the limits of what was politically possible; the release during the election was intended to achieve maximum political influence.[85] This approach, however, created significant tensions between Leap supporters and the NDP, which culminated in an intense conflict at the 2016 federal convention in Edmonton.

From the beginning, the Leap was grounded in grassroots activism. It called for "town hall meetings across the country where residents can gather to democratically define what a genuine leap to the next economy means in their communities."[86] Many took this call seriously and activists began to organize at the local level; some worked with their local NDP riding associations to support resolutions calling for the adoption of the Leap Manifesto as party policy.[87] As word of these resolutions began to spread, some long-time NDP organizers raised concerns that this "holus bolus approach" was "profoundly undemocratic";[88] the party, they argued, should be provided an opportunity to discuss the contents of the manifesto rather than adopting an external document wholesale.[89] These party activists, then, proposed a revised motion that would provide the NDP with a "meaningful opportunity to debate the Leap Manifesto in riding associations across the country" while stating that the Leap Manifesto is "a high-level statement of principles that speaks to the aspirations, history, and values of the party."[90] Throughout the process, the organizers worked with Thomas Mulcair's office and with the Alberta NDP, who were hosting the convention;[91] according to Avi Lewis, both supported the inclusion of the resolution if only because they understood the need to debate the issue without belabouring the point.[92]

The Alberta NDP, which took a pro-pipeline stance in order to maintain electoral support in a province dominated by the oil and gas industry, was particularly resistant to the Leap Manifesto and its calls for an immediate transition to clean energy. Their concerns were exacerbated by a pre-convention interview between Mulcair and Peter Mansbridge; following numerous deflections, Mulcair eventually conceded that, if the party membership voted to adopt a more radical approach to fossil fuels, he would accept their decision.[93] Infuriated by this position, the Alberta NDP sent Cabinet ministers to speak out against the Leap resolution, despite their previous (passive) participation.[94] In the end, although some believed there was significant confusion over the resolution—was it an adoption of the Leap Manifesto or simply the initiation of a discussion in riding associations?[95] – a significant majority of those at the convention voted in favour of it.[96]

Although the resolution passed, opposition to Leap remained fierce, especially in Alberta. "I'm spitting angry," said Alberta labour leader Gil McGowan.

> These downtown Toronto political dilettantes come to Alberta and track their garbage across our front lawn . . . They didn't give any thought to the political problems they're creating for NDP in Alberta . . . They didn't give any credit for the work the Alberta government has been doing on climate change . . ."[97]

The concerns appear to be twofold. On the one hand, the Alberta NDP and its allies were anxious that the manifesto did not respect the realities in the province and would hurt it economically and politically.[98] There was a sense that the government was "going to wear this now and it's going to be used by our opposition in Alberta that we're anti-oil."[99] On the other hand, those supporting the resolution were portrayed as outsiders, or "downtown Toronto political dilettantes," who frequently criticized the party and did not demonstrate a commitment to electoral politics. As Janet Solberg explained, "how people felt about this document in some measure had to do with who signed it." Opponents argued that these were individuals, such as Avi Lewis and Naomi Klein, who were "happy to undermine the party even as they're in the party."[100] Thus, as with the Waffle and the NPI, there was a sense that external social movement activists were trying to undermine the processes and policies of the party.

Supporters of Leap, though, also raised concerns about the process. For social movement actors who had decided to work with the NDP, the debate over Leap demonstrated the "hostile environment of the NDP," grounded in its focus on electoral success and "political opportunism."[101] Avi Lewis insists that Leap supporters demonstrated their willingness to compromise with the party; high-level NDP supporters worked in "lockstep" with the leader's office and the Alberta NDP to get the compromise resolution to the floor.[102] However, the convention demonstrated to some that the party was not really open to debates over policy or process.[103] The compromise resolution was viewed by some as a way to defer discussion of the Leap Manifesto so that it would cease to be a problem for the party.[104] Although there appeared to be support from the grassroots members of the party, as evidenced by the various resolutions proposed by riding associations, some within the party proved resistant to these demands.[105] Once again, it proved difficult to create common ground between the party and social movements.

Social movements and electoral parties have different roles in the Canadian political system. The former work outside the established systems of power to effect social change, while the latter attempt to influence public policy by electing candidates to public office. As Judy Rebick summarized, "A political party wants to get elected . . . A social movement is trying to change society's attitude[s]."[106] Together, social movements and political parties can contribute to a fundamental transformation of society; "movements," argued Avi Lewis, "need an electoral expression and [left parties need] the social movement energy and creativity and radicalism and ambition."[107] And, yet, "neither . . . have successfully figured out how to combine electoralism with extra-parliamentary social change activism."[108] Instead, tensions continue to emerge that will not be easily resolved.[109] These conflicts are particularly apparent in the NDP, the only left-wing party in Canada. It faces incredible pressures: activists demand that it be bold and inspiring, presenting an alternative vision for the country, while party loyalists insist that it be electorally viable, promoting policies and practices that are digestible for ordinary Canadians. This led to significant controversies in the 1960s, in 2001, and in 2016. Each time, the NDP has resisted the demands of social movement actors, and activists have failed to fully support the party, to the detriment of both. While, as Bill Blaikie argued, "the idea of the NDP, and the CCF before, was to get elected, to actually be in Parliament,"[110] without support from left-wing activists, this goal may continue to prove elusive. At the same time, social movements will struggle to achieve their objectives without support from elected representatives who can pass transformative legislation. Unless these tensions are resolved, fundamental change will be difficult to achieve.

CHAPTER 11

FROM CONTENDER TO THE MARGINS AND BACK

THE NDP AND THE FOUR HORSEMEN OF THE APOCALYPSE

Bill Blaikie

My goal here is to provide insight on the past forty years of the NDP from the perspective of one who lived a lot of that forty years of social democratic politics very intensely, as an elected NDP Member of Parliament interacting with the electorate, the party, and the media. It was not, I would say, the best of times to be a New Democrat, but I am grateful to have had the chance to participate in the way that I did, for as long as I did.

As for the Four Horsemen of the Apocalypse, my suggestion is that four issues—neoliberalism, the constitution, the culture wars, and social movements—all intensified in the 1980s and 1990s in a way that helped thwart the hopes the federal NDP had for itself in the late 1970s and early 1980s. And I want to further suggest that it was only after all four of these problems were either diminished, significantly resolved, or discredited that the federal NDP was able, in 2011, to finally not only return from the margins, but to make a breakthrough.

Neoliberalism is the first horseman, often associated with images of pestilence and false prophesy, not to mention the anti-Christ. As many of you know, it could be said of neoliberalism that, although it may have begun as a probably sincere academic attempt in Chicago to critique the shortcomings of the dominant post-war Keynesian and welfare state paradigm, it was soon hijacked and marketed as a way to revive affections for the unfettered marketplace that many thought had been put to rest. Particularly in the Anglo-American political universe, with the rise of Ronald Reagan and Margaret Thatcher, and the era of free trade, privatization, and deregulation, it was as if we were living an ideological version of Jurassic Park.

In Canada, this did not kick in fully until the election of Brian Mulroney in 1984 and the negotiation of two trade deals, the Canada-US Free Trade Agreement (CUSTA) and the North American Free Trade Agreement (NAFTA), both of which were early forms of constitutionalizing beyond the reach of sovereign national and democratically elected governments not just low tariffs and greater market access, but also a particular way of looking at the world. Only a few years later, this view would be globalized via the ethos of the newly formed World Trade Organization, whereby a perverse moral hierarchy was established that privileged investor rights, but marginalized labour rights and the environment. Further efforts at entrenching this kind of unregulated corporate globalization were made via failed attempts like the MAI and the FTAA, and, more recently, via the as yet undetermined CETA and TPP.

How did all this play out within and without the NDP? One of the legacies of the 1988 election was a narrative about how the NDP had tried to duck the free trade issue; on the first day of the campaign, during an event in Quebec, it is alleged that NDP leader Ed Broadbent didn't mention the FTA. This was brought up time and time again, not just then, but for years to come, as if it was proof positive that the NDP was not as totally opposed to the FTA as it should be. This narrative was aggravated by the fact that Ed had, before the election, refused to agree that the Senate should stop the agreement, even though his reasons for doing so were democratically impeccable.

The story about the first day of the campaign may or may not be true. I have never been able to determine what actually happened. But if it is true, I can understand that a tactical decision may have been made in consideration of the fact that the FTA was not as big an issue in Quebec, or in consideration of the fact that the economy was not seen as a strong issue for the NDP and that, therefore, leading with something like the environment might be in order. If the latter was the case, it was a decision that needed re-evaluation during the campaign when the FTA became THE issue; unfortunately, no such re-evaluation seemed possible. To top it off, Liberal leader John Turner did a better job of emotionalizing the nationalist political argument in the debates, despite the fact, known to all who were paying attention, and evidenced by everything that happened subsequently, that, though Turner may have meant it, there were plenty of Liberals, including Paul Martin, who were silently cheering for the FTA.

And then there was NAFTA, and the election of 1993, in which, despite efforts to have it otherwise, the fact that the NDP was the only party in Parliament to oppose the NAFTA seemed to have little or no traction with the deal's critics, who were either voting Liberal to kick the Tories out, or voting for the National Party formed by Mel Hurtig and Bill Loewen on the basis that the NDP position was somehow not good enough. There were enough ridings in which the National Party vote was strong enough to cause the defeat of sitting New Democrats, which led to the loss of official party status. The 1993–1997 Parliament would have been different if we had had party status and there had been a party in the House that was critical of the trade agreements and the neoliberal worldview. Instead, at a very critical time, when the neoliberal worldview was being consolidated, there were no contrary voices, or, more accurately, none being reported.

To make a potentially long story short, the neoliberal paradigm was so strong that it spawned many political offspring, as parties of the centre and of the left tried to deal with its all-pervading effect. Thus was born, for instance, the various but not identical Third Way politics of, to name a few, Tony Blair, Bill Clinton, and Gerhard Schroeder. Though I tended then, and still do, to regard the Third Way politics of that era as a politics less of accommodation to reality and more as a form of supine acquiescence to corporate power, it was nevertheless true that it posed a problem for the federal NDP.

The problem was twofold. The neoliberal paradigm was so strong that those who refused to genuflect were written off, as indeed we were by many, as people stuck in an earlier paradigm, unwilling or unable to adapt to the times. This was what we heard from our political opponents. I used to take this criticism as a compliment of sorts, because I believe the record will show that the federal NDP did not genuflect and maintained its critique and opposition to the dominant worldview at a time when many were giving up. We were, in my view, the last best left. Nevertheless, from many of our friends we were often unfairly under suspicion of somehow giving up and accommodating instead of resisting the prevailing worldview. This had to do, in part, with the perception of NDP provincial governments at the time and, in part, with the role of the social movements of the time whose way of speaking about Parliament and politicians often obscured the differences. But more on that horseman later.

Another frustration was the way the media, while often character-izing the NDP as stuck in the past, treated every rumour of change as the imminent and irredeemable corruption of an admirably principled political party.

In any event, with the financial crisis of 2008, and the ongoing realization that many of our predictions have come true about inequality and the loss of good jobs that would result from leaving everything to the whims of a global marketplace, dominated by corporations seeking only shareholder value, and not even the national interest, let alone the public interest, we have arrived at a time when the neoliberal world order is discredited. Unfortunately, it is mainly the political right, in the form of US President Donald Trump that has so far benefited from this. But it is also the case that Bernie Sanders did as well, and this I believe is part of a changing narrative about neoliberalism that has promise, if only the left can come up with a convincing alternative. Otherwise we are left with the choice that French voters had in 2017, between an inappropriate resistance to globalization, and inappropriate support of globalization.

The second horseman is associated with war and the spilling of blood. The second horseman here is the Canadian constitutional saga that runs, for our purposes, from the 1980 referendum and subsequent patriation controversy through to the Meech Lake Accord, the Charlottetown Accord, the 1995 referendum, the Clarity Bill, and the Sherbrook Declaration.

The patriation controversy was a source of division within the NDP. Saskatchewan NDP Premier Allan Blakeney was one of the leading provincial opponents of the unilateral nature of Trudeau's initiative, while Ed Broadbent was so supportive that he declared for the package within minutes of its proposal, without even talking to his caucus. Eventually, four Saskatchewan MPs would break ranks with Broadbent. Blakeney was also a Charter sceptic and would be instrumental in obtaining the notwithstanding clause that caused some NDP MPs to ultimately vote against the final patriation package. There are a lot more stories to tell about the patriation controversy, but it was not all that damaging to the NDP in the short run. In the long run, it could certainly be argued that it was, in so far as it created the conditions for the attempt at constitutional reconciliation with Quebec that resulted in the now infamous Meech Lake Accord, which did create a lot of problems for the federal NDP.

Broadbent was an early and avid supporter of the Meech Lake Accord. I recall him walking across the floor to congratulate Mulroney immediately after the announcement of the agreement in the House, something that would probably take place elsewhere these days. Initially, it was not

a source of division or controversy within the party. The only NDP premier at the time, Howard Pawley, was on side, but there was a problem in
Yukon with the provision in the accord for the creation of new provinces.
This might have been less important, had it not been for the fact that in
the summer of 1987, after the accord had been reached in June, there were
three by-elections. One of them was in Yukon, having been precipitated by
the resignation of long-time Tory MP Erik Nielsen. Our candidate was a
woman by the name of Audrey McLaughlin, and she was given a special
dispensation by Broadbent to voice opposition to the Meech Lake Accord,
in order that her electoral efforts might be less suicidal and more prone
to success. She succeeded and ultimately had an edge on others who had
initially supported what was by 1989 a deeply unpopular accord.

The accord was unpopular with Aboriginal leaders because it didn't
address their concerns, even though initially it had been greeted as a way of
getting the Quebec issue off the table so as to maybe finally have the provincial critical mass to reach an agreement on Aboriginal concerns. It was
unpopular because of growing anxiety about the distinct society clause, an
anxiety fatally aggravated by Robert Bourassa when he used the notwithstanding clause to strike down a court ruling favourable to English-lan-
guage rights in Quebec. I remember the phone call I got from Gary Doer
the day after, telling me that the Manitoba NDP, now in opposition after
the fall of the Pawley government in 1988, would have to abandon Meech
because of what Bourassa had done.

Recall that Manitoba was one of the birthplaces of opposition to
the Meech Lake Accord, courtesy of Liberal leader Sharon Carstairs, who
had made a breakthrough in Manitoba, in part as a result of her opposition to Meech. Federal Liberal leader John Turner supported Meech, but
Carstairs was acting in concert with fellow Liberal Jean Chrétien, who
would ride the division within the party over Meech to a victory over Paul
Martin in the dying days of the accord in June 1990.

The Meech Lake Accord was unpopular on the left because of growing anxiety about the language regarding the creation of new national
social programs; it talked about shared objectives instead of national standards for provinces opting out to create their own version of any such
programs. And unpopular on the left because, by 1989, Mulroney was
not seen as a constitutional conciliator. Instead he was seen as the politician who had foisted the Canada-US Free Trade Agreement on Canada
by virtue of his popularity in Quebec, English-speaking Canada having
voted in the majority against it. Meech came to be seen in some quarters

on the left as further evidence of Mulroney's plan to render the national government powerless.

Despite the divisions within the NDP political universe, the party was nevertheless widely perceived as supportive of the accord, which, in western Canada, where most of our seats were, was problematic. It shouldn't have been, with the other two parties in the House also being supportive, but that would ignore the fact that, in 1987 in Winnipeg, a convention was held to create the Reform Party of Canada.

The Reform Party was opposed to the Meech Lake Accord for a number of reasons, not the least of which was their doctrine of the equality of the provinces that made any distinct society clause, or any form of asymmetrical federalism, anathema. In this, there was a strange similarity to Pierre Trudeau's view of the provinces. But the Reform Party coupled this with a gathering together of every cultural and regional complaint that had accumulated since the 1960s. Some were addressed directly, some by that most excellent of dog whistlers, Preston Manning. Salient among those regional complaints was the decision to award the CF-18 contract to Montreal instead of Winnipeg, which set the stage for all further characterizing of policies that were favourable to Quebec, regardless of their merit.

By 1990, the NDP support for Meech was under attack from all sides, with few coming to its defense. The accord failed, finally, in Manitoba, where arguably it had first started to unravel, and the Bloc Quebecois was the result, a result which also had ramifications for the NDP. The most damaging thing to come out of the Meech Lake Accord, and its failure, was the subsequent attempt at constitutional reconciliation known as the Charlottetown Accord.

The NDP supported the Charlottetown Accord, not because of a unilateral decision by the leader, but due to a lengthy party process that included the federal council of the party. The accord was supported by both the Liberals and the Conservatives, but there were dissenting Liberals, like Sharon Carstairs. The Reform Party did not support the Charlottetown Accord and, in so doing, was able to characterize the NDP as in bed with the elites who were trying to foist something on the people. One of those things was the guarantee for Quebec of 25 percent of the seats in the House of Commons, which complimented the Reform critique of the CF-18 decision and of Meech as too concessionary to Quebec.

In any event, it is my view that the Charlottetown Accord, albeit in combination with some other factors, contributed greatly to the way in which our base collapsed in western Canada and went to the Reform Party.

The next problem in this file for the federal NDP was the *Clarity Act*, or Bill C-20. The *Clarity Act* followed from the ruling of the Supreme Court on a reference made to it by the Chretien government concerning whether Quebec had the right to unilaterally secede from Canada. It was a response to the near-death experience of the 1995 referendum. Another response was a motion in the House recognizing Quebec as a distinct society, put forward by a Liberal government after all the grief the Liberal Party had caused over that issue.

We had opposed the Supreme Court reference, but when C-20 was brought forward we decided, after much internal debate, to support it at second reading. Federal Council urged the caucus to vote against it at third reading. Ed Broadbent appeared as a witness before the committee in support of the bill. Michael Oliver, of Montreal, and a founder of the NDP, presented in support of the *Clarity Act*. And the then-new NDP premier of Manitoba was also supportive.

We almost did what Federal Council wanted, except that after my speech lamenting the unwillingness of the Liberals to support our amendments to recognize the Quebec Cree as players in the process, Stephane Dion offered to amend the bill if we would support it as amended. The bill was amended, and we voted for it at third reading, which led to the resignation of the Quebec NDP executive and vilification of yours truly, as I was the lead caucus critic on the file. The issue would resurface a few years later in the 2004 campaign, when Jack Layton said he would repeal the *Clarity Act*, and I, among others, publicly disagreed with him. Whatever one might think of the *Clarity Act*, I do not think that it is a coincidence that shortly thereafter Lucien Bouchard departed the scene, and the cause of Quebec separation began to wane, although the reasons for that are certainly multiple in nature.

One of the other amendments I moved on behalf of the party was to make 50 per cent plus one the definition of a clear majority. Although the amendment was unsuccessful, this would later become a key element of the Sherbrook Declaration adopted by the NDP in 2005, which also included a recognition of asymmetrical federalism. In some ways, this affirmation of asymmetrical federalism was old news. It was always the NDP view, going back to the founding convention when the adoption of the "deux nations" view of Canada caused CCF stalwarts like Eugene Forsey to leave.

I want to suggest that the Sherbrook Declaration, the decline of the threat of another referendum, and of separatism itself, the recognition by the House under Harper of Quebec as a nation within Canada, and no doubt other factors have all contributed to a context in which the NDP, for the time being, is not vexed in the way it was for so many decades about the Constitution. Proof of this is arguably the fact that, although Quebec issues like the niqab affected the NDP in the 2015 election, the Tories and Liberals never seriously employed the NDP position on the *Clarity Act* in their campaign against New Democrats.

The third horseman is associated with famine, and so perhaps it is not entirely inappropriate to use it as a metaphor for the way that the culture wars often starved the NDP of votes it would likely otherwise have gained, or kept, as the case may be.

When I use the term "culture wars," I am primarily referring to the evolution of the debate about sexual orientation and abortion, which began with the omnibus justice bill that was passed in 1969, legalizing homosexuality and providing a framework for legal abortions. The omnibus bill commenced a political era that one can argue finally ended with the decision of Prime Minister Harper not to revisit the issue of same-sex marriage or to reignite the debate about a woman's right to choose. It also ended when the Liberal Party of Canada, under Justin Trudeau, decided that the Liberals would no longer be a big tent on the abortion issue and required Liberals to support choice.

Without going into all historical details, suffice to say that at all times, with varying degrees of intensity and uniformity, the NDP was front and centre in advocating the next steps along the way to where we are today. The NDP did tolerate some diversity, but not to the same degree, and certainly not as a political strategy. It was seen, at least early on, particularly with respect to abortion, as a matter of conscience. MPs like Fr. Bob Ogle and Fr. Andy Hogan were not expected, or pressured, to be pro-choice. But after numerous court decisions on issues of sexual orientation and abortion, and the interpretations of *Charter* rights that were often integral to such decisions, the perception of these issues changed.

Canadian philosopher George Grant criticized modern liberal pluralism for putting the question "what is a right" ahead of the question "what is the good" and, as the so-called rights discourse took hold in earnest, those who dissented were seen not as holding a different moral position but as holding an immoral position, one that denied the rights of others to their proper autonomy. The *Canadian Charter of Rights and Freedoms*, and rulings that flowed from it, became sacred, particularly for those who agreed with the rulings, but also for other Canadians less partisan on such issues.

All this might have been more navigable without the Reform Party, and ultimately the new non-progressive Conservative Party; having a credible political party giving voice to certain opinions amplified things in a way that made it difficult for New Democrats to hope that such issues would not affect voting. Instead, from election to election, and issue to issue, we lost support from some of our base, especially when these issues combined with the narrative that the NDP was cavorting with the elites, who not only had questionable constitutional views, but also looked down on those with more traditional social views.

In my view, the intensity with which the left and the liberal elites embraced the culture wars was not unrelated to the dominance of neoliberalism. The culture wars were how progressives maintained their self-esteem as progressives, when they either had nothing to say anymore or were being ignored on economic issues. This was understandable, but the comfort so derived may well have distracted from the needed effort to come up with an alternative to neoliberalism.

In any event, the culture wars have simmered down. They may arise again, or continue in debates over bathrooms, but it is unlikely that they will ever be what they were from 1969 to 2006, and it is no coincidence that, after 2006, the NDP was able to regain some of its traditional strength.

The fourth horseman is associated with death, and it is therefore appropriate to discuss the issue of social movements in the context of such a metaphor, especially when you consider the New Politics Initiative (NPI) in 2001 that called on the NDP to euthanize itself in the name of a decidedly unclear vision of what the political future of the left might look like. But I am getting ahead of myself.

The place to start with social movements is with the peace movement, especially the movement opposed to cruise missile testing on Canadian soil in the years 1982 and 1983. The protests against testing would be attended by NDP MPs, who spoke for their party, and by a few Liberal or Tory MPs, who didn't. Yet, the rhetoric and organizational dynamic of the movement treated all of us the same, watering down or neutralizing the presence of New Democrats and exaggerating the hope associated with the token Liberals and Tories. In 1984, the pro-cruise Tories swept to power.

This pattern would repeat itself over the years on other issues. I wish I had a dime for every time I went away from a rally against NAFTA, or the MAI, or the WTO, or on several other issues, frustrated that the speakers had called on politicians generically to support a particular policy, without any acknowledgement of the fact that there was already a political party, in

Parliament, who agreed with them and could use some support, instead of being treated like the ally whose name dared not be alluded to, never mind spoken about.

This came to a head to a degree in the aftermath of the 1994 election when the anti-NAFTA Council of Canadians and the Action Canada Network were thought by many New Democrats to have been devastatingly silent on whom to vote for if you wanted to nix NAFTA. The Liberals won, NAFTA went ahead, and Chrétien said if people didn't want NAFTA they should have voted NDP. Liberal criticism of NAFTA did not mean that they were actually against it, as is the case with many other things.

In the meantime, as the neoliberal worldview became more entrenched, it became commonplace, as I alluded to before, for some on the Canadian left to complain that the NDP, mostly represented by the caucus, was drifting to the right. I don't believe we were, but, when what you say is never reported, people are left to their own imaginations and observations of other social democratic governments and parties. Alexa McDonough started her leadership campaign in 1995 by making just such a charge against the caucus. But, by 2001, she was being charged, again unfairly, with the same rightward drift.

To make a long story way too short, in 2001, on the heels of very high-profile and well-attended protests like the Battle in Seattle in 1999, in which I participated as NDP Trade Critic, the NPI was proposed. At the federal convention that year I was brought to the microphone by my friend and colleague of many years, Svend Robinson, who accused the party of being in the mushy middle.

Having just led the party through our solitary opposition to Bill C-36, the anti-terrorism bill that followed 9/11, I outlined to the convention a number of issues where we had stood alone, on the left. The motion to support NPI was defeated, 60–40, but it was enough to save the NDP so it could go on, under Jack Layton, to eventually make the breakthrough of 2011.

I fancy myself a movement person. There is something about the CCF and the NDP that is movement. There is also something about being a political party that can win seats or win governments, and, in all cases, have some measure of influence for the common good that would not be possible otherwise. It was the inadequacies of movements that caused people from various movements to come together in Calgary in 1932, and Regina in 1933, to form a political party. This insight seems to have reasserted itself, and I am glad of it. But as I previously said, the political right seldom had such problems. Preston Manning didn't start a movement. He started a political party, and it, although somewhat morphed, went on to govern.

There were other issues that vexed the NDP during my years in Parliament. NATO membership, the Middle East, and reaction to the Ontario NDP government come to mind, but I believe that, broadly speaking, the four things I have talked about here were the greatest challenges and greatest obstacles to electoral success. To the extent that they no longer exist in the same form, new opportunities for unity and forward progress present themselves. But then of course, there are pipelines to debate. But that is for another time and place, and certainly not here in Alberta.

CHAPTER 12

FROM TRADITIONAL SOCIAL DEMOCRACY TO THE THIRD WAY

AN ASSESSMENT OF FEDERAL NDP PLATFORMS, 1988–2011

Matt Fodor

During the 1990s, social democratic parties around the world underwent a process of ideological moderation known as the "Third Way." The federal New Democratic Party (NDP) has often been viewed as an exception to this broader pattern. Indeed, the NDP in the late 1990s and early 2000s resisted the Third Way tide. Yet, as this chapter will argue, while the Third Way had a delayed effect on Canadian social democracy, the NDP ultimately followed suit and underwent a Third Way alignment under the leadership of Jack Layton. This ideological shift is evident through an examination of the party's election platforms between 1988 and 2011.

This chapter is organized as follows. It begins by touching briefly on the realignment of social democracy in general and in the Canadian context. The core of the chapter examines changes in four areas: economic priorities, taxation, policies aimed at workers and unions, and social policy. It will conclude by bringing the analysis through to the most recent 2015 election and beyond.

The traditional social democracy that prevailed during the post-war period was characterized by a commitment to redistribution, democratic economic governance, and social protectionism.[1] Through the mechanism of Keynesian economics, post-war social democrats were able to pursue policies that benefited their working class constituency (full employment, extensive welfare state, income and wealth redistribution, support for trade unions) while supporting the "national interest" of sustaining economic growth.[2] However, it was evident by the end of the Cold War that social democracy had reached an impasse. Neoliberalism, fundamentally at odds with traditional social democracy, had displaced Keynesianism as economic orthodoxy among policy-makers in the 1980s.[3] The shift to a "post-industrial economy" eroded social democracy's base in the industrial working class, while globalization placed constraints on the ability of states to pursue traditional social democratic objectives.[4] The Third Way emerged in the 1990s as the strategic response of social democratic parties to these challenges.

The Third Way represented social democracy's shift to the political centre. While most closely associated with Tony Blair and New Labour in Britain, virtually all social democratic governments elected in the 1990s pursued a Third Way approach. According to leading proponent Anthony Giddens, the Third Way represented "an attempt to transcend both old-style social democracy and neoliberalism."[5] The Third Way embraced fiscal conservatism and rejected the levels of progressive taxation and extent of state intervention in the economy proposed by traditional social democracy.

The Third Way, then, represented a break from traditional social democracy in that it rejected the idea that the market needed to be constrained in order to achieve fundamental social goals. Rather, it seeks to work "with the grain of the market"; while supporting a "safety net" for the poor and marginalized, it seeks to work within the market wherever possible.[6] Altogether, the Third Way should be seen as a compromise between traditional social democracy and neoliberalism, or social democracy's accommodation to neoliberalism.

The federal NDP's shifting policies and priorities reflect the party's attempt to adapt to the competitive pressures of the Canadian party system, as well as to the changing composition of the social democratic electorate, economic change, and the ideological trajectory of social democracy worldwide. The NDP's ideological trajectory can also be seen in the context of what Bryan Evans refers to as the two structured refoundations of Canadian social democracy. The first structured refoundation was the creation of the NDP in 1961, which embraced a regulated capitalism. While there was no formal second refoundation, "in the wake of the free trade election of 1988, the NDP went through various internal debates, providing evidence that a second refoundation did take place."[7] This second refoundation represented the NDP's integration into neoliberalism.

In the 1980s, the NDP, under the leadership of Ed Broadbent, was able to secure the support of 20 percent of the electorate with a rather traditional Keynesian approach. By the 1990s, however, traditional strategies had proven inadequate.[8] The federal party suffered a near-wipeout in the 1993 election (receiving 6.9 percent of the vote and nine seats), saw a partial recovery in 1997 (11 percent and twenty-one seats), and fell back again in 2000 (8.5 percent and thirteen seats). However, a fundamental overhaul of policy and strategy did not come easily to the federal NDP. Under the leadership of Alexa McDonough, the NDP debated its future direction. In 1998, the party leadership expressed an interest in learning from the success of European leaders such as Tony Blair and Gerhard Schröder. However, this move was resisted by the party membership. At the 1999 federal convention, delegates overwhelmingly rejected the Third Way and the party leadership retreated, opting instead for a more vaguely defined "Canadian way."[9] For the most part, the party's 2000 election program "stayed remarkably true to its mainstream Keynesian roots—advocating significant programme spending in several key areas."[10] At the party's 2001 convention, two options to fundamentally change the party—the New Politics Initiative on the left and another attempt at the Third Way on the right—were rejected. It was only after Alexa McDonough was replaced by Jack Layton in 2003 that a fundamental transformation of the federal NDP took place.[11]

A media-savvy former Toronto city councillor with a pragmatic streak, Layton was known for his advocacy on environmental and urban issues. Elected with a decisive majority on the first ballot cast in the January 2003 leadership race, Layton had the support of key figures in the left-wing NPI as well as establishment figures like Broadbent. Layton enjoyed wide support in all wings of the party throughout his tenure, including the party's left. Yet Layton modernized the party's campaign operations and subtly moved the party to the political centre.[12] During his tenure as leader, the party increased its share of the popular vote and seat count in four consecutive elections, culminating in the stunning breakthrough of 2011, which brought the NDP to Official Opposition for the first time.

Seeking to reverse the erosion of the party's electoral base, Layton's NDP sought to appeal to a broader constituency. Traditional concerns such as labour and employment issues and democratic control of the economy became less salient in party platforms.[13] Layton also sought to distance the NDP from its "tax and spend" image.[14] By 2008, the NDP had regained its traditional constituency, having received 18 percent of the vote in that year's election. Layton's team then sought to appeal to the next "tier" of voters.[15] By the 2011 election, a Third Way realignment of the federal NDP had occurred.

Why was the Third Way initially resisted, but eventually adopted by the federal NDP? Quite simply, the NDP in the late 1990s was in no position to break from traditional social democracy. It could ill afford to alienate what remained of its political base. Furthermore, the governing Liberals comfortably occupied the Third Way "space." By the Layton era, however, the Canadian political landscape had changed. The decline of the Liberal Party—who were reduced to a minority government in 2004, were defeated in 2006, fell further again in 2008, and ultimately reduced to third place in 2011—created an opening for the NDP on the centre-left. Furthermore, Layton's modernization project was not explicitly presented as the Third Way, and he retained the trust of leftists and social movement actors who backed his leadership throughout his tenure. With a heightened profile and increased support over four consecutive elections, party members gave Layton a wide leeway to remake the party.

In examining the ideological evolution of the NDP over time, it seems appropriate to start by comparing the main economic priorities expressed in party programs. Reflecting a traditional social democratic view, the 1988 platform stated that an NDP government would "make full employment the guiding principle for all its policy decisions."[16]

The platform in the 1993 election, which appeared during the recession of the early 1990s, was entirely framed around a full employment strategy that would create 500,000 jobs nationwide. It expressed a goal of "building a high-wage, high-skill, high value-added and knowledge-based economy—a 'smart' economy—that serves the interests of working people."[17] However, ceding ground to growing concern about the national deficit, it stated that its program "will lead to a gradual but sure reduction in deficits and debt."[18]

The 1997 platform again stressed the centrality of full employment. With 10 percent of Canadians officially unemployed, it pledged to "make full employment the primary goal of government." This included setting targets to reduce unemployment by half in its first mandate and to reprioritize the goals of the Bank of Canada to emphasize job creation rather than fighting inflation. It took seriously but treaded carefully on the question of the deficit: "During periods of growth and prosperity, we . . . favour balancing the federal budget, and reducing the weight of federal debt on the economy . . . The question is how to do it, how quickly to do it and who should bear the cost." It pledged to eliminate the deficit in three years by expanding public services, higher taxation on the wealthy, and eliminating duplication.[19]

By the 2000 election, the governing Liberals had slayed the deficit and the government had a surplus of $130 billion. The 2000 NDP platform stated: "Working families made sacrifices in these seven years of cuts. Working families should be able to share in the benefits of the surplus."[20] The 2000 platform outlined the following goals of economic policy: full employment, good jobs, an equitable sharing of the opportunities and burdens of technological change, and sustainable development. It reiterated the call for reprioritizing the goals of the Bank of Canada to "require that monetary policy works toward targets for both employment and inflation."[21] It also maintained that its economic policies would not add to the national debt.[22]

By 2004, the party's traditional goal of full employment was abandoned. That year's platform made clear its support for balanced budgets, noting that: "Over the last 20 years, NDP provincial and territorial governments are less likely to have run deficits than governments of any other party." However, it also rejected "deficit reduction for deficit reduction's sake," stressing instead the need to "invest in innovation to meet our economic, social and environmental challenges."[23]

The 2006 platform noted that the NDP "is as serious about prosperity as it is about social justice" and outlined four key economic priorities: (1) annual balanced budgets; (2) creating a competitive tax regime; (3) a twenty-year program of infrastructure development based on investment in cities and regional economic development; and (4) reduction in provincial trade barriers. It stated that: "These commitments along with our continued emphasis on health and education are a powerful expression of the NDP's commitment to wealth creation."[24]

The 2008 platform pledged that an NDP government would "implement a prudent and sensible plan to keep good jobs in Canada, encourage innovation, and get the Canadian government engaged in creating good jobs in the new energy economy."[25] It also stated that it would "[i]ntroduce and maintain balanced budgets in each and every year of a mandate."[26]

The 2011 platform emphasized more small-scale and practical measures than NDP platforms of the past. Its emphasis on "rewarding the job creators" signaled a shift in emphasis toward the private sector in terms of job creation.[27] The Great Recession of 2008 saw a return to government deficits. The 2011 platform expressed that it would "maintain Canada's commitment to balance the federal budget within the next 4 years, as per the Department of Finance projections."[28]

With regard to tax policy, progressive taxation and tax fairness have long been a cornerstone of NDP policy. Pointing to the tax advantages enjoyed by wealthy Canadians, the 1988 platform called for a minimum tax on profitable corporations, closing loopholes, a more progressive tax code, and a reduction of sales taxes.[29] However, it presented more policy aspirations than policy specifics.

Tax policy became more specific in the 1993 election. That year's platform pledged to eliminate the Goods and Services Tax (GST) within five years.[30] The GST would be replaced by the elimination of various deductions for business, a minimum corporate tax of 14 percent, the creation of new tax brackets of 35 percent and 40 percent for taxpayers earning more than $100,000 and $135,000 respectively, a wealth tax on the top 10 percent of income earners, and the taxation of private trusts.[31]

The 1997 platform called for the immediate removal of the GST from books, magazines, and children's clothing and repeated the call for eventually phasing out the GST altogether. It included measures to increase taxes on wealthy Canadians, including new rates of 32 percent and 35 percent on incomes above $100,000 and $150,000, a "millionaire's tax" on inheritances and taxing capital gains at the same rate as employment income (exempting small business and family farms), and a wealth tax. It also called for curtailing corporate tax deductions, a minimum corporate income tax, increasing the GST credit by 30 percent, eliminating federal surtaxes on low-income Canadians, increased taxes on tobacco, and hiking the corporate tax rate by two points.[32]

A notable shift in 2000 was the NDP's embrace of "targeted" tax cuts,[33] where the NDP promised to maintain the Liberals' income tax reduction on middle income earners from 26 percent to 23 percent. Nor did it propose new personal tax brackets for wealthy individuals. The 2000 platform called for doubling the Child Tax Benefit to $4,200, elimination of federal income tax on incomes below $15,000 a year, increasing the GST credit by $200, and the removal of the GST on books and magazines. It treaded more carefully on the question of the GST, warning that "ending the GST/HST will have to be done gradually and with reference to the need to reinvest in the public services we need." Other measures included an excess profits tax of 20 percent on financial institutions when rates of return exceeded 10 percent, a "millionaire's tax" on estates over $1 million, treating capital gains the same as other income, disallowing corporate exemptions on political lobbying and entertainment expenses, extending the GST to brokerage fees, and increased taxes on tobacco products.[34]

The 2004 platform included similar measures to 2000, including the elimination of federal income taxes on incomes below $15,000, removing the GST from family essentials and increasing the Child Tax Benefit to $4,900 (while permitting poor families that do not pay federal income tax to qualify), and treating capital gains the same as employment income. While it proposed an inheritance tax on estates over $1 million, this was abandoned during the campaign. It also called for the indexing of tax brackets and credits to protect taxpayers from inflation, the reversal of corporate tax cuts, and closing tax loopholes.[35]

The 2006 platform saw a more explicitly conservative turn on taxation. While calling for prioritization of public investments over tax cuts, it ruled out further tax increases. It stated that: "The federal government will have enough money over the next four years to do its job inside of balanced budgets. With billions of dollars in surplus, Ottawa doesn't need new tax revenues. Accordingly, New Democrats won't be proposing to raise new tax revenues during the next Parliament." It called for stopping the Liberals' $10 billion corporate tax cut while supporting increases in the basic personal credit amount rates and the cutting of the lowest personal tax rate.[36]

The 2008 platform focused on corporate taxes rather than personal income taxes. It raised concern about "wasteful and unproductive corporate tax breaks" and called specifically for a return to the 22.12 percent corporate tax rate that had existed before Stephen Harper's Conservatives took power. It also called for simplifying the tax code and removing loopholes, ending special tax breaks for the tar sands and the oil and gas industry, and cracking down on international tax havens.[37]

The 2011 platform called for raising the corporate tax rate to 19.5 percent. Remarkably, it also pledged to "keep Canada's corporate tax rate competitive by ensuring that our combined federal/provincial Corporate Tax Rate is below the United States' federal corporate tax rate."[38] Its call for "rewarding the job creators" meant tax cuts for small business. It pledged to "reduce the small business tax rate from 11 percent to nine percent to support a sector of our economy that creates half of all new jobs in Canada."[39] It also emphasized tax credits for jobs and investment, including a Job Creation Tax Credit of $4,500 per new hire.

As a social democratic party with a traditional base in the working class and institutional links to organized labour, the NDP has long included several policies targeted specifically at workers and unions. However, like other social democratic parties, it has also moved away from specific "class" appeals to try to appeal to a broader share of the electorate.

The 1988 platform included calls for improved workplace health and safety laws, a higher federal minimum wage, and ensuring that part-time workers received benefits on a pro-rated basis. The main issue of the 1988 election was the proposed Canada-US Free Trade Agreement (FTA) and that year's NDP platform explicitly aimed its opposition to the FTA at working people: "Ed Broadbent and the New Democrats have stood up for working women and men in Canada ... Most importantly, New Democrats have consistently worked against the Mulroney-Reagan trade deal: it threatens Canadians' control over our own economic future, threatens Canadian jobs and threatens social programs like Medicare and unemployment insurance."[40]

As noted, the 1993 platform was entirely framed around job creation. It included a national infrastructure program to immediately kick-start job creation across the country, a National Investment Fund to create high-skill jobs, and a national training strategy. It promised to reverse changes to Unemployment Insurance by the Conservative government. It also called for the abrogation of the FTA and not proceeding with the proposed North American Free Trade Agreement (NAFTA).[41]

The 1997 platform explicitly pledged to "defend and promote the rights of workers in the new economy" and stated that: "The New Democratic Party believes that it is a centrally important objective of public policy to strengthen the position of working people by making trade union representation more widely accessible, and by helping trade unions become more effective organizations." Its proposed labour reforms included ending discrimination against part-time workers in pensions and unemployment insurance, requiring employers to pay benefits to part-time workers, redistribution of work times in order to create jobs, ensuring workers the right to refuse overtime, enforcing employment standards for temporary and contract workers, and banning the use of replacement workers. It also criticized the Liberal government's cutbacks to unemployment insurance and called for a new program with benefits based on an average of two-thirds of average earnings and restoring the maximum benefit of fifty weeks. The 1997 platform also criticized trade agreements such as the FTA and NAFTA, "which encourage corporations to go where wages are lower, benefits are lower and environmental regulations are weaker" and expressed support instead for trade agreements that "improve wages and working conditions" and contain "real, enforceable and progressive social, labour and environmental standards."[42]

The 2000 platform stressed the need to "ease worker and community adjustment to change" by improving the links between Employment Insurance (EI) and giving workers advance notice and severance pay during layoffs, and the prioritizing of workers' claims over all others in bankruptcy proceedings.[43] It called for federal government leadership in job training through the creation of a national training fund, as well as increasing training funds for short-term and seasonal workers and social assistance recipients.[44] It also called for restoring EI benefits to two-thirds of weekly pay and expanding coverage to at least 70 percent of unemployed workers, for federal legislation to provide part-time workers the same pro-rated benefits and job security prospects as full-time workers, and the reintroduction of a minimum wage for federally regulated employees.[45] Notably, it did not call for outright abrogation of NAFTA but rather of specific elements (the investor-state dispute mechanism and water exports). It pledged to work with progressive legislators to obtain the necessary changes to NAFTA, and, failing that, to replace NAFTA.[46]

The 2004 platform outlined a plan to modernize Canada's Employment Insurance program, noting that less than one-third of unemployed workers qualified. Measures to reform EI included allowing unemployed workers undergoing retraining to receive EI benefits, easing EI eligibility requirements, restoring benefits to two-thirds of former salary, and making the EI a separate trust fund.[47] It pledged to work toward a shorter work week, longer paid holidays, and more flexible retirement options. Other measures specifically aimed at workers and unions included outlawing the use of replacement workers during strikes and lockouts, a federal minimum wage, and a national training strategy and support for lifelong learning for workers to adapt to skills shortages.[48] The NDP continued to moderate its position on NAFTA, with the 2004 platform calling for renegotiation (particularly Chapter 11, the investor-state dispute mechanism) rather than abrogation and for working for fair trade agreements.[49]

The 2006 platform proposed reforming the Employment Insurance program to facilitate job and skills training, and broadening eligibility for EI training benefits to include employee benefits and unemployed workers who do not qualify for EI. It repeated the call for requiring all EI premium revenue to go to benefits, and also called for increasing the percentage of unemployed covered by EI from 40 percent to 80 percent and using the best twelve weeks to determine benefits. The 2006 platform also called for a $10 per hour national minimum wage for workers under federal jurisdiction, and repeated the previous call for banning the use of replacement workers.[50] With regard to NAFTA, the 2006 platform called for "trans-forming NAFTA to make it work in the cause of free trade" and for "a public review of every aspect of NAFTA on the Canadian economy and Canadian public policy," raising particular concern again with Chapter 11.[51]

The 2008 platform called for the creation of a Green-Collar Jobs Fund to train and retrain workers for the renewable energy sector and for the appointment of a Job Protection Commissioner to investigate lay-offs and shutdowns and to work with workers, business, stakeholders, and communities to ensure good jobs for Canadians.[52] It pledged to "[r]espect the right of workers to organize and bargain collectively." It also called for an action plan to address work-life balance issues and nonstandard employment relationships.[53] It repeated several planks from 2006, including a $10 an hour federal minimum wage, outlawing the use of replace-ment workers, and reforms to EI.[54] It also spoke of the need to renegotiate NAFTA, particularly Chapters 6 (energy) and 11, as well as its dispute resolution mechanisms.[55]

The 2011 platform put less emphasis on labour and employment issues. It called for extending EI stimulus measures in the face of the reces-sion and amending the Employment Insurance program to raise benefits to 60 percent of former salary (as opposed to two-thirds), basing benefits on the best twelve weeks, and improving training and retraining programs. It also repeated the call for a national minimum wage.[56] There was no mention of unions and the previous call for banning replacement workers was abandoned. Free trade agreements had also ceased to be an issue; there was no mention of abolishing or reforming NAFTA.

The NDP has traditionally advocated for universal social programs and a more extensive welfare state (health care, childcare, housing, pen-sions, etc.). And with the emergence of neoliberalism in the 1980s, the NDP also defended the post-war welfare state in the face of cutbacks from Conservative and Liberal governments.

The 1988 platform included a call for "an affordable, quality child-care program that puts the emphasis on new childcare spaces" as well as a national housing program to expand affordable and co-operative housing. It also called for increasing Old Age Security (OAS) and the Guaranteed Income Supplement (GIS) for seniors, the re-indexing of family allow-ances, and increases to the child tax credit.[57]

The 1993 platform, focused on job creation, had less to say on welfare state measures. It did, however, include a national childcare program that it estimated would create 40,000 jobs. It set a goal of doubling the number of childcare spaces nationwide to 600,000. The federal government and the provinces would each pay 40 percent of the cost ($1.5 billion) with parental fees (assessed by income) paying the remainder. It would be administered by the provinces.[58]

The 1997 platform called for the reversal of the Liberal government's cuts to social services. It also called for expanding medicare to include a national prescription drug plan and homecare, greater enforcement of the Canada Health Act to ensure universality and accessibility, and guaranteeing a $15 billion floor for the Canada Health and Social Transfer. It also included a ten-year plan to eliminate child poverty in Canada (with a target of cutting child poverty by half in six years) and a national strategy to combat hunger and homelessness. A national childcare and early education program would create 150,000 spaces by 2000. The 1997 platform also called for a long-term plan to strengthen the Canada Pension Plan (CPP), and for starting non-profit and co-operative housing programs.[59]

Defense of medicare fared particularly prominently in the 2000 platform. It called for increasing the federal share of shared health spending from 13.5 percent to 25 percent and for amending the Canada Health Act to withhold transfers from provinces allowing private, for-profit healthcare. It repeated the call for including pharmacare and homecare under medicare.[60] It pledged to work with provinces to build a comprehensive childcare and early childhood education program, backed by a fully funded National Early Years fund of $3.5 billion by 2004. It also called for a national housing strategy, where the federal government would spend 1 percent of the federal budget on building 25,000 units of affordable housing annually.[61]

The 2004 platform proposed a ten-year housing program that would build 200,000 units of affordable and co-operative housing.[62] It repeated previous calls for pharmacare and homecare, to increase the share of federal funding of health care to 25 percent within two years, and amend the Canada Health Act to prevent funding of private, for-profit hospitals.[63] It pledged to work with provinces to provide funding to create 200,000 childcare spaces within four years.[64] It also called for setting nationwide goals and ensuring federal funding for social assistance, establishing a federal pension insurance system, improving access to the CPP/QPP for women, and a review of the adequacy of the pension system.[65]

The 2006 platform pledged to enact a National Childcare Act to establish a national framework for childcare and early childhood education, creating 200,000 spaces in the first years and an additional 25,000 spaces annually over the next three years. It repeated the previous call for a ten-year housing program.[66] It pledged to enact national pharmacare and expand homecare coverage and to enact a Protection of Public Healthcare Act to stop privatization of health care, as well as to train 16,000 new health care providers.[67] It vowed to protect pensions through a pension benefits system for federally regulated employees and to reform bankruptcy laws to protect workers. It also pledged to undertake an annual review of seniors' income needs and to amend the CPP benefits formula in order not to penalize caregivers.[68]

The 2008 platform pledged to enact the NDP's Early Learning and Childcare Act (which passed second reading in the House of Commons) that would create 150,000 spaces in the first year and rise to 220,000 spaces in the fourth year. It proposed a rather ambitious Poverty Elimination Act that would aim to end poverty in Canada by 2020, with initial targets of eliminating child poverty and overall poverty by 50 percent and 35 percent in five years respectively. It also called for the creation of a $5,000 per year Child Tax Benefit and a pledge of 1 percent of federal spending to affordable housing.[69] In terms of health care, the 2008 platform pledged to increase the number of Canadian-trained doctors and nurses by 50 percent and repeated its commitments to pharmacare and homecare and prohibiting federal funding of private, for-profit delivery.[70]

The 2011 platform was more modest in terms of welfare state measures. For instance, it did not call for the expansion of health care into new, previously uncovered areas.[71] Pharmacare did not appear in the 2011 platform. Rather, it stressed that it would train more health care professionals (giving specific figures of 1,200 doctors over ten years and 6,000 nurses over six years), as well as designate transfers for homecare and long-term care for seniors, work with provinces to lower drug prices (bulk buying, enhanced price reviews, etc.), and negotiate a new ten-year health accord with the provinces.[72] The 2011 platform promised to eventually double (with no specific date) CPP/QPP, increase the GIS to take seniors out of poverty, increase funding for affordable housing, and set targets for poverty reduction. It also pledged to combine existing supports into a single non-taxable Child Tax Benefit of up to $700 per child over four years, on top of the existing Universal Child Tax Benefit. And while it did call for a national childcare program, its goal of adding 25,000 spaces per year was much more modest than previous platforms.[73]

In examining federal NDP platforms between 1988 and 2011, it is evident that a movement away from traditional social democracy occurred.

The party moved away from more ambitious spending initiatives and became more accepting of the market as it sought to appeal to a broader share of the electorate beyond its traditional working-class base. It increasingly accepted the parameters of neoliberal capitalism.

A rethinking of Canadian social democracy had begun in the 1990s—this was apparent in the party's embrace of balanced budgets in 1993 as well as some concession to Liberal tax cuts in 2000. But it was really in the Layton era that a shift to Third Way social democracy was evident. The Layton era can itself be divided into two periods. In the 2004, 2006, and 2008 elections, the NDP, seeking to regain its traditional constituency, included several progressive planks and policies in such areas as health care, childcare, housing, and labour rights. However, this coincided with a fiscal conservatism that included balanced budgets and holding the line on taxation—placing constraints on the ability to pursue a traditional social democratic program. In 2011, having secured its base and seeking to appeal to a broader constituency referred to by party strategists as "Layton Liberals,"[74] the NDP moderated and simplified its policies further, and placed more emphasis on the private sector. Hence by the 2011 election, the NDP had undergone a Third Way realignment.

Following Layton's untimely death shortly after the 2011 election, the NDP membership elected Thomas Mulcair to lead the party. A former Cabinet minister in the Liberal government of Jean Charest in Quebec, Mulcair was seen as an experienced hand who was best poised to solidify the gains of 2011 and even lead the NDP to power. While perceived by many party activists as being on the right of the party, for most members his perceived ability to win and maintain the party's recent gains in Quebec took precedence.[75]

The content of the 2015 platform cannot be viewed in isolation from the electoral strategy. With a lead in most national polls when the election was called in August, Mulcair and the NDP sought to reassure voters sceptical of the party's "tax and spend" image. Mulcair firmly rejected tax increases on the wealthy and pledged to balance the budget in his first year in office. This positioning allowed a revitalized Liberal Party under Justin Trudeau to successfully outflank the NDP on the left with pledges to increase taxes on the top 1 percent and run short-term deficits to pay for major infrastructure spending.[76]

The 2015 election was the longest campaign in Canadian history and the NDP did not release its platform until October 9, just ten days before election day. Hence by the time of its release, the general tone of the campaign had already been set and the NDP had fallen back to third place. The 2015 platform did seek to regain disappointed progressive voters and in several respects was more progressive than the 2011 platform. For instance, it expressed support for trade union rights and a ban on the use of replacement workers,[77] which did not appear in 2011. It pledged to work toward universal drug coverage[78] as well as a national childcare program that "would be the first major new social program in Canada in generations."[79] Some supporters of Mulcair even went as far as to suggest that this was "the most ambitious and progressive platform we have put forward in decades."[80] However, this was clearly not the case.[81]

Perhaps importantly, the 2015 platform went even further in terms of fiscal conservatism. As in 2011, it again pledged to keep the combined federal/provincial corporate tax rate "well below the United States, and below the G7 average."[82] However, this time the federal corporate tax rate would be 17 percent rather than the 19.5 percent proposed in 2011.[83] Furthermore, the 2015 platform took a more austere position in terms of balancing the budget. While the 2011 platform promised to balance the budget within four years, the 2015 platform stated that "we will balance the federal budget in all four fiscal years under an NDP government."[84] Such a commitment to balanced budget orthodoxy, if taken seriously, would place severe constraints on pursuing a progressive program, particularly if the fiscal situation proves less optimistic than projected.

The recent election of the young, charismatic Jagmeet Singh has generated new excitement in the NDP. Singh has signaled a break with the fiscal orthodoxy of the past and expressed a willingness to run deficits in difficult economic times.[85] During the leadership race, he also expressed support for some tax increases on wealthy individuals and estates.[86] However, his plan to merge OAS and other existing seniors' benefits suggested a break with the party's long-standing commitment to the universality of OAS and universal social programs in general.[87] Furthermore, Singh was backed by much of the party establishment and his appeal had more to do with his perceived ability to win than with ideology.[88] While the type of program the NDP runs on remains to be seen, a full reversal of the Third Way turn that accelerated during the Layton era seems unlikely.

CHAPTER 13

THE NDP IN QUEBEC BEFORE AND AFTER THE ORANGE WAVE

Karl Bélanger

Before the 2011 Orange Wave, Quebec had been out of reach for Canada's New Democrats, a pipe dream. From 1935 to 2006, no CCF/NDP MPs were ever elected in Quebec in a general election. Everything changed when Jack Layton convinced Quebecers to vote en masse for the NDP and elected fifty-nine Members of Parliament, a success that was beyond the wildest dreams of his NDP and CCF predecessors.

It was not for lack of trying, but the CCF had been founded and was led by Protestant westerners, a certain drawback in the very Catholic Quebec. The clergy, strongly supportive of Maurice Duplessis' Union Nationale, was not shy about warning their flock against the socialist hordes. Still, a small base of activists believed in CCF principles and that the message of solidarity would appeal to Quebecers. In its first federal election after forming in 1932, the CCF ran candidates in Quebec. It was far from being a full slate, as was the case elsewhere in the country. The upstart party ran only three candidates for sixty-five Quebec seats. That number grew to four candidates in 1940 and twenty-nine in 1945.

Meanwhile, the CCF was also trying to establish itself on the provincial scene. A candidate ran as "CCF candidate" in the 1936 Quebec general election, although the Quebec section of the party had not yet been founded. That happened in 1939, when the Fédération du Commonwealth Co-opératif was established. The party only ran one candidate in 1939. In 1944, led by Romuald-Joseph "Doc" Lamoureux, the CCF ran twenty-one candidates and elected the first—and only—CCF/NDP Member of the National Assembly (MNA): David Côté in Rouyn-Noranda.

Côté was a labour organizer with the workers' unions in the mines of the Rouyn region and was later recruited by the Congress of Industrial Organizations (CIO). Côté was elected with only 21 percent of the vote and a majority of 250 votes over Bloc Populaire candidate Maurice Caouette. There was a lot of discontent in Quebec following the Great Depression, as was the case elsewhere, and smaller parties from the far right to the far left were trying to emerge and build a base of support. The election of Côté allowed the CCF to dream about a possible breakthrough because, until then, the CCF was clearly seen as marginal among French Canadians. Alas, David Côté ended up fighting with party officials and left to sit as an independent in July 1945. The party only ran eight candidates in 1948.

In 1946, Thérèse Casgrain joined the CCF; she became vice-president in 1948. A feminist well ahead of her era, Casgrain became the first woman in Canada to become leader of a political party, leading the Quebec wing of the CCF from 1951 to 1957. While she was leader, the party tried to "Frenchize" its brand and became the Parti Social Démocratique (PSD) in the mid-1950s. Under Casgrain, the party grew a little and ran twenty-something candidates in 1952 and 1956, including candidates like Gaston Miron, a poet who would later become a Parti Quebecois (PQ) icon. In 1960, under the leadership of union leader Michel Chartrand, the PSD announced that it would not contest the provincial election and would dedicate its meagre resources to the creation of a new democratic party. Chartrand invited "les dégoutés" to void their ballot.

In its entire existence, the CCF-PSD in Quebec did not have a significant electoral impact, never even reaching 3 percent of the popular vote either federally or provincially. The lone shining light was the election of Côté—but also, in Thérèse Casgrain and Michel Chartrand, the emergence of key characters who would become historic figures in Quebec.

When the New Democratic Party of Canada was founded in 1961 by the CCF and unions affiliated with the Canadian Labor Congress (CLC), the French-Canadian issue was part of the debates at the founding convention. Chartrand, the leader of the Quebec wing of the party, wanted the new organization to recognize the French-Canadian nation in a special way by removing the word "national" from the party structures and constitution and replacing it with the word "federal." Delegates accepted the request but also adopted a resolution stating that the new party believed in the federal system as the only one that could ensure the joint development of the two nations.

Similar to the CLC's involvement in the birth of the NDP, in Quebec the Fédération des travailleurs et travailleuses du Québec (FTQ) was involved in the creation of the new party. The goal was to build a wider alliance with the active Quebec labour movement and other progressives in Quebec. Several renowned Quebecers got on board: Robert Cliche, Gérard Picard, Fernand Daoust, Charles Taylor, and many others. This occurred while Quebec was undergoing very transformative changes: the Quiet Revolution of Liberal Premier Jean Lesage, who significantly expanded Quebec's safety net, creating social programs that would slowly erode the influence of the Catholic Church. Meanwhile, Lesage mandated René Lévesque to nationalize hydro-electric power. But many Quebecers wanted something more and wanted it faster: this led to the emergence of two independentist parties, le Ralliement Nationale (RN) and the Rassemblement pour l'indépendance nationale (RIN).

It is in this context that the New Democratic Party was born in Quebec. It was a difficult process. Radical disagreements emerged during the convention in June 1963. The disagreements were mostly about the constitutional future of Quebec and the links to the New Democratic Party of Canada. The convention ended with the creation of two distinct entities: a provisional council of the Socialist Party of Québec (PSQ) and a provisional organizing committee of the federal NDP in Quebec (NPDQ). The NPDQ would concentrate its efforts on the federal scene, while the PSQ would focus its attention on provincial policy. The FTQ, which was supportive of the initial project and had provided a strong contingent of organizers to support the NDP of Canada, took its distance and never assisted the PSQ. The PSQ, which never managed to become an officially registered political party, ran five unofficial candidates in 1966, garnering a little more than 1,000 votes combined. The party dissolved in 1968, with many joining the newly formed Parti Québécois, while others came back to the NDP.

The federal NDP was immediately more successful than its CCF-PSD predecessor, gathering over 4 percent of the vote in Quebec in its first election in 1962. A year later, the NDP obtained over 7 percent. By coincidence more than by design, the NDP was bringing forward policies that were aligned with many voters in Quebec, especially in intellectual circles. The creation of medicare, for instance, or opposition to the deployment of the Bomarc nuclear missiles were popular positions. A young Pierre Elliott Trudeau was an early member of the party. NDP leader Tommy Douglas demonstrated an openness to the emerging Quebec nationalism—partly out of principles and partly because the Quebec wing of the NDP was naturally populated by nationalists. The party adopted early on the two nations conception of Canada.

The Quebec-wing leader was Robert Cliche, a charismatic lawyer from Beauce. The NDP had a lot of hope for Cliche and invested a lot of resources in him. Many, in fact, saw in him a potential successor to Tommy Douglas. In the 1965 federal election, Cliche ran in Beauce and obtained almost 30 percent of the vote. Cliche had recruited a strong slate of candidates to contest the 1965 election, including TV star Laurier LaPierre. Meanwhile, Trudeau betrayed his friend Charles Taylor and ran as a Liberal against him in Mount Royal, winning easily. The NDP was shut out again. Still, the 1965 election showed the NDP as a serious player in Quebec, receiving over 12 percent of the vote—a high mark that would last over twenty years.

An opportunity arose in 1967 when the Liberal MP for Outremont-St-Jean, Maurice Lamontagne, was called to the Senate. A by-election was triggered and the NDP recruited Deniz Lazure, the founder of the infant psychiatry department of the Sainte-Justine hospital. Thérèse Casgrain previously had respectable showings under the NDP banner in that riding in 1962 and 1963, and the party had finished second, albeit distant, in 1965. The Progressive Conservatives did not run a candidate and Lazure came within 1,500 votes of wrestling the riding away from the Liberals. Lazure left the party and later joined the PQ, becoming a minister in René Lévesque's government.

Disappointed by the defeat in 1965, Cliche ran again in 1968, but in the new riding of Duvernay, in Laval. The Liberals, who had been battling the Social Credit Quebec-wing, led by Réal Caouette on the right of the spectrum, did not want the upstart NDP, with a very autonomous Quebec wing, to be successful on the left. They convinced Eric Kierans, a popular former provincial Liberal minister, to run against Cliche. Cliche lost again, this time with 43.85 percent of the vote. The 1968 election saw the NDP's vote share in Quebec drop back to 7 percent. Cliche was done; he quit politics shortly thereafter and was later appointed judge to the provincial court.

The federal NDP, which had gone quite far in its support of Quebec nationalism and the need for asymmetrical federalism, recognizing in 1967 that "Quebec is different from the other provinces" and that this difference called for a different relationship with the federal government, decided to backtrack somewhat. The anti-nationalist Trudeau was winning the public opinion battle, while the NDP was failing to make inroads in Quebec.

The Quebec NDP's first attempt to elect MNAs was in 1970, when it fielded thirteen candidates under the leadership of Roland Morin. A young unionist activist, Morin had been president of the party since 1967. Morin was elected leader in March 1970, while the Quebec election had already been called for the end of April. The party hastily adopted a program. It steered away from linguistic and constitutional issues that were at the heart of Quebec's political life in these tumultuous years. Morin wanted to focus on unemployment, the economy, poverty, and health care. There was some reference to the theme of Quebec's economic independence—but within the Canadian federation. Short on time and candidates, the party did not register with the electorate, while the social-democrat and pro-independence PQ elected seven MNAs on its first attempt.

A few months later the traumatic events of the October Crisis occurred; members of the FLQ kidnapped provincial minister Pierre Laporte and British diplomat James Cross. The government of Premier Bourassa formally requested that the Government of Canada grant "emergency powers" to allow police to arrest suspicious individuals without due process, a request that Montreal Mayor Jean Drapeau had also made. Prime Minister Trudeau responded by implementing the War Measures Act. In Ottawa, the NDP was the lone voice for sanity, with outgoing leader Tommy Douglas stating, "The government, I submit, is using a sledgehammer to crack a peanut." Politically, this was seen by many as political suicide. The party did not have a real base of support in French Quebec, and this position was a major problem for the Anglophone community. Elsewhere in the country, the implementation of the War Measures Act was seen as necessary to crush the separatists apprehended during the uprising. The courageous position taken by the NDP was noted by a young Quebecer named Jack Layton, who joined the party in the aftermath.

David Lewis succeeded Douglas at the 1971 leadership convention, when the radical faction known as the Waffle was at its peak. The Waffle's candidate James Laxer gave Lewis a run for his money, pushing the voting to four ballots. The Waffle was also active on the policy front, even proposing a resolution supporting Quebec sovereignty; however, the resolution was not adopted. Lewis issued a stern warning to the Quebec NDP, stating that they could continue to debate Quebec's constitutional status, but the NDP was a federalist party. Lewis spoke some French, but that was not enough to convince Quebecers, and the NDP fell further in Quebec in the 1972 federal election, below 7 percent, despite an increase in support in the rest of the country—and holding the balance of power in Ottawa.

Provincially, the NPDQ, under new leader Henri-François Gautrin, decided to sit out the 1973 election, refocusing the work of the Quebec wing on the federal scene, which was rather unstable. But the party failed to make any gains in Quebec during the 1974 federal election, which saw the NDP lose seats nationally (including Lewis') and lose the balance of power.

Gautrin was courted by the Regroupement des militants syndicaux (RMS), a political organization founded in 1974 by members of the three main Quebec unions, the FTQ, CSN, and CEQ, to rally trade unionists into political action. The RMS, which had been quite active in the creation of the Rassemblement des citoyens de Montréal at the municipal level, convinced Gautrin to enter into a coalition in time for the 1976 Quebec general election. Gautrin himself ran against Liberal premier Robert Bourassa in Mercier. The NPDQ-RMS coalition fielded twenty-one candidates, mostly in Montreal. Change was in the air, but it was René Lévesque and the PQ that benefited, forming its first government in history. Only one candidate from the NPDQ-RMS coalition received over 1 percent of the vote.

The arrival of the PQ government removed all oxygen from the NDP; the majority of Quebec's progressive activists were attracted to the PQ. Quebecers still involved with the NDP were pushing the party to support Quebec's right to self-determination, which was not well received by the federal NDP leadership. A resolution on the issue failed to pass at the 1977 NDP federal convention. Newly elected federal leader Ed Broadbent spoke little French, and when he did he had a very strong accent. In the 1979 federal election, which saw Joe Clark take power from Trudeau, the NDP fell to 5 percent support in Quebec. The PQ was tacitly supporting Social Credit, which elected a half-dozen MPs and prevented Joe Clark's Progressive Conservatives from making inroads in Quebec, allowing the Liberals to almost sweep Quebec. Joe Clark's government survived only nine months, and another federal election was triggered, with a looming Quebec referendum on secession as a backdrop.

The 1980 federal election set the stage, with Trudeau's Liberals winning seventy-four out of seventy-five seats in Quebec. As the non-establishment party, Broadbent's NDP benefited from the implosion of the Social Credit and saw its support in Quebec almost double. Still, the NDP was not seen as particularly relevant ahead of the upcoming referendum, even though it sided with the "No" camp.

After the defeat of the referendum, Prime Minister Trudeau embarked on a path to unilaterally repatriate the constitution. NDP leader

Ed Broadbent was quick to back the plan, as long as Trudeau would allow more provincial control over natural resources. This support proved unpopular with the NDP caucus and with the Quebec wing of the party. On June 4, 1981, following the re-election of the PQ government in April, an election where the NDP did not field candidates, the repatriation process culminated with what is known in English Canada as the "Kitchen Meeting," but has been dubbed "la nuit des longs couteaux" in Quebec. New Democrats will forever be associated with this event, as it was Saskatchewan's New Democratic attorney general, Roy Romanow, who teamed up with Jean Chrétien to isolate Quebec and to convince the provinces allied with Quebec to change sides and accept a deal to repatriate the constitution. René Lévesque was informed of the deal the next morning. He refused categorically to sign it and immediately left.

In the mid-1980s New Democrats attempted a real breakthrough in Quebec. At the time, not unlike today in 2018, New Democrats saw a political vacuum in Quebec, with many orphaned voters left behind by both the PQ and the Liberal Party. In July 1983, the NDP convention affirmed the right of the Quebec people to self-determination, thus becoming the first Canadian federal party to do so. Federally, though, the NDP under Broadbent fell short once again in 1984, but still received over 8 percent of the vote in Quebec. The party also came close to overtaking the Liberals as Official Opposition to the Mulroney government. In 1985, with former Ontario MP Jean-Paul Harney as leader, the NDP ran ninety candidates in the Quebec election. The party became the third party in Quebec in votes cast, but since voters were highly polarized between the PQ and the Liberals, no NDP candidate was elected and the party ended up with a disappointing 2.42 percent of the vote—though this remains, to this day, a high mark.

In 1986, Terrebonne Tory MP Robert Toupin was very critical of the Mulroney government and left the Progressive Conservatives to sit as an independent, citing many policy differences. Toupin, who hailed from the ranks of the Quebec Liberal Party, tried to join the Liberal Party of Canada but the local riding association would have none of it. NDP leader Ed Broadbent, sensing an opportunity, approached Toupin and played a full court press operation. Seven months later, Robert Toupin became what Ed Broadbent called "a Christmas gift to us" who would be a "strong voice for Quebecers." New Democrat strategists at the time insisted that Toupin was brought in only after careful scrutiny, to make sure that he would fit in. But Toupin didn't quite fit in—he never did, wherever he had been. He would soon openly challenge the leadership of the NDP in Quebec, over many issues, which ultimately led Toupin to leave the party, claiming the party was infiltrated by communists and far-left extremists.

Still, the NDP was moving forward. A federal convention was held in Montreal in March 1987, and the party launched a Quebec charm offensive. A resolution recognizing Quebec's unique status and the National Assembly's responsibilities regarding the French language was adopted. The party was on a roll in Canada and in Quebec, as Ed Broadbent was for a time the most popular politician in the country.

A few months later, Brian Mulroney's attempt to resolve the constitutional crisis caused by patriation resulted in the Meech Lake Accord. At first, the Meech Lake Accord received widespread support within the NDP, with all sections onside—except for Quebec. Soon however, opposition to Meech started to rise inside and outside the party, especially about the Distinct Society clause. This clause would have recognized the differences of Quebec from the rest of Canada in regard to its legal regime, its language, and its culture. Concerns were raised about Aboriginals, western alienation, and the north.

While Meech was indeed stewing on the backburner, it was not really an issue during the 1988 election, which focused instead on free trade. Despite promising polls, the federal NDP failed to breakthrough in Quebec. The Quebec campaign was marked by divisions in the ranks, notably about the issue of language. Still, the NDP achieved unprecedented support in Quebec with 14 percent of the vote. Seven candidates finished second: Rémy Trudel with 37.8 percent of the votes in Témiscamingue, Phil Edmonston with 31.4 percent in Chambly, and Claude Rompré with 30.1 percent in Saint-Maurice. A good number of other candidates obtained between 15 and 30 percent of the votes.

Provincially, the Quebec NDP was coming dangerously close to overtaking the Parti Québécois for second place. Buoyed by the popularity of federal leader Ed Broadbent and by the division that consumed the PQ at the time, the Quebec NDP was polling reasonably well, at around 15 percent, with a peak of 22 percent in October 1987. Jacques Parizeau, who was then leader of the PQ and the Official Opposition, made several moves to neutralize the NDP.

Rémy Trudel, who was seen as a rising NDP star, was offered a safe seat by Parizeau and possibly a seat at the Cabinet table if the PQ was elected. Trudel agreed to join Parizeau's party, and the riding of Rouyn-Noranda was made available for him. Parizeau then went to see François

Beaulne, vice-president of the Quebec NDP and a federal candidate in Laurier-Ste-Marie in 1998. He had just lost his job as vice-president of the National Bank and Parizeau offered him an office in the Parti Québécois headquarters, until he found a job. A good PQ riding was soon made available for Beaulne. Both he and Trudel were elected as PQ MNAs in 1989. This was the equivalent of cutting the head off the Quebec NDP.

Infighting ensued. In a move reminiscent of the 1963 Founding Convention, the Quebec NDP convention held in the spring of 1989 adopted a resolution in favour of severing the NPDQ's structural links with the federal NDP. Meech Lake, free trade, language; it was believed there were too many differences for the delegates, though they still wanted to keep a "fraternal link" with the federal party. The Quebec NDP also changed leaders during that convention: Roland Morin, who had succeeded Jean-Paul Harney in 1987, was defeated by Gaétan Nadeau. The new leader of the NDP was a former PQ activist and was relatively unknown. The party fell in the polls from its 1987 peak. With no money and no resources, and with a loose pro-sovereignty platform, the Quebec NDP ran only fifty-five candidates in the 1989 election under Nadeau, falling to fifth place behind the Anglo-rights Equality Party and the Greens. On election night, Nadeau mused about merging with the Green Party.

Federally, though, the NDP was still doing well in Quebec. After the resignation of Progressive Conservative MP Richard Grisé in May 1989, following a conviction for corruption, fraud, and breach of trust, a by-election was held in Chambly in February 1990. After years of Liberal reign under Pierre Trudeau and the rampant corruption of Mulroney's Progressive Conservative government, voters had had enough and were looking for something completely different. The NDP, under new leader Audrey McLaughlin, was poised to benefit, and Phil Edmonston was elected with almost twenty thousand votes more than his Liberal opponent.

Then, everything changed with the death of the Meech Lake Accord. The final nail in Meech's coffin came from NDP MLA Elijah Harper, who, on June 22, 1990, denied the unanimous support required by the Manitoba Legislature to proceed with ratification on the very last day that ratification was possible. In the wake of its collapse, Lucien Bouchard, along with other disappointed Progressive Conservative and Liberal MPs, walked away from Mulroney's government to form the Bloc Québécois. McLaughlin's NDP, which until then was still polling well in Quebec, saw its support collapse overnight.

When the newly formed Bloc announced it would run a candidate in the upcoming by-election in the riding of Laurier-Ste-Marie, triggered by the passing of Liberal MP Jean-Claude Malépart, NDP candidate Louise O'Neill, who was seen as a favourite, saw her support collapse and her volunteers disappear. She even tried to distance herself from the federalist position of the NDP, but to no avail. The remnants of the NPDQ announced their support for Gilles Duceppe, the Bloc candidate, and urged O'Neill to step down. Any remaining ties were severed between the federal NDP and its former Quebec wing, which was urged to change its name. In August, Duceppe won handily with 67 percent of the vote, ahead of Liberal candidate Denis Coderre at 19 percent. The NDP finished third, with 7 percent of the vote. The party's hopes in Quebec were over for the foreseeable future. By the time the 1993 federal election came around, the federal NDP was in full save-the-furniture mode, and, since there was no furniture to save in Quebec, the party fell to 1.5 percent in the province on election night, its worst results since the CCF days.

Meanwhile, the relationship with its former Quebec party was getting worse. In November 1991, the Quebec NDP, by then a full-blown separatist party, announced that former FLQ leader Paul Rose would be their candidate in a by-election in Anjou, set for January 20, 1992. This created tremors in the federal NDP, which did not want to be associated with a terrorist. Rose would end up being barred from running because of his criminal convictions. The Quebec NDP ran forty-one candidates in 1994. Following the election, Rose became leader of the Quebec NDP. The federal NDP sought legal means to force the NPDQ to stop using the name, but it became moot when the party changed its name in 1995 to become the Party of Democratic Socialism (PDS). Eventually, the PDS joined the coalition of the Union des Forces Progressistes (UFP) in 2002, along with the Rally for the Progressive Alternative and the Communist Party. The UFP merged in 2006 with Option Citoyenne to create Québec Solidaire. Québec Solidaire is therefore a great-great-great-grandson of the NDP.

The federal NDP replaced Audrey McLaughlin with Alexa McDonough. Her first task was to bring the party back from the dead, and the road to do so was not through Quebec. The party chose to simply rely on a small group of activists working as the Quebec section of Canada's NDP. The upcoming 1995 referendum was, however, the main political issue and the party was struggling to find space. During the *Commission on the Political and Constitutional Future of Québec*, set up by the Parizeau PQ

government, the New Democratic Youth of Quebec were the sole federalist party representatives participating, the others boycotting the process.
The referendum was lost by the PQ, Lucien Bouchard left the Bloc to
take over from Parizeau, and Gilles Duceppe took over from Bouchard in
Ottawa. The Bloc adjusted its strategy and became a very effective progressive opposition in Ottawa. There was little room for McDonough's NDP
in Quebec, which registered 2 percent of the popular vote in the 1997 and
2000 elections. It was not that people disliked the NDP. In fact, the NDP
was regularly seen as the second choice of most Quebecers, a number that
actually grew with the arrival of Jack Layton. On most issues, the BQ and
the NDP were aligned and voting together, so there was no real reason for
voters to abandon their first choice for the NDP.

That slowly changed with the arrival of Jack Layton at the helm of
the NDP in 2003. Layton was the first Quebec-born leader of the federal
New Democrats. Layton had grown up in Hudson, outside of Montreal.
His father, Bob Layton, had been a Quebec Tory MP who had also been
active with the provincial Liberals. His grandfather, Gilbert, had been a
Cabinet Minister for the Union Nationale government of Maurice Duplessis. Never before did an NDP leader have such a background and understanding of Quebec politics. Though his French was rusty, it was colloquial.
Layton connected with Quebecers immediately. His first appearance on
the popular talk show *Tout le Monde en Parle* had an immediate effect on
his recognition in the province. He connected with the show's host, and
more importantly, with the audience.

Even though Quebec was not the top priority of the party, Layton's
oft-repeated thesis was that in order to build a house, you needed a solid
foundation. The NDP had tried to build a house but was missing a big
piece without Quebec. Layton worked tirelessly on his French, spending
time in immersion in Jonquière and Montréal, and agreeing to all French
media requests from across the country. Support for the NDP started to
rise slowly but steadily, to 5 percent in 2004 and to almost 8 percent in
2006. One of the reasons for the slow rise was the party's support of the
Clarity Act, a piece of legislation that was quite unpopular in Quebec.
However, Layton's popularity remained higher than the party's.

The other missing piece of the puzzle was to find a strong Quebec
leader who could help bring the party to higher heights. An opportunity
arose when environment minister Thomas Mulcair quit Jean Charest's
Liberal Cabinet over a dispute regarding condo development in a provincial park. The party's 2006 convention was held in Quebec City; Mulcair

was invited as a keynote speaker and the NDP did a full court press. At that convention, the party adopted the Sherbrooke Declaration, which Layton had asked Pierre Ducasse to produce, and which would form the basis of the NDP's policy to "create the winning conditions for Canada in Quebec." Layton and Mulcair established a strong relationship and, a few months later, Mulcair joined the NDP as Layton's Quebec lieutenant.

When popular Liberal MP Jean Lapierre stepped down in 2007, the opportunity was too good to pass up. Internal polling showed that Mulcair's name was resonating well in Outremont. It was show time. From that point on, the party's communications team made a point of offering Mulcair, instead of Layton, for media interviews and events. Meanwhile, tone-deaf Liberal leader Stéphane Dion barred Justin Trudeau from running, installing instead Jocelyn Coulon, an academic. New Democrat canvassers went hard after Bloc voters, who knew the BQ could not win Outremont. Mulcair won, and the NDP became immediately unavoidable for the Quebec media. Then, in 2008, Mulcair made history by becoming the first NDP MP ever elected in Quebec in a general federal election. The party also took over 12 percent of the vote in La Belle Province, the best results in twenty years. These results were bitter-sweet for the party, since it was still unable to convince Bloc voters to switch to the NDP at the same rate as they had in Outremont.

Layton's NDP numbers rose steadily in Quebec following his attempt to replace Stephen Harper by a coalition government in December 2008. The coalition was nowhere more popular than it was in Quebec. The NDP was polling consistently in the mid-to-high teens in Quebec, finding itself regularly in second place, though still significantly behind the Bloc Quebecois.

Lessons from 2008 had been learned, and when the 2011 election came around, the party was ready—and so were Quebec voters. The NDP campaign began slowly, with Layton recovering from hip surgery. Good performances on *Tout le Monde en Parle* and in the TV debates turned the tide. A panicked Gilles Duceppe was holding unplanned news conferences to tell Quebecers not to trust the polls. The Bloc turned their guns on the NDP, and the more they did, the more the party climbed in the polls. On May 2, the NDP won fifty-nine seats in Quebec alone and became Official Opposition for the first time in its history.

Layton passed away sixteen weeks later. Despite his illness, this came as a shock and a blow to New Democrats. The grieving members entered a leadership race with stakes higher than ever for the NDP: the next leader

would be prime minister in waiting. New Democrats elected Thomas Mulcair to lead them to the New Jerusalem.

Following the Orange Wave of 2011, many Quebec New Democrats
wanted to take advantage of the popularity of the NDP brand in Quebec
to resurrect the provincial party. A poll suggested that over half of Quebecers could vote for a provincial NDP. Activists, led by Pierre Ducasse,
were hoping that there was enough orphaned voters who would like to vote
for a progressive, federalist party: voters too progressive to continue voting
for the governing Liberals or to consider the even more right-wing CAQ;
voters for whom separation was not relevant or no longer topical, which
would exclude the PQ, Québec Solidaire, and the even more radical Option
Nationale. As this demonstrates, Quebec needs the New Democratic Party.

In Ottawa, Mulcair led the New Democrats with aplomb in the
House of Commons, shaking the Harper Conservatives with his pointed
questioning. The arrival of Justin Trudeau shook things up, but by the time
the forty-first Parliament came to an end in June 2015, the NDP was leading in the polls. In fact, from early June to mid-September, the NDP was in
front of the pack, thanks in large part to a significant lead in Quebec. Never
before had an NDP leader been so close to becoming prime minister.

On September 15, the niqab entered the campaign via a ruling from
the Federal Court of Appeal quashing the Harper government's attempts
to ban face coverings at citizenship ceremonies. Mulcair's NDP supported
the ruling. A September 17th Nanos poll had put the NDP in first place;
this would be the last time in the 2015 campaign. The Conservatives and
the Bloc went on a relentless offensive against the NDP over the niqab
issue. The Liberals, which had a similar position, were not targeted the
same way, as they were behind in the polls and not seen as a primary target.
Mulcair, however, was dogged by the issue wherever he went, all the way to
Nunavut. On the ground, NDP candidates in Quebec saw their volunteers
quit and their fundraising dry up. Many simply stopped door-knocking
because of the furor they received. By the end of September, the NDP
had lost over twenty points in Quebec; the party never recovered. By the
time the niqab storm had calmed down, the NDP was no longer seen as
the party able to defeat Harper's Conservatives. Voters instead flocked to
the Trudeau Liberals, which won a majority. Despite this turn of events,
Mulcair was able to lead the NDP to its second-best results in the party's
history, with forty-four seats across the country, including sixteen in Quebec. Still very disappointed, however, delegates to the 2016 convention in
Edmonton called for a leadership race, effectively giving the boot to the

most successful rookie leader ever to lead the CCF/NDP in a federal election. Their high hopes and expectations had not been met.

Provincially, the newly formed NPD Québec, with no formal links to Canada's NDP, announced they were going to be back on the provincial scene in time for the 2018 Quebec election. In a by-election held on October 2, 2017, former MP Denis Blanchette became the first candidate to run under the Quebec NDP banner in twenty-three years. He finished seventh out of ten, with 1.35 percent of the vote. Many other former MPs, defeated in 2015, are involved. Interim leader Pierre Ducasse announced that, while the party would run candidates, he would not lead them in the campaign. Members of the New Democratic Party of Quebec were set to elect a permanent leader on January 21, 2018, and two candidates were in the running: Former Beauport-Limoilou MP Raymond Côté and Raphaël Fortin, a two-time federal candidate. Of 588 members, 397 voted in the contest. Fortin won 62 percent of the vote against 37 percent for Côté. "People who feel like political orphans have a home now," Fortin said after his victory.

On the federal scene in Quebec, the NDP remains the second political force behind Justin Trudeau's Liberals. Yet its membership fell following the 2015 defeat and Mulcair's departure, and, despite a small uptick during the federal leadership race that ensued, there were less than five thousand Quebec NDP members eligible to vote for the next leader. The sole Quebecer in the race, MP Guy Caron, finished last with less than 10 percent of the vote. During the race, issues surrounding religious symbols and identity occupied a prominent space in Quebec media, as they have over the past fifteen years. NDP members courageously decided to go with Jagmeet Singh, a religious Sikh wearing turban and kirpan. Singh, who is bilingual, is asking Quebecers to see the politics behind the turban and the beard. The next NDP chapter in Quebec rests with this leap of faith.

CHAPTER 14

THE CCF/NDP AND POPULISMS OF THE LEFT AND THE RIGHT

Murray Cooke

We are living in a populist era. This specific populist moment began in the aftermath of the global economic crash of 2008. In the United States, the Tea Party movement emerged as a right-wing populist movement, and then Occupy Wall Street emerged on the left. The American presidential election cycle of 2016 witnessed the rise of left-wing populism in the form of the Bernie Sanders campaign but culminated in the shocking victory of the right-wing populist Donald Trump over the establishment Democrat, Hillary Clinton.

In Europe, far-right populism seems a constant threat in country after country. In May 2017, Marine Le Pen of the far-right, anti-immigrant National Front received over 10.5 million votes, and over one-third of the vote in the second round of the French presidential election. On the left, Syriza, which rose to form the government in Greece, and Podemos, which has challenged in Spain, are two notable left-populist parties that grew dramatically amid the economic crisis. In the UK, Jeremy Corbyn came from seemingly nowhere to unexpectedly win the leadership of the Labour Party. Then, in 2016, a majority of UK voters endorsed leaving the European Union in the stunning Brexit referendum.

What does this mean for Canada's New Democratic Party (NDP)? The contemporary NDP's relationship to left populism is uncertain. Jack Layton was credited with having a populist touch during the Orange Wave of the 2011 federal election when the party became the Official Opposition for the first time.[1] Yet, during the 2014 Ontario election, the provincial NDP leader Andrea Horwath was criticized by some on the left for running a campaign that was negatively categorized as "populist."[2] Federally, the NDP waged an uninspiring campaign in 2015 and is now trying to reinvigorate itself.

For anyone with a passing familiarity with the history of the NDP and its predecessor, the Co-operative Commonwealth Federation (CCF), this apparent unease with the concept of left populism is jarring. Populism was a crucial element of the CCF from the beginning and has remained an aspect of the NDP throughout its history. Similarly, the contemporary challenge of right-wing populism is hardly unprecedented in Canada. In the 1930s and 1940s, the newly formed Co-operative Commonwealth Federation was rivalled by the emergence of the Social Credit. In the 1990s, the New Democratic Party was undermined by the rise of the Reform Party. More generally, the shift to neoliberalism involved a prominent role for the kind of right-wing, anti-tax, free-market populism typified by Ralph Klein and Mike Harris.

All of this leads to important questions. What is populism? What has been the CCF/NDP's relationship to populism? How has right-wing populism challenged the NDP and left politics? Is there potential for a renewed left-wing populism in Canada?

Unfortunately, contemporary discussions of populism in Canada have tended to lack clarity about the concept or an appreciation of the history of populism in this country. When observers question whether the NDP could stake out a populist position or they criticize the NDP for attempting to do so, one can only wonder if they have ever heard of Tommy Douglas. Similarly, when observers point to the current threat of right-wing populism and its challenge to progressive politics, it is useful to keep in mind various Canadian examples from Social Credit to recent Toronto mayor Rob Ford. This chapter, then, will examine the concept of populism, focus on the CCF/NDP's relationship to left and right populism, and conclude with a few tentative observations about the current context.

As David Laycock, among others, has pointed out, "populism is a notoriously ambiguous concept."[3] The term is used in a variety of ways by academics, journalists, and political observers. In journalistic shorthand, it sometimes appears to be no more than a leadership style or image, such as being (or presenting an image of being) folksy, down-to-earth, friendly, relatable, approachable, or a "regular" person. This does not get us very far. Populism is more than just a leadership style.

The academic literature on populism is vast and includes a variety of approaches and ongoing debates. There seem to be two main academic debates over populism; authors differ over how precisely or loosely to define the concept and whether populism is inherently dangerous.[4] I am going to use a simple and straightforward definition of populism because it is useful and credible, and it has been the most common usage within the academic literature on populism in Canada.[5] I use the term populism to refer to an approach to politics that pits "the people" against "the elite."[6] Populist movements are not inherently anti-democratic, dangerous, or harmful. Such movements can take a variety of forms and appear on the right or the left of the political spectrum. As such, the meaning of those categories, "the people" and "the elite," are politically and socially constructed and therefore can differ widely between different populist movements. Defining "the people" and "the elite" is a matter of ideological interpretation, but it is also an active political project of framing, or constructing, these social categories.

The Co-operative Commonwealth Federation was formed in 1932 as a coalition of different groups. One of the primary constitutive elements of the new party, especially in Saskatchewan, was prairie populism, which had emerged in the early twentieth century.[7] The "Ginger Group" of MPs, who played a role in the formation of the CCF, included individuals originally elected as progressives.[8] Moreover, populist farmer organizations, such as the United Farmers of Alberta, the United Farmers of Canada (Saskatchewan Section), and the United Farmers of Ontario, were active participants in the formation of the CCF. The party's full name, the Co-operative Commonwealth Federation (Farmer, Labour, Socialist), reflected the fact that, at least initially, it was truly a federation of existing farmer organizations, labour parties, and socialist parties.[9]

Populism was even significant for the British Columbia CCF, which is often depicted as more working-class and Marxist-influenced than the other provincial wings. Robert A. J. McDonald has suggested "that the rise of the [BC] CCF can be explained as much by populism as it can by socialism."[10] McDonald argues that, "reminiscent of the populist rhetoric of the western farmers' movements leading up to and during World War I, speakers ranging from local CCF candidates to elite members of the movement . . . defined the problem of capitalism as the inordinate power of big industries and banks."[11]

On the prairies, the CCF became the main political vehicle for what Laycock describes as "social democratic populism."[12] The CCF was populist in the sense that it attempted to represent a broad alliance of people, especially farmers and workers, struggling against powerful corporate interests amid the Great Depression of the 1930s. In 1933 at the Regina convention, CCF leader J. S. Woodsworth described the party as "essentially a drawing together of the common people."[13] Referring to the Saskatchewan CCF, Lipset argued that "the party conceives of the people for whom it speaks as farmers, laborers, and small businessmen."[14]

The CCF depiction of the elite reflected the historic populist grievances of prairie farmers; "the railroads, banks, grain exchanges, and manufacturers who increased prices . . . have been highly visible exploiters of agrarians."[15] However, influenced by the desperate economic conditions and pushed by the labour and socialist currents, the CCF represented a more radical form of populism than its predecessors on the prairies. Rather than a piecemeal critique of big corporate interests, the CCF's anti-elitism was, nominally at least, anti-capitalist. The CCF's Regina Manifesto famously vowed that "no CCF government would rest content until it had eradicated capitalism."[16]

The CCF was not the only populist party formed on the prairies in the 1930s. The Alberta Social Credit League was formed in 1935 and soon won the provincial election. In retrospect, and based on its record as government, particularly after 1940, Social Credit is usually depicted as a right-wing populist party, but this was not so clear cut in the mid-1930s.[17] Led by Christian fundamentalist preacher, William "Bible Bill" Aberhart, Social Credit initially developed as "a loose coalition of reformers" with both rural and urban support.[18] While monetary reform was its central and most famous proposal, Social Credit attracted a wide range of social reformers desperate for relief and solutions to the economic turmoil of the times. Alvin Finkel demonstrates that "the early Social Credit movement shared programmatic and rhetorical similarities with the CCF."[19] Social Credit's founding platform statement from 1935 included the slogan, "Let us end poverty in the midst of plenty."[20] While the banks and the financial system were seen as the primary culprits, a more general critique of big business could also be heard within Social Credit circles. As Laycock points out, "the Social Credit League started out as an antagonist of corporate interests—not their policy ally."[21]

Initially, the CCF and Social Credit were both attempting to attract the populist social reform or protest vote in opposition to the traditional parties. This raised the issue of whether to compete or co-operate. As Lipset noted, "a movement developed, both within and without the CCF, for unity between the two third-party western groups."[22] In some cases, this involved local co-operation. In the most notable example, Tommy Douglas, as the federal CCF candidate for Weyburn, Saskatchewan, in 1935, was also endorsed by Social Credit.[23] There was some commonality in language. Some prominent CCFers and many grassroots supporters were advocates of monetary reform.[24] As McDonald notes, the tendency of some leading CCFers to mix socialism and social credit demonstrates "the fluidity of political thinking across the west in the depths of the Great Depression."[25]

In the 1940s, led by Ernest Manning, Social Credit dropped its populist monetary reform proposals and solidified its position as a right-wing conservative party. As Finkel describes, "the original radicalism of the Social Credit League later gave way to conservative and often reactionary ideology."[26] Social Credit populism was increasingly directed at communists, socialists, bureaucrats, and social planners, including the CCF.

There are two points to highlight here. First of all, in times of economic anxiety, populism can take different forms. The CCF and Social Credit offered different populist responses to the crisis. In doing so, they conceptualized the people and the elite in different ways, and their policy prescriptions diverged significantly. Both movements presented cross-class appeals, but the CCF had stronger connections to labour and working-class organizations than Social Credit. CCFers considered the elite to be big business or the capitalist class, while members of Social Credit were more focused specifically on the banks and the financial elite, including sometimes a supposed international Jewish financial conspiracy.[27] With their different conceptions of the people and the elite, the CCF and Social Credit had different political programs. In the 1930s, both favoured social reforms, but the CCF's ultimate stated goal was the eradication of capitalism, and Social Credit's goal was a fairer market economy.

Secondly, the populist characteristics of the CCF have been a matter of significant debate. Most agree that the CCF was populist but disagree on the effect of that populism on the party. For some, the coalition of farmer and labour interests in the CCF, and the presentation of a populist discourse, was a necessary adaptation to local social conditions and political culture, and was a strength of the CCF.[28] For others, usually writing from a Marxist perspective, the CCF's cross-class, farmer-labour populism led the party to become ideologically muddled and moderate.[29]

Populism in the CCF may have been strongest in Saskatchewan, but it had an ongoing influence on the federal party. In their book, *Make This Your Canada* (1943), David Lewis and Frank Scott struck many a populist chord.[30] While not shying away from describing the CCF as socialist, Lewis and Scott frequently refer to the party as a "people's movement." Most strikingly for today's readers, Chapter 7 was entitled "Political Action for the 99%." In it, Lewis and Scott use a version of the populist rhetoric that we now associate with Occupy Wall Street and Bernie Sanders:

> The industrial workers, the office and professional workers, small business people and the farmers together comprise the vast majority of Canada's population. Only a tiny proportion of the people own and control the big corporations, the huge monopolies and most of Canada's wealth-producing resources ... The basic struggle today is between the 99% who are reaching out for the economic and political power which the 1% now effectively control.[31]

After the Second World War, amid the post-war boom and the Cold War, social democrats shifted their goal (perhaps a distant goal) from a non-capitalist future to a dramatically reformed capitalism. The ideological climate and the prosperous economic times led these individuals to emphasize Keynesian fiscal policies, economic planning, and the development of social programs over public ownership. These changes were signaled by the CCF's moderate new Winnipeg Declaration, passed in 1956 to supersede the more radical Regina Manifesto, and the creation of the New Democratic Party in 1961.

Unlike the Regina Manifesto, which vowed to eradicate capitalism, the Winnipeg Declaration promised to break "the stranglehold of private monopolies" while acknowledging "there will be need for private enterprise." Clearly, there had been a shift from achieving socialism to reforming capitalism. Yet some populist themes remained. In 1956, the CCF still pointed to the gap in wealth and power between the many and the rich.[32] And the New Party Declaration passed at the NDP's founding convention in 1961 still pointed to an economic system that "operated chiefly for the benefit of the few owners of great corporations."[33]

There is no doubt that the CCF/NDP continued to think in terms of "the people" in a broad sense. However, class-based appeals became increasingly uncommon. The transition from the CCF to the NDP involved a closer and more formalized relationship with the labour movement but paradoxically also involved an electoral pitch to "liberally minded" members of the middle class. In 1961, the NDP also proclaimed that "everyone in Canada is a consumer" and that the NDP "truly represents the consumers."[34] At the same time, "the elite" was less of a focus. Certainly, inequality was recognized as a problem, but it was understood as a challenge of including all within the booming economy and the growing consumer society. During the post-war boom, populist notions seemed old-fashioned.

Post-war social democracy, with its Keynesian policy prescriptions, saw the "mixed economy" and the welfare state as win-win scenarios for workers and business. Social democrats often appealed to voters as the enlightened party that could run capitalism even better than the capitalists. Sure, corporations would have to pay their fair share of taxation, but the goal was now robust economic growth and a friendlier form of capitalism, not the eradication of capitalism.

The political turmoil of the late 1960s and the emergence of the Waffle movement within the NDP shook up this managerial and technocratic form of post-war social democracy. The "people," redefined once again, now included a prominent role for students.[35] The Waffle also voiced the themes of participatory democracy, "community democracy," and "worker participation." Even more significantly, there was a renewed focus on, and new understanding of, the elite. To some extent, this was a return to classic left populism with references to the "corporate elite." The Waffle's declaration that "corporate capitalism is characterized by the predominant power of the corporate elite aided and abetted by the political elite" could have been uttered by a prairie populist in the 1930s. However, there was a new twist to the rhetoric. The Waffle presented a left-nationalist understanding of Canadian political economy. In doing so, the Waffle Manifesto pointed to "American corporate capitalism" taking the form of American multinational corporations and their investments in Canada. Meanwhile, "the Canadian corporate elite has opted for a junior partnership with these American enterprises."[36]

Influenced by the Waffle and the wider political climate, the NDP did take up some left-populist issues in the early 1970s.[37] During the 1972 federal campaign, NDP leader David Lewis railed against "corporate welfare bums" and their government grants, tax concessions, and tax loopholes that shifted the tax burden onto the "ordinary Canadian taxpayer."[38] As Whitehorn describes:

> In speech after speech, Lewis hammered away at the "corporate welfare bums," each time pointing out another glaring example of corporate tax avoidance and government handouts for the rich. Left populism at its oratorical best, it was a campaign backed up by a steady barrage of statistics and striking examples of corporate rip-offs.[39]

The campaign resulted in a record number of seats for the CCF/NDP (to that point) and helped reduce the Liberals to a minority government.

The subsequent federal NDP leader, Ed Broadbent, frequently used populist rhetoric, appealing to "ordinary Canadians" and describing his Liberal and Conservative opponents as the "Bobbsey twins of Bay Street."[40] However, during the 1988 federal election, the NDP failed to prioritize the fight against the Canada-US Free Trade Agreement and allowed the Liberals to become the standard-bearer for the opposition forces. In doing so, the NDP downplayed a left-populist attack on the corporate trade and investment deal in favour of a leadership-based campaign focused around Broadbent.[41]

For the most part, the NDP under Broadbent and subsequent leaders became associated with the defence of social programs, especially public health care. Populism became a secondary current within the NDP. It remained a dormant part of the party's political discourse, ready to be dusted off and trotted out when considered useful. Some have suggested that the NDP's left populism was renewed under Jack Layton,[42] but this was primarily a question of leadership style, particularly in the 2011 election, rather than populist content. The NDP's moderate 2011 platform did begin with a populist note: "For too long Ottawa has focused on the priorities of the well-connected, not the priorities of your family. Together we're going to fix that."[43] But beyond that, the platform proceeded to offer tax credits to business, tax cuts to small business, and promises to keep Canada's corporate tax rate lower than the Americans. Still, the NDP did promise to increase the corporate tax rate to 19.5 percent. This small nod toward economic populism proved popular among voters.[44] During the 2015 campaign, Tom Mulcair and the NDP again proposed a modest corporate tax increase, but this was overshadowed by the Trudeau Liberals' promise to raise personal income taxes on the top 1 percent and lower taxes on the supposed middle class.

If populism was relatively dormant within the NDP in the late twentieth century, it was about to explode on the right of the political spectrum. This was consistent with developments elsewhere. As Michael Kazin has shown in his history of populism in the United States, over the twentieth century, populism shifted from the left to the right of the political spectrum.[45] In North America and Western Europe, a New Right emerged as a backlash against the Keynesian welfare state and the labour and social movements pushing for social change. The New Right combined free-market economics with a variety of socially conservative policies, such as law-

and-order and anti-immigrant sentiments, in a potent brew that Stuart Hall termed "authoritarian populism."[46]

There were notable precursors to the dramatic rise of right-wing populism in Canada in the 1990s. As shown above, Social Credit had shifted to the right by the 1940s. In the late 1950s, "the western base of the CCF crumbled under the onslaught of the Saskatchewan populist [John] Diefenbaker."[47] In 1962, Social Credit unexpectedly won twenty-six federal seats in Quebec and would retain a presence until 1980.[48]

But, in the 1990s, right-wing populism became a major force in Canada. During the serious economic recession of that decade and the slow employment recovery, there was considerable anxiety and anger among Canadians. Meanwhile, the political class seemed pre-occupied with constitutional issues. Opinion polls and research studies showed that Canadians were in a very foul mood.[49] The Citizens' Committee on Canada's Future, set up by the federal government and chaired by Keith Spicer, reported in 1991 that:

> Overwhelmingly, participants have told us that they have lost faith in the political system and its leadership. Anger, disillusionment and a desire for fundamental change is very often the first issue raised in discussion groups . . . Canadians are telling us that their leaders must understand and accept their visions of the country—that their leaders must be governed by the wishes of the people, and not the other way around.[50]

Survey data indicated a "decline of deference" among the Canadian public.[51] The anger of Canadians was on full display in the 1992 constitutional referendum and the 1993 federal election. And, at the provincial level, sober, cautious Ontario turfed the Bob Rae New Democrats after one term in office and elected a right-populist "Common Sense Revolution."

The failures of the left helped create the conditions for the rise of right-wing populism. The NDP had followed up the relative electoral success of the 1988 federal election with provincial victories in Ontario in 1990 and in British Columbia and Saskatchewan in 1991. However, not only were the NDP provincial governments in Ontario, BC, and Saskatchewan unable to provide workable social democratic solutions to the recession, they and the federal leadership of the NDP aligned with the increasingly unpopular Prime Minister Brian Mulroney and the rest of the political establishment in favour of the Charlottetown Accord.[52]

Long before Brexit, in 1992 Canada had its own angry populist referendum vote against the establishment, as Canadians rejected the Charlottetown Accord, supported by the political, economic, and social elites, including the NDP.[53] At the time, observers compared it to the Danish rejection of the European Union's Maastricht Treaty earlier that same year. As journalist Jeffrey Simpson pointed out:

> [T]he élites were part of the problem rather than the solution just as they were in Denmark, where the élite support was just as overwhelming and as inconsequential for the Maastricht treaty. As in Denmark, so in Canada, people took out their anger and frustration at politicians by kicking their constitutional baby.[54]

With its opposition to the Charlottetown Accord, the Reform Party was well-placed to take up the mantle of populist champion, especially in western Canada. This helped set the stage for the rise of Reform and the collapse of the NDP in the 1993 federal election. That election was one of the most tumultuous in Canadian history. The governing Progressive Conservatives were reduced from a majority government to two seats. The NDP fell from forty-four seats to nine. The Reform Party won fifty-two seats and would go on to become the Official Opposition after the 1997 election.

Right-wing populists Ralph Klein[55] and Mike Harris came to power in Alberta in 1992 and in Ontario in 1995. The Reform Party, Ralph Klein, and Mike Harris all projected themselves as representing the "common sense of the common people."[56] For these right-wing "authoritarian populists," the people were usually referred to as "taxpayers" and the enemy was identified as big government and "special interest groups." The elites were old-line politicians, bureaucrats, unionized public sector workers, and representatives of particular groups of Canadians, such as Quebecers, Indigenous peoples, ethnic minorities, women, gays, and lesbians, who sought recognition and/or equity. The right-populist solutions focused on downsizing welfare states, cutting taxes, and undermining equity policies, while strengthening the coercive aspects of the state. For example, the Conservative government of Mike Harris cut social assistance rates by 21.6 percent, introduced workfare, reduced income taxes by 30 percent, scrapped the *Ontario Employment Equity Act*, and passed the *Safe Streets Act* to criminalize squeegeeing and panhandling.[57]

The Reform Party was Canada's federal version of rising right-wing populism throughout Western Europe and North America.[58] The Reform Party undercut the NDP, appealing to many former NDP supporters, including union members and low-income voters. It is estimated that 13 percent of NDP supporters from the 1988 election switched to the Reform Party in 1993.[59] The right-wing threat of Reform also helped shore up support for the Liberal Party among progressive voters.

As the Reform Party evolved into the Canadian Alliance and then merged with the Progressive Conservatives, it left elements of its populism behind.[60] Long gone were the Reform Party's democratic reform proposals, such as referenda, recall mechanisms for elected officials, and parliamentary free votes. Even during his time in the Reform Party, Stephen Harper always was more of a right-wing ideologue than a populist.[61] In government, however, the Harper Conservatives did maintain significant elements of right-wing populism, such as reducing taxes, defunding arts, culture, and equity groups, promoting a law-and-order agenda, stoking anti-Muslim sentiments, and dismissing expert opinion and scientific research. As Clark Banack summarizes, "Harper essentially conceives of society as being divided between the 'real people' and those left-leaning 'special interests' that seek to block the advance of neoliberalism by enhancing the welfare state."[62] Thus, the Harper government developed a kind of technocratic populism that harkened back to Social Credit governments in Alberta and had clearly authoritarian populist tendencies.

The most remarkable right-wing populist in Canada in recent years was Rob Ford, mayor of Toronto from 2010 to 2014. Just as the collapse of the Bob Rae government led to the election of Mike Harris, the mayoralty of social democrat David Miller in Canada's largest city was followed by the election of Rob Ford.[63] In many ways a classic right-populist, Ford portrayed himself as a champion of the "little guy" taking on the "downtown elites" and their tax-payer funded "gravy-train." Bureaucrats, city workers, union members, cyclists, and streetcars were just a few of his targets. Erratic and outspoken, Ford's rhetoric was often sexist, homophobic, and/or racist.[64] Despite his controversial statements and seemingly out-of-control behaviour, Ford retained the passionate support of much of his "Ford Nation" political base.

Left populism is a long-standing, if sometimes dormant, element of the CCF/NDP tradition, and based on the current political and economic context, left populism seems highly viable, almost a necessity.[65] Occupy Wall Street succeeded in raising the issue of economic inequality and the power of the financial elite. Bernie Sanders' campaign took up these left-populist themes, inspiring considerable enthusiasm and support, especially among young people, and opening room for left-wing ideas in a way not seen for a long time. The Canadian context seems ripe for another populist movement. Study after study has highlighted the issue of income inequality in Canada; census data shows that "income inequality rose from 2005 to 2015, with the highest income groups continuing to pull away from the broad middle class and poverty continuing to increase."[66] There is widespread anxiety over youth unemployment, precarious work, housing affordability, and rising student and household debt. Feelings of economic insecurity and anxiety are populist issues that the NDP could address differently than the other parties. There seems to be widespread awareness in the NDP that they missed a golden opportunity in the last federal election by being too cautious and too moderate and not inspiring voters. A jolt of left populism seems like a useful tonic.

Thinking about left populism and the NDP raises an important question: who are the people? First, a left populism needs to be explicitly inclusive, unlike the xenophobic populism of the right. It would need to recognize, defend, and support difference and diversity within the people by confronting and challenging racism. Diversity was not a strength of the Sanders campaign or Occupy Wall Street.[67] It is a major challenge for the NDP. But it is a necessity for confronting intolerant and racist right-wing populism and building a broad left-populist movement.

Secondly, contemporary left-populists are confronted with the challenge of finding the language to unify the diverse working class. Diversity here refers both to the social composition of the working class and the different sectors and forms of work. A sincere populist strategy would raise the issue of whether the NDP can actually work for, include, and represent the most precarious and marginalized members of the working class. Genuine left populism would attempt to reach and inspire those who feel alienated and disconnected from politics, do not currently see their interests represented, and, in many cases, do not vote.

A renewed left populism would also raise the question—who are the elites? Left populism needs to be anti-austerity, anti-neoliberal, and anti-free market, but it needs to be anti-corporate as well. Neoliberalism and globalization need to be analyzed, but they may be too abstract to mobilize people. A left-populist NDP might need to revisit that 1972 campaign in which David Lewis went after the corporate sector and named specific corporations. Left populists should seriously target business subsidies, tax loopholes, and off-shore tax havens.

What can populists do in office? The experience of Syriza in Greece since 2015 is not encouraging, to put it mildly. There is a wider crisis of left politics and social democracy without easy answers. At least populism offers a conceptual terrain, even a vague one, for understanding that the people are confronted by economic, social, and political elites that need to be challenged.

There is an oft-noted contradiction of populist governance. Once populists gain office, are they not now the elite they once railed against? Social democratic populists need to emphasize and explain that the economic elites remain in their position of dominance. Social democrats need to think of themselves as governing on behalf of the people, their base, rather than all of society. In other words, left-populist social democrats should remember which side they are on and strive to govern in a way that begins to erode the power of economic elites.

One final note: from a Marxist perspective, populism surely remains much too vague and confused. Rather than speaking of "the people" and "the elites," Marxists insist we should recognize social class and class relationships. The problem, from a Marxist perspective, is not accountability, greed, or a few nasty corporations. It is capitalism. And capitalism needs to be superseded, abolished, smashed, or replaced. Lacking such clarity of analysis and end goals, populism is highly frustrating and limited to many Marxists. Populism is dismissed as bad analysis and muddled politics. But, frankly, the options for the NDP are not populism or Marxism. The NDP's alternative to populism is a non-populist progressive liberalism. And if those are the choices, populism seems like the best direction for the NDP.

CHAPTER 15

MEDICARE AND SOCIAL DEMOCRACY IN CANADA

Erika Dyck & Greg Marchildon

For Canadians, the introduction of universal, publicly funded health care was cause for celebration. But for social democrats it has been a particularly cherished achievement. A pan-Canadian policy that was, at the same time, implemented by provincial and territorial governments of differing ideological stripes, medicare nonetheless reflects social democratic values. In particular, the element of universality embedded in medicare, that all citizens have access to medically necessary health care on uniform terms and conditions, differs in important respects from the underlying values of pro-market liberals and conservatives in Canada who tend to see health care as a welfare-based program rather than as a right of citizenship.[1] In fact, one-tier medicare is a uniquely social democratic contribution. This dimension goes beyond the sentiment that access is based on medical need rather than ability to pay and a limited insurance concept. It is the right of all citizens to access the same services in the same facilities without a private class or tier of higher quality health services relative to the public services offered under medicare. This single-tier aspect of Canadian medicare sets it apart from most, perhaps all, other health systems in the world.[2]

However, it is important to note that single-tier in this context does not mean a single Canadian standard for all health services. Canada is a highly decentralized federation in which the lion's share of responsibility for health care falls to the provincial governments. As a consequence, citizens receive services based on provincial or territorial residency. Although the Canada Health Act stipulates that access must be based on uniform terms and conditions, it is up to provincial and territorial governments to administer their own health systems and regulate this one-tier access. It is also up to these same governments to decide on the extent to which private for-profit and private not-for-profit providers and facilities are used to deliver medicare services. There is no assumption that private providers and facilities are problematic as long as these services are provided within a publicly regulated environment in which access is based on medical necessity rather than ability to pay. The social democratic design of medicare precludes a separate tier of private coverage and privately funded services in order to prevent faster access or better quality based on the ability to pay. While contemporary social democrats may be divided in their views on these aspects of Canadian medicare, the original social democratic conception of medicare was based on a decentralized and pluralistic delivery model.[3]

At the same time, the social democratic originators of the Canadian model of medicare never intended the model to be frozen in time. They considered medicare as an ever-evolving aspiration. The Co-operative Commonwealth Federation (CCF) government in Saskatchewan under Tommy Douglas started with universal hospital coverage in 1947 because it could not afford more. When Ottawa introduced federal cost-sharing programs for universal hospital coverage in 1958, only then could the Douglas government consider extending universal coverage to physician services. However, the Douglas government wanted medicare extended to prescription drugs, rehabilitative care, homecare, and long-term care, elements that have yet to be incorporated to this day. In addition, Douglas realized that the delivery system itself should be changed once tax-based financing replaced private health insurance and out of pocket payment, but he also knew that this would be an even more difficult change than the financing reform. He well understood that health care would evolve beyond hospitals and doctors and that other services, such as prescription drug therapies and social care (i.e., homecare and long-term care), would become more important over time. Moreover, these services would have to be more highly organized to ensure effective care across the continuum of health.[4]

However, unlike Douglas, we have often not experienced medicare as an evolving policy in our historical and cultural consciousness, and medicare today is often perceived as a program and set of policies that must be defended and preserved, held sacrosanct, and untouched by reformers. The politics of health care reform in Canada have moved across the political spectrum. Whereas the social democrats of the 1940s, 1950s, and

1960s were the reformers bucking conservative trends of insurance-bound policies and health for payment services, many on the left have become the ardent defenders of the status quo, cherishing the tradition and values associated with medicare. Reform has become a project of the right and an assault on left-wing values, including safeguarding universal, single-payer health care. Perhaps it is necessary for social democrats to eschew this ideologically characterized notion of reform and instead begin imagining how a social democratically reformed health care system might look in the twenty-first century.

In a pre-medicare era, the Canadian institutional health care landscape involved a variety of services that differed according to disease type, geography, and demographics, along with the range of governing authorities, whether federal, provincial, municipal, or even religiously run institutions. Canada was not alone in offering different kinds of health care facilities, some based on payments, others supported by charities or religious orders, and others still built around working conditions and workers' insurance schemes. Moreover, the style of care differed across the variations in geography and population density. Provincially run tuberculosis (TB) sanitaria dotted the landscape throughout much of the country, making them a recognizable and more or less standardized facility across the country, but run by provincial health authorities. Other institutions were strategically located on the margins of the country and run through federal agencies, such as leprosaria and quarantine hospitals. Meanwhile, the federal government paid for Indian hospitals, which often relied on provincially trained staff and inadequate facilities on loan from others, whether discarded military barracks or empty schools.[5] Newfoundland maintained cottage-style health care facilities as well as a marine-based set of traveling physicians tending the isolated communities of Newfoundland and Labrador.[6] Religious orders ministered to sick and chronically disabled populations, and some of these relationships helped to foster fruitful research and training institutions outside of the federalist landscape. Provinces, research institutes, regions, and ethno-religious communities contributed to this institutional tapestry, in part by establishing facilities that tailored their needs to the regional priorities of the local residents, while the federal government continued to provide services in aid of the military or quarantine care at points of immigration or in states of national crisis.[7] Mental health care took place in purpose-built facilities, often segregated from other health units.[8] Municipalities also played their part in providing services, oftentimes under the umbrella terms of health or relief, which combined economic and health priorities.[9] Before medicare, the design and operation of health care facilities represented a blending of local initiatives and national priorities. Importantly, patients faced a patchwork of services, payments, and expectations for care, much of which depended on their ability to pay for services or seek upgraded luxuries, like privacy, pharmaceuticals, bedding, or a hospital bed close to home. Health care options had more to do with geography, disease, social class, and race than a more generalized or universalized notion of seeking health care as a citizenship right or as a shared social responsibility.[10]

This varied set of options also required different mechanisms for funding, whether through tax-supported systems or direct payments from patients. Collecting payments burdened both patients and physicians, who were often uncomfortable extracting payments from sick and dying clients.[11] In 1915, now somewhat famously, the rural municipality of Sarnia, Saskatchewan, boldly collected money from its residents to offer a retainer to secure the services of a physician. The provincial minister of health swiftly amended the law to allow municipalities to use taxes to pay physicians a retainer to ensure coverage, particularly in smaller or rural regions. This pooling of resources expanded over the next two decades and offered an alternative to the standard practice of doctor-patient private payment plans.[12]

The Great Depression of the 1930s led to a major rethinking of health care and the role of the state, as many families were rendered unable to pay for even the most basic forms of health care.[13] Canada's first social democratic party—the CCF—emerged out of this crisis. Adopted at the CCF's first national convention, the Regina Manifesto of 1933 called for the public financing and systematic organization of health, hospital, and medical services.[14]

The opportunity to implement such a vision did not present itself until the CCF was elected in Saskatchewan in 1944, where it held power for the next two decades. It constructed a welfare state that one political scientist later described as the sole Swedish-style social democratic outpost in North America.[15] In the early post-war years, the CCF in Saskatchewan and the rest of the country became the chief proponent for universal health coverage, the policy program that most party leaders and activists saw as fundamental to the social democratic version of the welfare state. Drawing upon an immense brain trust of administrative and policy talent, the provincial CCF government designed, implemented, and then managed single-payer hospital and medical care coverage programs—programs that were so effectively run that it was much studied by other governments for years afterwards.[16] Ultimately, the national CCF, as well as provincial CCF parties, used the successful example of Saskatchewan to promote the model outside of that province.

Tommy Douglas is the key figure in this narrative, and deservedly so. He was a pragmatic idealist, who saw politics as the art of the possible in which he had to contend with the many forces opposed to his government's ideological direction and work within the severe financial constraints under which the provincial government operated.[17] At the same time, the distance between the status quo and the ideal of the "New Jerusalem" he desired was enormous, and he drove his government to change the policy landscape to what he considered the edge of what was politically and fiscally feasible.[18] He prioritized health care reforms over other areas of social responsibility and assigned himself the role of minister of public health, in addition to his responsibilities as premier. He invited international experts to comment on and survey the provincial health needs. In 1944, Johns Hopkins University professor Henry Sigerist visited the province and recommended a series of principles from which to guide the establishment of a socialized system of health care.[19]

Douglas purposely raised public discourse on the subject in order to determine what might be politically feasible. He knew that some of Sigerist's recommendations were unacceptable to physicians and even to some of his supporters and focused instead on making a major change to the financing of hospital care, the one area that was more immediately acceptable and therefore capable of more immediate implementation. It is significant, however, that he not only championed a form of universal health care, unrestricted by one's ability to pay, but that he also made the issue one of considerable public debate. Drawing international attention to the plight of sick residents of Saskatchewan, Douglas' reforms were as much about culture as they were about politics. In other words, by raising the level of public discourse on the issue, Douglas engaged in a process of changing the way people thought about their health and their collective responsibility to invest in our health as a society.

There was no inevitability in the Douglas government's achievements in establishing universal health coverage. Although the CCF government managed to avoid a major confrontation with the existing hospital and medical associations over its introduction of universal hospital coverage in 1947, the program taxed the fiscal capacity of the government, which was forced to tighten its purse strings in other areas, as well as create a unit that would systemically search for administrative efficiencies.[20] It also faced policy competition and comparison from a non-universal hospital scheme in Alberta.[21] First established in 1950 as a purposeful counter to the universality of the Saskatchewan plan, the Alberta plan publicly sub-sidized the purchase of private hospital insurance for low-income individuals and instituted compulsory daily user fees. However, in 1958, this plan was grudgingly abandoned in favour of a universal program that mirrored the Saskatchewan plan, in response to an offer of shared-cost financing from the federal government based on federal standards.[22]

These federal standards were set out in the *Hospital Insurance and Diagnostic Services Act of 1957*, a law that was the product of considerable struggle within the Liberal government of Louis St. Laurent—no great fan of universal social programs—and an activist health minister, Paul Martin Sr., who was highly impressed with the administrative effectiveness of the Saskatchewan plan. Although not a social democrat, Paul Martin saw the benefits that flowed from Saskatchewan's "compulsory" plan, in terms of covering the entire provincial population, and the problems associated with Alberta's "voluntary" plan and its inevitable gaps of coverage. Martin was eventually able to convince St. Laurent and his Cabinet colleagues to provide cash transfers to encourage other provincial governments to implement universal hospital coverage, but on the standard of universality set by CCF government in Saskatchewan, since their model was adminis-tratively inexpensive and, unlike the Alberta model, designed to cover the entire population.[23]

The provision of federal cost sharing for universal hospital coverage allowed the CCF government in Saskatchewan to move to the next stage—the introduction of universal coverage for all physician care.[24] However, implementing universal medical care coverage would prove much more difficult, precipitating a doctors' strike and forcing major concessions on the part of the government.[25] The conflict also revealed a sharp division within the social democratic movement, between those who wanted the government to fundamentally alter the mode of delivery as well as financ-ing, and those, many serving in the Saskatchewan government, who felt the financing reform was difficult enough and that any major attempt to change the delivery system in the immediate term would generate so much opposition that it would simply ensure the failure of the financing reform.[26]

By the early 1960s, organized medicine had come under the con-trol of specialists, some of whom were self-described refugees from the National Health Service (NHS) in the United Kingdom. These doctors were uncompromising in their opposition to any sign of what they interpreted as socialized medicine. They were convinced that, if the doctors rejected the CCF's proposed bill on universal medical care coverage, the government would be forced to back down. In contrast, Douglas felt that his government's reform, limited to changing the mode of payment from patients (either out-of-pocket or through private health insurance) to the public purse in order to remove all financial barriers from access, should have been more than palatable to the medical profession. Both sides miscalculated and the result was a twenty-three-day doctors' strike in July 1962 that would capture the attention of the country as well as observers from around the world.[27]

The strike mobilized social democratic activists in Saskatchewan and the rest of Canada. Community activists established primary care clinics in a dozen centres in the province, hiring doctors supportive of public financing and the principles of group practice involving non-physician health providers. During the strike, the CCF government supported the community clinics and helped airlift supportive doctors' from the United Kingdom as a way to put pressure on the striking doctors. The government, nonetheless, soon felt compelled to back away from its support of the community clinics as part of the terms of the deal that brought the strike to an end; while the so-called Saskatoon Agreement was not explicit about the community clinics, the deal implied that the dominant form of physician practice would remain an independent fee-for-service business contrary to the salaried doctors in the community clinics. This result angered many left-wing activists within the CCF. For years (and in some cases, for decades), this left a residue of distrust for the government members and the party establishment.[28]

The resulting governmental arrangements subsequently enacted to administer the new medical plan facilitated the continuation of traditional practices to the detriment of salaried group practice.[29] The Saskatoon Agreement then became the template for medical care plans in all other provinces. Even assuming the Saskatoon Agreement was an essential pre-condition to the implementation of universal medical care coverage, it nevertheless shaped the way health care evolved in Canada for the next half century. The episode also illustrates the very contingent nature of medicare and the extent to which the policy was a compromise between what social democrats, especially the leftist activists within the CCF, actually wanted, and what was politically possible, at least as perceived by the Saskatchewan government at the time.

In Esping-Andersen's typology of conservative, liberal, and social democratic welfare states, Canada is generally classified as liberal.[30] However, as is the case with the United Kingdom, the considerable influence of social democratic parties, such as the CCF/NDP in Canada or the Labour Party in the UK, particularly when they have held power for substantial periods of time, means that the character of the welfare state is more mixed than this simple typology might imply. Both countries' universal health coverage policies owe far more to a social democratic than a liberal or conservative ethos. This can be seen in the principle of first-dollar coverage for all necessary hospital and medical care and a single-payer funding mechanism. However, unlike Canada's strong form of single-tier universality, the UK's NHS has always permitted a private tier. Roughly 10 percent of the population have used this private tier for at least some of their health care needs since the 1990s.[31]

At the same time, there are liberal and conservative elements that survive in Canadian medicare, including the continuation of medical liberalism—the independent contracting position of physicians—in the decades following the Saskatoon Agreement.[32] Even in countries such as Sweden, the most obvious social democratic welfare state based on Esping-Andersen's typology, there are significant conservative and liberal elements, such as the prevalent use of (albeit modest) user fees for almost all necessary hospital and medical care.[33]

Canadian medicare, despite its more unique single-tier quality, also represents the triumph of compromise and negotiation that mirrors the work of other countries in their attempts to blend ideological values into public policy. Much like these other systems, there is a marriage of the concepts of health as a right and health care as a service. Given Canada's geo-political relationship with the United States, the comparisons with American health care are difficult to ignore; arguably, the intensity of the health care debates in the United States serves to distort our understanding of what Canadian medicare represents. Compared with European nations, Canada's single-payer system stands out and underscores the affect of social democrats on the founding of medicare.

Social democrats in Canada often celebrate medicare as proof of what they can do when in charge and as proof of a humane public policy that institutionalizes a set of values in a universal system. Simply put, they see it as the left's gift to Canada. But far beyond a victory for social democrats alone, the story of medicare has become part of what it means to be

Canadian, because it is a story of compassion, leadership, and a concern for human welfare, values that have become part of the Canadian ethos.

Successive commissions established to review the program have not only reinforced this idea, that medicare is somehow uniquely Canadian, but have also furnished us with language (sometimes, but not always, ideological) to further embellish our ideas of what medicare means to our identity as Canadians.[34] Made-in-Canada medicare, therefore, was not only a bold demonstration of what social democrats can do, but of the kind of public policy they can create working together in a pluralistic federalist system that creates opportunities for working with federal, provincial, and territorial governments led by non-social democratic parties (but that have at least some members who share a social democratic vision), as well as diverse citizen groups and organizations without party affiliation. In the twenty-first century, as we look ahead to medicare's future, while cherishing it as an accomplishment of the past, we might also consider the role of social democrats in stimulating debates about health care reform. Celebrating medicare has perhaps made us complacent about reinvesting in the *process* that was at least as important as the product.

CHAPTER 16

CHANGE THE GAME

THE SOCIAL
DEMOCRACY PROJECT

Jonathan Sas

I'd be remiss if I didn't begin with a tip of my hat to the incredible achievements of the Notley government—here at the conference in Calgary, Alberta, the beating heart of contemporary Canadian social democracy.

In the midst of an economic crisis, natural disasters, and an emboldened and hateful misogynist right, the government has brought in a carbon tax, moved to aggressively phase out coal, transition affected workers, and invest massively in solar and wind renewable power. They brought in progressive income taxation and raised corporate taxes. They've raised the minimum wage, the first provincial jurisdiction on a path to $15. They are investing in affordable child care, in mental health, and in education. And while much hard work and making progress remains, particularly on respecting Indigenous rights and reducing the impact and emissions of the oil sands, this all happened in two years. I can't think of a social democratic government in Canada that has done more.

In this chapter, I want to focus on the window that has opened, both here in Canada and abroad, for the renewal of social democracy, as a political philosophy but ultimately as a political project interested in state power. I will argue that social democracy, not liberalism, can and must be the response to rise of the right and the answer to the wreckage of four decades of unfettered free-market capitalism. For social democracy to rise to the occasion, however, I will suggest it requires a thorough reimagining, and one that contends with its shortcomings and blind spots.

I'd like to start by setting some context for this historical moment as I see it, and to explain both the background of the Broadbent Institute and the work we are engaged in.

The institute was founded in 2012, but really got going in 2013. I joined four years ago, in May 2013, wet behind the ears, a disgruntled journalist and political theory grad.

My, what a different moment that was.

Stephen Harper was well into his first majority government and had been prime minister for seven years, most of my adult life at the time.

I am reminded of a telling passage in a seminal book of political economy, edited by Leah Vosko and Wallace Clement. Coming after the lean and austere Paul Martin finance years, the 2001 book detailed the retrenchment of the welfare state and scaling back of redistributive programs. Mel Watkins' chapter mused that perhaps Canada's "neoliberal moment" would soon come to a close.

Of course, we know that "moment" was not short lived. Harper would oversee a shrinking of federal fiscal capacity that threatens to tie the hands of all future federal governments for decades unless bold progressive tax reform is put back on the table. Harper continued to pursue neoliberal policies mixed with his own brand of mean-spirited attacks on equity seeking groups, environmentalists, and the lot. Good riddance.

But there is an important political dimension to Canada's inequality story here worth re-emphasizing. The surge in income inequality occurred primarily in the 1990s and has since plateaued. In Canada, of course, this was the result of Liberal government policy, more so than globalization or technological change, the Third Way's popular excuse.

Across the OECD, the response to growing inequality in market incomes has varied, reflecting differences in the domestic politics of member countries. Many countries have found ways to mitigate the growth in inequality. In Canada, however, the policy response reinforced, rather than offset, it.

Since the mid-1990s, the social role of government has been reduced dramatically. By 2007, the year before the economic meltdown, OECD data indicated that the traditional difference between Canada and the United States in social spending (as a proportion of GDP) had disappeared. In addition, public revenues in Canada have declined from the middle of the OECD pack in 1992 to the bottom quintile by 2012. The progressivity of the tax system has been reduced, and social transfers such as Employment Insurance and social assistance have been deeply retrenched. As a result, the tax-transfer system is much less effective in reducing inequality than in the past.

According to the OECD, government taxes and transfers in the late 1980s and the early 1990s narrowed the gap between rich and poor the most in Canada, Denmark, Finland, and Sweden. By the late 1990s and early 2000s, Canada had joined Switzerland and the US as the countries with the smallest redistributive impact.

As leftists, of course, we must interrogate from a critical perspective what prompted this turn in Canadian policy. There is good evidence to point to the well-organized and well-funded influence of right-wing think tanks, corporate media, and a knowledge production and distribution machine that successfully united the right in the form of the Conservative Party and that continues to colour our national political discourse to this day. From the Fraser Institute to the Manning Centre, the Frontier Centre to the Macdonald Laurier Institute, the budgets of the right far outweigh those of the CCPA, Caledon, and a comparatively modest progressive cohort of research organizations.

At the time of the Broadbent Institute's launch, Canada was in the midst of Harper's politically motivated audits of progressive charities, including the CCPA, Tides, David Suzuki's, and others.

The Broadbent Institute was launched to be expressly political in its social democratic advocacy and agitating. We are registered as a not for profit, not a charity, precisely so we can be political. This designation allowed us, for example, to release two scathing reports exposing the CRA's politically motivated tax audits of left-wing charities, an analysis that showed the Fraser Institute and nine other right-wing charities were claiming 0 percent political activity in their tax filings and yet were not under audit. Funny that.

So, what do we do? What does a social democratic think tank look like in practice?

Our work is made up of four key pillars.

First is our training and leadership program, geared to providing backbone support for left organizing across the country. We've trained thousands of activists and campaigners, providing the skills and tools for winning both issue and political campaigns and contributing to broader movement building and leadership development. Our Online Leadership School ensures trainings are accessible across Canada. I'm proud to report we were very active recently in helping to train key campaigners in the successful progressive mayoralty win of Charlie Clark in Saskatoon!

The second pillar of our work fits the more traditional think tank image. The institute has released over thirty pieces of original research on critical public policy issues since 2014, including research on: the dynamics of income and wealth inequality, including our wealth gap study; pensions and seniors poverty referenced almost daily in news reports on Canada's seniors' savings crisis; stagnant youth unemployment and a proposed youth job guarantee. We've also made the case for public investment in innovation and infrastructure, emphasizing fair returns that are socialized not privatized, and we have looked at workplace democracy and worker voice, and social democratic approaches to climate action.

Perhaps the clearest example of the impact of our policy work came in the publication of studies on the regressive nature of income splitting and the expansion of TFSAs (Tax-Free Savings Accounts). Widely covered in the media, these reports helped convince both the opposition federal NDP and Liberals to campaign against the policies (that they both had tacitly supported initially) in the 2015 election, and both died in Trudeau's first budget.

This brings me to our third pillar. Four years ago, we took a risk and started a conference called the Progress Summit. The conference, which convenes trade unionists, activists, academics, community leaders, policy-makers, and politicians in Ottawa, has become core to what we do. It is a space for critical policy discussions, yes, but also for organizing and networking on the left, learning from progressive wins and tough conversations between different movements. We had no idea that one thousand people would show up each year to an annual conference of progressives.

This year saw some really difficult conversations, as Indigenous, black, Muslim, and other communities of colour challenged the myths of the progressive left in what remains a stubbornly white space.

Last, but not least, the institute launched a news media project called *Press Progress* that has become perhaps our most far-reaching and effective endeavour. *Press Progress* is read by tens of thousands of readers every day and reaches millions every year. Using listicles, video montages, graphic art, and other web-friendly media, our traffic has grown to be higher than many daily newspapers across the country.

Press Progress breaks news and covers stories from an accessible but boldly left perspective. The attractive digital-first format, combined with a feisty, muckraking journalistic style, has meant a daily check on the political right, one that contributed to sinking Kevin O'Leary, Stephen Harper, and their ilk.

We've also made a habit of dutifully challenging the machinery of the right, fact-checking their research, and exposing their methodological flaws and the biases in their ideologically motivated studies.

Thanks are due in large measure to the support of the trade union movement and tens of thousands of individual donors across the country; five years on we are now a steady feature in the Canadian political landscape and a powerful voice on the left. We have offices across the country, a huge digital media presence, and, I think, we can argue credibly to have helped shift the politics in the country.

Sunny ways, right, my friends? I'm afraid this is the point in the narrative arc of my presentation that the villain must reappear.

Like everyone else on the left, the institute has felt the urgency of grappling with the political-economic climate that elected Trump, as we witness the rise of the Front National and other far right parties across Europe, and, indeed, a rabid white nationalist movement at home.

As Ed Broadbent argued recently, a number of democratic countries have turned to the populist right and its false promises to turn back the clock and return to ethnically homogenous and economically self-reliant nation states. Concurrently, many social democratic parties in these countries have lost the confidence of voters to provide an alternative economic and social agenda.

Of course, the inequality story I spoke to above in Canada is critical to understanding what is going on elsewhere. In the West, the left has failed in many ways to put forward an economic agenda that regulates rather than abandons workers in a globalized economy, and we've failed to find effective policy levers to create decent jobs for all, to promote greater equality, and to build an environmentally sustainable economy.

But the inequality story, the very real politics of winners and losers in today's economy, is but one piece of what is underpinning the rise of the right.

I wrote recently that the speed, scale, and ferocity of racist attacks across the United States and in Canada in the wake of Trump's victory are revealing. They are doubly revealing, in fact.

First, they reveal what most people of colour know plainly through lived experience—whiteness, and indeed white supremacy, continue to explain power dynamics in society. The violence that underpins white supremacy, subtler and blunted at times, is only expressing itself more fully and honestly today.

The second revelation emerges from the first, albeit for white folks. Our shock and surprise at the outbursts of racist violence are unfounded, ahistorical, and plainly insufficient. In fact, our very "shock" is evidence of our comfortable perch atop the social location hierarchy.

White progressives have in large part not differed from most whites in becoming dangerously self-assured that racism had abated, held few people back, and only really thrived on the fringes.

White supremacy was conjured in the mind's eye as the KKK, or maybe a holdover of the religious rural right. In any event, it is imagined as a marginal force unrelated to that "white privilege" thing we can joke about, but only in passing and without doing anything differently.

Trump was elected despite (or because of) explicit appeals to white supremacy. The Trump "white lash," as Van Jones referred to it, normalized at every turn by mainstream media, has put mass deportations of Latin Americans on the table and now regressive law and order policies that will surely further terrorize black communities.

Of course, the normalization of this bigotry over the past year cannot be understood without confronting how whiteness currently operates. It is not about the existence of the emboldened racists at Trump rallies or in Alberta at Rebel rallies. No. It is about the stunning silence from most white people, progressives included, who have been comfortable with the status quo to date.

There is, of course, a complex tangle of causal explanations for Trump's election that go beyond race. Prominent voices on the left, such as Naomi Klein, have written compellingly and plausibly of the centrality of the wreckage of neoliberalism, and the Democrats' disastrous abandonment of their progressive-labour base that Bernie Sanders had so obviously brought to light.

But her account, like many others, falls short. Its call for a resurgent left remains, in large measure, colour-blind or at least colour-shy. Racism is acknowledged and deplored but is explained as more of a byproduct of the dark underbelly of global capitalism.

Political liberals in Canada believe they have the antidote to the right. Our telegenic prime minister has become a global brand in this regard. He's taken the torch from Obama and is hailed by the Center for American Progress as the great hope for global liberalism.

We must acknowledge that throughout the West, liberals have at various times supported social democratic reform, whether it be through expanding parts of the welfare state, such as public pensions and medicare, or supporting progressive taxation in order to pay for public services and other social goods. However, as historian Tony Judt has remarked, "whereas many liberals might see such taxation or public provision as a necessary evil, a social democratic vision of the good society entails from the outset a greater role for the state and the public sector."

It is my contention that Trudeau embodies the managerial, technocratic approach to politics, with an enduring and unshaken faith in markets, and a shallow notion of representative diversity rather than equity. Trudeau's convincing win, I propose, masks that this liberal project, what is ultimately still the status quo, is in serious crisis.

I want to cite a passage written by Charles Taylor in 1970 in *Pattern of Politics*, about a different Trudeau leader. It remains, as my colleague Luke Savage has pointed out, a devastating critique of liberalism's shortcomings. Imagine this is being written today.

> The NYL—the New Young Leader—is said to be attuned and responsive to the issues which preoccupy young urban dwellers. He is said to have the courage to dispense with the double-talk and circumlocution of the Old Guard . . . All this may have little relation to reality, but it is the myth rather than the reality of the NYL we are examining here: and this myth firmly rests upon the consensus view of politics. Those who promote the NYL make up the highly successful new elite . . . Lawyers, professors, businessmen are not at all at odds with the structure of our society. What they look for in the NYL is the crystallization and expression of a consensus.

> This is why his goals must remain without real content. He expresses "changes," "innovation at our highest political level," everything except a clear program of reform, which he contemptuously dismisses as "old fashioned promises." But this is more than mere equivocation, because the role of the leader is to remain flexible and pragmatic, to respond to problems as they arise. To do this, the embodiment of the supposed new technological elite must be an exponent of the main thesis of consensus politics: that politics is the domain of problems and solutions, and not the confrontation of fundamental questions. He must embody the end of ideology.

> At the same time, if the NYL is courageous in eschewing the language of equivocation, he speaks out not to break the consensus but to present more effectively the goals that are hidden in the gobbledygook of the traditional politician or bureaucrat. In short, the NYL is supposed to be discovering and articulating the demands of our society. He "personifies all of the exciting changes in our society." But does he?

What is totally missing in the argument is any inkling that there are important and fundamental conflicts in our society which make any claim to consensus specious. It is impossible for one person to represent the demands of the whole.

In the saga of the new leader, the battle is exclusively between the young and "with it" and the old with their outworn ideas and sensibilities. But this in no way involves a critique of the structures of our society or an attack on the privileges they entrench. Instead, the attack is launched in the name of these structures or on behalf of their ideal image of themselves as the breeding ground of enlightened, technocratic innovators.

The myth of the NYL is a kind of parody of the modern idea of progress, in which the latest thing is always right and always wins effortlessly over the old. The idea that progress requires struggle, so prominent in earlier theories, both liberal and socialist, finds no place here—because the myth takes no account of structures.

With liberalism clearly not up to the task of tackling the fundamental conflicts, what political project legitimately stands in the way of rise of the right?

The Sanders movement offers important lessons.

Though a self-described democratic socialist, Bernie almost won the Democratic ticket on what is a rather standard fair of social democratic offers: free tuition, universal health care, respect for workers' rights, and a fair wage. This is not Waffle Manifesto stuff. But it was critical of corporate power and named income and wealth inequality.

It put the lie to the notion that progressive parties cannot capture the imagination of a broad cross-section of voters and build constituencies of support for universal programs, not endlessly targeted and means tested ones.

The left has forgotten, as Tony Judt rightly pointed out, how to talk about these things. To remind people that social democracy transformed democratic politics in the twentieth century. Believing that markets should be regulated and put in the service of social aims, social democrats fought for state investments in the common good and for the idea of citizenship that included not only political and civil rights but also social and economic rights. And I truly believe the Sanders movement suggests new constituencies of support can be found on these commitments.

Unlike liberalism, we have a tradition, and critical orientation to power, and, I hope, the willingness to confront the most pressing contradictions of today—those that go beyond economic inequality to social democracy's blind spots.

Celebrating past successes is clearly not enough. In a very real sense, the election of Trump pushed us at the institute to confront the fact that social democracy will have to be fundamentally renewed if it is to regain momentum and be fully relevant to today's challenges. Any successful left offer will have to be connected to and a champion of contemporary struggles for justice.

There is no alternative to neoliberalism which does not centre anti-oppression and take intersectionality seriously.

It is now undeniable that we white progressives must dispense with mythologies about cosmopolitan diversity, inclusion, and meritocracy in a deracialized and plural society. It's time to question the tunes of the liberal universalist songbook we've sung from for decades. How white supremacy will or will not be challenged on the institutional left—in progressive movements, political parties, unions, the academy, etc.—is pivotal to whether the left will be able to counter Trump and the whiteness he represents with a broad and diverse left coalition.

Will white progressives struggle for anti-racism alongside people of colour and make it a central strategy and analytical tool in organizing change? Or will we obfuscate and equivocate and provide cover for the privilege we know we accrue through our skin colour?

The feminist philosopher and critical race theorist Linda Alcoff has put the challenge clearly in her indispensable recent book, *The Future of Whiteness*. With demographic changes promising to make white Americans a minority by 2050, Alcoff asks whether whites will "adapt to a multiracial, decentralized society in the same basic way that others have, by not assuming a right of presumptive entitlement to political leadership, cultural domination, or comparative economic prosperity—by learning, in short, to share, to take a turn on the periphery now and again . . ."?

Key to answering these questions is whether whiteness as an identity can be disentangled from supremacy and from its history informed by subjugating others. It certainly won't evolve positively if white social democrats aren't leading agents in defining its path.

Social democrats are fools to ignore the reality of white supremacy and the legacy of our own violent colonial past and present here in Canada. An honest political economy account demands it.

When it comes to justice for Indigenous people, the gap between words and actions today is unconscionable. It is a challenge the progressive left must fight for vigorously.

This will be difficult. Confronting Canada's colonial history means acknowledging that even celebrated social democratic achievements left out Indigenous peoples along with other groups, and that much of the wealth created and enjoyed came through violence and dispossession.

It means discomfiting discussions about how whiteness animates official Canadian history and dominant understandings of *being* Canadian.

Importantly, it also means confronting how on the left, too, white privilege continues to shape power dynamics and social location and whose voices get heard, including, in the institutional left, at organizations like the Broadbent Institute.

Indigenous leaders, activists, artists, and movements have been calling out for a different way. Indigenous scholars like Val Napoleon, Hayden King, Pam Palmater, and Glen Coulthard are shining light on a different path forward.

Moreover, groups like Black Lives Matter are making clear the connections they see between anti-black racism and the struggle for Indigenous justice. Black-Canadian scholars like Rinaldo Walcott are underlining the imperative of moving past colour-blind economic policy.

Work too has changed. Social democrats can't rely on outdated notions of industrial democracy. Worker rights and voices and a robust trade union movement remain absolutely central to any transformation, but we must have answers to protecting workers in contingent and precarious work that go beyond a neoliberal spin on a basic income.

Of course, we also face an ecological crisis and the challenge of economic transition. I think we can draw on the long tradition on the Canadian left of grappling with the staples trap. This left approach, once out of vogue, has much to offer communities, and workers cannot be left behind in any climate plan. And social democrats are uniquely placed to grapple with the implications of transition, not only for ecological integrity of the planet, but for the economic opportunities and job security for communities and workers.

This year, the Broadbent Institute launched its project: "Change the Game." The project invites a critical look at the history of social democracy in Canada, so that we can learn from the successes and challenges of the past in order to build the best possible path forward.

The project will begin by exploring major themes, including Indigenous rights and decolonization, the ecological crisis, economic inequality, the rise of the populist right, as well as pluralism, feminism, and systemic racism.

The second phase of the project will look more closely at the legacy of social democracy in various regions in Canada and local innovations.

The final phase of Change the Game will look forward, imagining an inclusive path for renewing social democracy in Canada. Based on the critical analysis from the first two phases of the project, it will propose avenues for social democracy to pursue in four key areas: inequality, trade and the economy, the environment, and equity and inclusion.

Together, we will change the game.

www.broadbentinstitute.ca/change_the_game

CHAPTER 17

EVALUATING THE 2017 NDP LEADERSHIP CAMPAIGN

Jillian Ratti

On October 1, 2017, New Democrats watched Jagmeet Singh win the federal NDP leadership on the first ballot with 53.8 percent of the vote. This was a surprise to most, who assumed that it would take at least two ballots for any of the candidates to get to the 50 percent plus one mark. Charlie Angus, in particular, was polling well, especially among those who had been members of the party for a long time. As the results were announced live on television in alphabetical order, the shock was clear among viewers and social media followers that Angus had failed to get anywhere close to making it a competitive race. Having said that, the rumours out of Singh's campaign in the lead up to the first ballot results were consistent: they knew they had it in the bag and were planning the party. They had signed up 47,000 new members across Canada. They had raised 53 percent of all money donated during the campaign. They had done their internal polling. They knew it was their win.

In the lead up to all of this, we had a stimulating and productive campaign between four excellent candidates: Charlie Angus, Niki Ashton, Guy Caron, and the ultimate winner, Jagmeet Singh. In contrast to the very nasty Conservative party leadership race this year, which saw the surprise victory of Andrew Scheer over Maxime Bernier, we saw a remarkably civil exchange of ideas between candidates. It took at least two debates before anyone was willing to suggest that they didn't all agree with each other. The worst of the infighting during a time of turbulence was a vague and indirect implication that one might be a bit too Liberal, with a capital L.

In another party, Niki Ashton's pregnancy, with twins, could have been an open topic for debate, and her male competitors could have taken the opportunity to challenge her fitness to lead. Not so here: we saw cheers, congratulations, and respect for the historic undertaking from her male competitors.

In another party, Jagmeet Singh would have been thrown under the bus by fellow candidates when Bloc Quebecois leader Martine Ouellette suggested that his visible religious symbols would never get him any traction in Quebec. Instead, we saw outrage at the suggestion, with a particularly emphatic "No" from Guy Caron, the only Quebec representative in the leadership race.

In another party, Charlie Angus might have lost ground while attending to his dying sister. It could have easily been used to undermine his perceived dedication to party leadership in subtle or not so subtle ways. Instead, support and love were the dominant messages to him during that time.

In another party, Guy Caron might have faced criticism for his accented English and endured accusations that he would never be palatable to the English-speaking majority in Canada. Language is an easy point of entry for those wishing to cut down a candidate.

In the grand scheme of Canadian politics, civility is a priority for the NDP. We are about solidarity, even in times of conflict: lifting each other up; looking for the best in people; and busting courageously through the walls that prevent progress. This is the New Democrat way, and it's one of many reasons I feel so at home in this political family.

Certainly, we are far from perfect in our own progressiveness, and much could be said about the many ways that ethnicity and gender played out over these past months. Specifically, there has been an ugly side to internal criticisms of Singh: it is said that he is unmarketable, not because of his ideas or policies, but because of his turban. Niki Ashton, and many of her supporters, have noticed she has received less attention, both inside and outside the party, than her male competitors, despite polling quite well among members. Sexism is likely part of that.

But overall, are we too nice? What has gone wrong? A federal NDP government has yet to be achieved, despite the fact that we could practically taste it in 2015. Many commentators yell loudly that we have no place in the political landscape, except as the conscience of Parliament. It seems nearly a sport in the political and media communities to dismiss and delegitimize social democracy and democratic socialism, which are so central to our sense of identity and solidarity. We are told we are not fit to govern because we are idealists who lack the strength of character to be appropriately responsible.

All of this is nonsense, of course, and, while that is completely obvious to me and many reading this, it is far less so to the voting public, which has been bombarded for decades by this messaging. To crack that egg, we need to do three things:

First, we need to turn back to our left-wing roots in social democracy and democratic socialism. We need to use those words, be proud of them, and articulate a vision of Canada that breaks the neoliberal mold and provides real means to address the growing problem of inequality.

Second, we need to get creative to overcome the major challenge of communicating our vision in the face of the dominant narrative. We have to tell new stories in new ways with new media. Can we get art, history, fashion, theatre, and community groups to join the advocacy project of campaigning? Can we better engage social movements as allies and supporters? A good and traditional ground game is critical, but we have to break beyond it in order to be heard.

Finally, we need to make our voices louder and more assertive. We can still act with kindness and civility, as is our default, but we need to turn the dial up and focus on directing the narrative instead of letting the narrative happen to us. Getting obnoxious in our creativity will help. We also need to carefully cultivate relationships with the media and be intentional with messaging every step of the way. When we are confidently and unashamedly wearing our identity and staying firm in our values, it will be easier to get loud and be heard. We have, indeed, tiptoed around our core beliefs for too long.

Regardless of who won, we would have seen more audacious policy and a clear realignment to the left side of the political spectrum. With Singh we certainly do see a leader who uses the word "nationalize" from time to time. We also see a leader who is a fundraising powerhouse with the potential to open up party membership in young and racialized communities. The greatest challenges ahead will involve working to unite the various leadership factions and to realize electoral success in the form of a majority government. In pursuing these goals, the new leader will do well to remind the membership, as Jack Layton did in his last letter, that the "cause is much bigger than any one leader." And we must push forward with a firmly leftist, newly creative, and assertively vocal campaign in 2019.

CHAPTER 18

SOCIAL DEMOCRACY AND THE LEFT IN CANADA

PAST, PRESENT, AND FUTURE

Avi Lewis

Good evening friends, conference organizers, fellow leftivists, legendary Legion bartenders, members of the Alberta NDP (here in disguise), and, speaking of disguise, a warm welcome to the security operatives posing as any of the above.

I think we are all afflicted with some measure of impostor syndrome—the suspicion that at any moment, the people around us will discover that we are unqualified—extravagantly, fraudulently so. That we are mere pretenders, that we have arrived at the exam to discover that we forgot to dress and are standing before judgment in abject nakedness.

I feel a little like an imposter right now. To be here, in this hallowed if hops-scented hall, where eighty-five years ago the electoral left in Canada began its national journey, at the outset of a three-day conference to interrogate and celebrate that history, to speak on a topic as outrageously ambitious as "The Left in Canada: Past, Present, and Future," well, let me just say, it is not assuaging my sense of cosmic inadequacy.

Unlike the other presenters at this conference, I have no expertise or academic credential in this field. If I have some notoriety in Alberta these days—and I understand it might be closer to the truth that my name has become an expletive for some—it is not because I carry the torch of the CCF/NDP as a lifelong partisan. In fact, I am, I think it is clear, seen as an outsider.

But I have had, through sheer accident of birth, a front row seat at some of the party's historic moments. And The Party—it was always spoken with capital letters in our house—was, for all of my upbringing, the family business.

My earliest memories are of committee rooms, shop floors, prop planes, and election day boards. Campaigns with six events a day. Plates of sandwiches with amputated crusts, festooned with neon pickles. The heaving, surging emotion and drama of convention floors and election nights, often beyond my capacity as a child to understand, but always, as an emotional being, overwhelming in their intensity.

So, what I'd like to do with you tonight, in a spirit both personal and political, is embrace the three-act structure—past, present, and future—which the title of this conference so neatly confers.

In reflecting about the past, I'll pick out three or four themes and tensions that have emerged from my recent dive into my grandfather's body of work. This is absolutely not a comprehensive survey—not even of his personal political philosophy—far less than of the CCF/NDP over the decades.

In a posture of sincere humility, I will leave the scholarship to the scholars and share with you tonight some themes from the past that, simply, resonate with me.

In terms of the present, I had the good fortune to be at the Canadian Labour Congress convention this week in Toronto. One of the excellent keynote speakers was Premier Notley. As the head of the only NDP government in Canada, I think she would be proud to represent the present of social democracy, and I'll share some critical reflections on this government and its approach that I think contrast in interesting ways with the past.

Also, in the present for me is the vision of the Leap Manifesto—a living document and continuing coalition that I have been involved with since its conception. I think some of the tensions in the left in Canada today can be seen in sharp relief in the way the Leap has been characterized, mischaracterized, and debated since its launch less than two years ago.

And finally, I'll wrap up with some brief thoughts on where I believe the future of the left lies in this land.

So, to the past. It is irresistible, on this occasion, to read the words that came out of the meeting in this very room eighty-five years ago and reflect on their eerie and infuriating relevance today. Let's just do the first paragraphs of the founding document of the Co-operative Commonwealth Federation, the Regina Manifesto of the CCF:

We aim to replace the present capitalist system, with its inherent injustice and inhumanity, by a social order from which the domination and exploitation of one class by another will be eliminated, in which economic planning will supersede unregulated private enterprise and competition, and in which genuine democratic self-government, based upon economic equality will be possible.

The present order is marked by glaring inequalities of wealth and opportunity, by chaotic waste and instability; and in an age of plenty it condemns the great mass of the people to poverty and insecurity. Power has become more and more concentrated into the hands of a small irresponsible minority of financiers and industrialists and to their predatory interests the majority are habitually sacrificed.

When private profit is the main stimulus to economic effort, our society oscillates between periods of feverish prosperity in which the main benefits go to speculators and profiteers, and of catastrophic depression, in which the common man's normal state of insecurity and hardship is accentuated. We believe that these evils can be removed only in a planned and socialized economy in which our natural resources and principal means of production and distribution are owned, controlled and operated by the people.

Every time I read these words, and I make a point of doing so every few years, I am struck by their continued relevance. By how little has fundamentally changed in the basic dynamics of our economy. Despite the fact that those words emerged in the early years of the Great Depression, we have not come nearly so far as we would like to think. For instance, let's look at the common person's "normal state of insecurity and hardship" today. Just this week, a study by a bankruptcy firm revealed that almost one-third of all Canadians don't make enough money to meet their monthly payments.

More than half of the country is within $200 a month of not being able to pay the bills. Almost three-quarters of Canadians would go underwater on their mortgage if their monthly payments rose just 10 percent.

As for "glaring inequalities of wealth and opportunity"? Well, since the 2008 financial crisis, the financial sector in Canada has racked up profits of $421 billion dollars. An average of almost $47 billion a year.

And this year's OXFAM wealth survey revealed that our two wealthiest citizens, Galen Weston and David Thomson, control as much wealth as a third of all Canadians. The wealth of two guys equals that of eleven million of us.

I don't know how that makes you feel, but for me it unleashes an insurgent tide of outrage. A 1930s-style desire to overthrow such a desperately unfair arrangement.

I've been reading another historic text of the left, *Make This Your Canada*, written in 1943 by my grandpa David Lewis, then national secretary of the CCF, and Frank Scott, the national chairman. It was effectively a popular account of the CCF's history and program—and it was a huge bestseller, coinciding with a surge in the party's popularity in the wartime years.

About halfway through, the authors review the distribution of income in Canada, and come to the following conclusion:

> Only a tiny proportion of the people own and control the big corporations, the huge monopolies and most of Canada's wealth-producing resources . . . The well-to-do group is merely a dot in proportion to the other figures and needs a magnifying glass to be identified. It is to this dot that the whole country pays tribute . . . The basic struggle today is between the 99% who are reaching out for the economic and political power which the 1% now effectively control.

Now I doubt that *Make This Your Canada* was required reading in 2011 at Occupy Wall Street in Zuccotti Park, New York City. But the basic dimensions of the crisis of capitalism have clearly not altered in the past eight decades.

But if the diagnosis feels like it was written today, the solutions are definitely more out of fashion.

A caveat: David's thinking, like the NDP's, obviously changed over time. In fact, from the Regina Manifesto in 1932 to the Winnipeg Declaration of 1956, which my grandfather had a strong hand in writing, there is an unmistakeable shift in rhetoric, emphasis, and policy. In other words, the process of the electoral left moving to the centre of the political spectrum did not start with Bob Rae in the 1980s.

In fact, David Lewis was unquestionably a factor propelling this trajectory—in particular, the step back from Regina's full-on embrace of nationalization of major industries to Winnipeg's explicit recognition that private enterprise can make a useful contribution, situating the party in a vision of a mixed economy.

But there are a number of really consistent themes in my grandfather's thinking—and I want to tease out a few of them for you because they seem so very relevant today, just as he and Frank Scott understood with such visionary clarity the framing of the 99 percent vs the 1 percent.

First: revisiting the historic texts, there is a consistent and passionate commitment to what is now the lost art of planning. In the Great Depression, the CCF espoused a planned economy to pull society out of existential crisis.

By the time of *Make This Your Canada*, though, it was no longer theoretical. In the Second World War, Canada's government had taken control of almost all sectors of the economy and enlisted them—directed and controlled them—in the service of an overarching national mission.

It was a flawed and unequal process, largely presided over by corporate titans, and I do not romanticize it. But it was incredibly successful on its own terms.

The national income more than tripled in the decade from 1932 to 1942. Massive joblessness in the 1930s gave way to full employment in the war years. Women went to work, and society and the economy surged forward on many fronts. The moral imperative to defeat fascism swept aside economic dogma and opened space for transformation.

> The reader will recall how during the depression Canadian governments rejected every suggestion for a works programme and every plea for more generous allowances to the aged, the blind, the unemployed and the impoverished farmers, on the excuse that the money was not available. In 1932 a million dollars a year could not be found for public works. In 1942 the federal treasury spent the huge sum of 13 million dollars per day.

So, the War Industries Control Board took over production of steel, lumber, oil, metals, and vehicles, and harnessed them to a single purpose. The Wartime Prices and Trade Board regulated quality and limited the choice of consumer goods (does that sound so bad?).

And there were massive public investments in new plants and machinery. New industries were built from the ground up, existing industries were transformed. It was clear that the private sector would never have done this on its own.

As Frank and David wrote:

> Hitler forced war on us and we at once had a national purpose—the total defeat of fascism. The people and the government became determined to achieve this objective.

> Monopoly could ignore it only at its peril. Big business had to submit to some curbs on its powers, for it dared not oppose the clear will of the Canadian people . . .

The basic lesson which our war experience has taught us is that, in order to achieve the production which the war needs of Canada and her allies required, even a capitalist government was forced to abandon the normal practices of capitalism and to substitute for them some degree of national planning and central control. The sheer urgency of the need imposed the adoption of a technique which in pre-war days Liberal and Conservatives would have rejected and condemned as socialistic and Bolshevistic.

The defining crisis of that generation was the rise of fascism. I don't think it's hyperbole to suggest that we may yet look back on our lives—on this very decade—and say the same thing.

But, in fact, we face multiple overlapping crises today: spiralling inequality, but also systemic, daily racism that devalues, demeans, imprisons, and visits violence and even murder on bodies that are not white. And a never-ending colonialism that continues to trample on the rights of Indigenous peoples, withholding and contaminating the services, water, education, and, most of all, the land that is the source of all life.

And underlying and surrounding all these is the climate crisis, the great existential threat to our future survival, which disproportionately affects those who are already living with the worst effects of all those other crises.

Do we really believe that these disasters can be met by anything less than a mission moment for all the peoples of this land? I resist military metaphors on principle, but I find the notion of wartime footing unavoidable, when I think of the depth and breadth of change so urgently needed at this point in history.

And so, the idea that the direction of society cannot be left to the chaotic and carnivorous ways of the market seems utterly logical to me. To achieve change on the scale required, we are going to need a plan, one that is democratic in its conception and accountable to all communities, especially those most marginalized under our current system. The call for an economy that operates according to some sort of plan is one that resonates profoundly in the present.

Second: Despite the CCF's commitment to a planned economy, there is another impulse that speaks across the decades to me from my grandfather's work. The project to win—to form a government that dares to control and direct, even take over industry—was always paired with a deep faith in the self-organizing powers of people.

Whether unions or farming collectives, co-operatives or broader social movements, the need for government intervention was always tem-

pered by a clear role for people's organizations, a sense that the project of
the left could never be fully captured solely by a political party that merely
sought government. It had to be, as the CCF was, a movement party.

Let me quote again from *Make This Your Canada*, and its account of
the founding meeting that took place in this room in 1932.

> On July 30th, 1932, the Western Labor Conference met in Calgary, Alberta.
> On August 1st, the labour delegates were joined by farmer representatives. The
> conference to form a nation-wide people's political movement was opened.
> The meeting took place in the Calgary Labour Temple. Over a hundred del-
> egates were present, representing all the labour, socialist and farmer political
> organizations of the four western provinces ...
>
> Naturally, there was great division of opinion among the delegates. This was
> the first major attempt in Canadian history to unite farm and urban peo-
> ple into one political party under one name and one programme. There was
> unavoidable suspicion and strangeness. There were provincial parties which
> had achieved some political success and were determined to retain their iden-
> tity. There were differences of social philosophy, ranging all the way from pure
> reformism to doctrinaire socialism. No one came to the conference with a cut
> and dried programme. Every group brought its particular approach.
>
> The opponents of the new movement saw in these differences a reason for
> rejoicing. This was short-sighted. The unity which emerges out of a recognition
> of differences is a real, dynamic unity instead of an artificial front. And the
> resulting political programme is a dynamic programme hammered out of the
> needs of the people, instead of an arbitrary collection of preconceived notions.
> In all this lay great democratic strength ...
>
> The Calgary conference decided to establish a federation rather than a unitary
> party. It decided also to find a name which would be distinctive and broad
> enough to convey the idea of an *all-in people's movement*. Hence "Co-operative
> Commonwealth Federation."

An "all-in people's movement." Wow.

The embrace of difference, the vision of a coalition with real tensions
but also unity of purpose—that I think is a defining characteristic of the
founding of the electoral left in Canada. And I believe it's a culture that
needs urgently to be recovered.

Now, some of you may be thinking that my grandfather was not
exactly famous for his embrace of difference. In fact, he was a well-known

and sometimes harsh disciplinarian. There are those who have even called it a family trait—and by those, of course, I mean members of the Waffle.

And I get it. It is an enduring irony of this story. My grandfather stood with Tommy Douglas and only fourteen others to oppose Pierre Trudeau's War Measures Act. But when he apprehended an insurrection in his own party, he metaphorically called the soldiers into the streets. And I guess that put my Dad in uniform.

I don't know how I feel about that episode, to be honest. I believe the Waffle was in some measure the ideological rebellion it claimed to be. But for some of its protagonists, it was—and astonishingly, almost fifty years later, continues to be—riven through with such ugly personal animosity that it is hard for me to see the schism as merely one of political difference.

But setting aside the history of attempted takeovers and purges, common to any political party, my point here is that the bedrock belief in the centrality of people's movements was there from the party's founding. And I believe it will either be a part of the party's future, or the party will not have one.

But before I leap to the end of my argument, let me tug on a third thread from the fabric of my grandfather's work: his understanding of the idea of incrementalism.

Again, this is one of those ideas that can be portrayed as part of the ineluctable march of the electoral left from the margins to the centre, from a 1930s politic of overthrowing capitalism to one of merely ameliorating its worst effects. But I don't think that really captures the truth.

In 1955, David Lewis gave a speech at Woodsworth House in Toronto called "A Socialist Takes Stock." The euphoric rise of the CCF in its first decade had given way to a plateau in the post-war period, and he was clearly in the mood to zoom out and name the big pillars of what he saw as democratic-socialist thought.

The first two sections of the speech are entitled "Socialist Ends" and "Socialist Means." I think it is significant that the ends come first. In other words, the vision of the world we're fighting for is always in view. And it is expansive, in fact, it's a frankly utopian view.

David defines the goals of democratic socialism as "the achievement of a classless or egalitarian society, a world free from imperialism, economic and social security for all, and a lasting global peace based on freedom and equality both within nations and among nations."

It is striking to utter those words in the cold light of 2017. Unlike the prescience of his analysis of the 1 percent and the 99, these goals sound positively retro today.

And yet, I think the fact of this vision, and its pride of place at the very top of his description of democratic socialism, speaks volumes.

He goes on to enumerate the means by which these ends must be achieved, and they include democratic process, of course, planning, of course, and public ownership, of course. And then he goes on to cite: "A constant and continuing improvement in the existing standards of living and in the social services provided by the state," followed by a very long list of the kinds of social programs with which the CCF/NDP is rightly associated in Canada: labour legislation, unemployment insurance, old age pensions, family allowances, housing, health care, and the list goes on.

What's striking for me is that the vision of change—patient, incremental, program by program, improvement by improvement—is not just rooted in a vision of the world we're fighting for: it is explicitly posed as a tool to get there.

In fact, it is a theory of change which proposes that immediate reforms—concrete, tangible changes, one after another after another—can build momentum and ambition for a leap to system change.

This is a vast difference from the electoral left today, which presents those minor moderations to the capitalist status quo as the end, the destination: the best that we can hope for, the limit of what is politically possible, lest we make the perfect the enemy of the good.

In fact, I think my grandfather and his comrades, from the 1930s until the 1970s, were pragmatic utopians. They fought for concrete policies that made people's lives better in the short term. But they pursued incrementalism *in the service of transformation.*

They understood well the narrow box of what was considered politically possible. But they didn't see their role as merely working within it. I believe they were clear that the purpose of working within the political constraints of the day was to build the constituency—the movement—that would have the power to radically change the political reality.

Finally, a huge difference between the electoral left of today and that of the David Lewis era was the appetite for bashing corporate power and skewering the propensity of Liberal and Tory governments to gift large chunks of the public purse to their golfing buddies.

My grandfather was incandescent when railing against the capitulation of governments to the priorities and profits of corporations. He excoriated corporate wealth and privilege with gusto, with verve, with precision, with research, and an ever-evolving litany of facts and figures that were caustic enough to strip the paint off a limousine.

It was energizing stuff. But again, it was not an end in itself—it was clearly harnessed to a positive agenda that used outrage as rocket fuel for positive change.

Here's the reason for all that corporation-bashing fervour, neatly encapsulated in a speech to the Kiwanis Club of Winnipeg in 1972:

> I refuse to be taken in by the myth that just because the government is spending a lot of money on incentives to industry, we should sit back in the belief that all is well, because it isn't . . .

> Instead of ladling out hundreds of millions of dollars to corporations in tax concessions and grants in the hope they may create jobs, let us build houses at prices and rents that the ordinary people can afford; let us build recycling and waste treatment plants to stop human pollution of the environment; let us provide decent daycare centres for the children of working parents, more homes for the aged, recreation centres for the young and dozens of other facilities to improve the quality of life for Canadians. Such a program would fill important needs and would produce jobs directly and immediately.

> At this point many of you will ask: Where will the money come from to meet all these social needs? And this is precisely my point. The tax concessions and grants to corporations add up to hundreds of millions of dollars a year that could be better spent. In the weeks ahead, my colleagues and I will be spelling out with facts and figures just how much is involved and how we believe it could be used.

I think this is a perfect transition to a consideration of the electoral left of the present day. We can advocate for green jobs, universal daycare, pharmacare, and other reforms. But before we can advance any major change, we have to address a vast mismatch in the balance of forces in society.

We live in a time of unprecedented wealth. The global economy is like an enormous rocky tide pool, with waves of capital sloshing back and forth, looking for places to hide and accumulate.

But those resources are not within the reach of governments anymore. And so, when the electoral left is fighting for reforms, if it does not seek to recapture the wealth being produced, it must shrink the size of its demands to what can be covered by the puddle that is left at the bottom the public pool.

And even that puddle continues to be sucked away. When Jean Chretien came to power in 1993, the federal corporate tax rate stood at 29 percent. A generation later, it has been cut in half, to 15 percent. And that generational corporate handout came equally from Liberal and Tory largesse.

Justin Trudeau, for all his progressive promises, and there have been many, presides over a government whose share of the GDP is at a sixty-year low. Just think about that. No wonder he doesn't talk, like his father did, about a Just Society. The federal government's capacity to lead—to change the direction of our economy and society—is at a sixty-year low. If there is a Trudeau philosophy of this generation, it is surely: Announce big—but dream small. And deliver smaller.

Meanwhile, what are corporations doing with all that extra money that they are capturing? We had to cut their taxes, we were told, so that they had the capacity to reinvest, to create jobs. My grandfather wouldn't put it this way but let me: bullshit.

In 2014, Canadian corporations were hoarding so much cash on their balance sheets, they could have retired the national debt. Just with cash on hand, some $640 billion.

People know this in their bones, especially after 2008. That's why Bernie Sanders got more than thirteen-million votes and captured the imagination of an entire generation of voters: by banging on, relentlessly, about inequality and the need to rein in the greed of Wall Street and the corporate class, and the need for immediate, dramatic action on climate change.

An in fact, the excitement on the electoral left these days is in precisely that kind of big, bold message. Because we face epic crises today, the crises created by this past century of ever-escalating corporate control of the economy and society.

We simply cannot get to a better place by tinkering.

But even if we could, the rapid acceleration of the climate crisis is a clear message that we need major change in an unprecedented hurry. When large parts of Fort McMurray are incinerated, when parts of Quebec are in the midst of a millennial flood, when the Great Barrier Reef is bleaching and dying from warmer waters—we just have to start hearing the message and acting with the kind of urgency and scale that this crisis demands.

But that is really outside the bounds of what is considered politically possible today on the electoral left in Canada. And nowhere is that truer than here in Alberta.

Okay, big caveat. I saw Rachel Notley speak this week, and I thought she was fabulous, as always. She is a great politician—she comes off with great authenticity. She spoke with real conviction about how her government is resisting intense pressure to impose austerity to deal with the economic crisis brought on by the oil price crash of 2014.

It is really historic, that for the first time, Alberta is not dealing with the bust part of the commodity cycle by cutting services for people—and is, in fact, building schools, freezing tuition, creating daycare spaces, and moving on a $15 per hour minimum wage.

But when the premier talks about Alberta's climate plan, she loses me. Again: it *is* indeed historic that Alberta has a climate plan, that there is a coal phase out in this province, that there is a cap on emissions from bitumen extraction.

But the fact—as the premier inevitably says with great pride—that oil company CEOs were on the stage with her when she announced Alberta's climate leadership plan tells you all you need to know about the efficacy of those plans. The Alberta NDP has made a decision not to take on the oil and gas industry in this province.

That's a decision that is no doubt reflective of a calculation of political survival. But it is certainly not a decision about climate policy.

Already, with 4.2 million people, Alberta has higher emissions than Ontario and Quebec combined, more than 22 million people. Under Alberta's historic climate leadership plan, that imbalance is going to grow, big time. The hard truth is that Alberta's emissions cap is set so high that it does not require any immediate emissions reductions at all. In fact, quite the opposite. New mines are still opening, production continues to rise, and the cap is in the distant future. Over time, the cap allows a 47 percent increase in emissions from the tar sands.

That's what it takes to get industry on board. Now, this posture of partnership with industry may be smart politics in the province of the Wild Rose. I'm not arguing that.

I am arguing that if this is the current approach of the electoral left in Canada, then from the perspective of climate policy, the electoral left is helping to preserve a deeply destructive status quo. One that will intensify regional resentments and erase the progress other provinces make on confronting the existential threat of climate change.

Let me just briefly back up that rather radical assertion.

Canada's current international climate commitment is to reduce emissions 30 percent from 2005 levels by 2030. It's the target set by Stephen Harper, so that should tell you all you need to know about its ambition. It's also the target that has been embraced by the Trudeau Liberals. So that clears up the state of their ambition as well.

When you look at it in terms of what Canada's fair share would be, as a member of a global community, as a rich country that built its prosperity on 150 years of burning fossil fuels, the target is so insufficient as to be offensive.

According to a major civil society review of all the pledges brought by countries to the Paris climate summit, it is roughly one-third of Canada's fair share. We should be doing three times more in getting off fossil fuels and shifting to a low- or no-carbon economy.

It is in that light that I want to test the assertion that Alberta's climate leadership plan is worthy of the name.

Last year, an earth scientist named David Hughes wrote a paper called "Can Canada Expand Oil and Gas Production, Build Pipelines and Keep Its Climate Change Commitments?" Now, David Hughes spent thirty years with the Geological Survey of Canada. He's one of our foremost experts on unconventional fossil fuels. David found that if you tally up the emissions increases allowed under Alberta's climate leadership plan, and just one of BC's twenty proposed LNG projects, the oil and gas sector would account for 40 percent of our entire country's allowable emissions by 2030.

That means that the rest of the economy—every other sector in every other region of Canada—would have to reduce its emissions by 47 percent in the next thirteen years. Just in order to reach our crappy, insufficient, Harper-Trudeau climate commitments.

That level of reduction has never been achieved anywhere on earth before. Not even after the collapse of the Soviet Union, when millions of people plummeted into poverty, disease, and dysfunction.

This is why we need a wartime approach to dealing with the climate crisis. An approach that brings forward the features of democratic socialism of the past and fuses them with a twenty-first-century mission: to transform our energy system in an incredibly short time, and take the opportunity, while we're at it, to deal with inequality by putting economically and racially marginalized communities first in line for the benefits of the next economy.

We need to expropriate a portion of the vast and unearned profits the corporate sector has extracted from the rest of the economy. We need to recover the role and capacity of government to manage a massive societal transition.

We need to rediscover the lost art of planning so that this transition off fossil fuels is not managed by the market, in a disruptive and traumatic way in which workers will be hurt first and worst—as they have been in the last few years here in Alberta.

And to marshal the kind of momentum required to confront this immense challenge, we need a movement of movements, including an electoral front, that can tip the balance of forces in a hurry.

In short, we need to Leap.

The emergence of the Leap Manifesto in 2015 was a direct product of this recognition—a surfacing of deep impatience among social movements with the failure of the electoral left to truly grasp this moment of epic, intersecting crises and the unprecedented political possibilities they have created.

The manifesto came out of an historic gathering in May 2015—a once-in-a-generation, silo-busting convening of movement leaders from across the country and a huge range of different issues. There were faith leaders, trade unionists, environmentalists, First Nations, from the tar sands to Kanesatake, feminist icons, food justice, anti-poverty, and immigrant rights activists.

While there was an equally broad spectrum of divergent political philosophies in the room—along with a heavy history of tensions and wounds from earlier struggles—there was also a tremendous sense of common ground when it came to defining the Yes, the vision of the Canada we are fighting for.

While the NDP has so far had a very mixed reaction to the manifesto (which I would characterize as virulent antipathy from party insiders and an energetic embrace from the grassroots), it is worth remembering that the NDP federal convention in Edmonton in 2016 passed a resolution that supported the very essence of the document. In the words of that resolution is, I believe, a glimpse of the future of the left in Canada. It is a future that could revive and modernize the founding principles of our past—if we can explode the impoverished political imagination of centrism in time to grasp it. The fact that the party has already democratically adopted these words gives me hope that this future is in reach:

> The NDP recognizes and supports the Leap Manifesto as a high-level statement of principles that speaks to the aspirations, history, and values of the party. We recognize and embrace the opportunity to confront the twin crises

of inequality and climate change with an inspiring and positive agenda—to transform society as we transition to an economy beyond fossil fuels.

The specific policies in the manifesto can and should be debated and modified on their own merits and according to the needs of various communities and all parts of the country, but the goal of transforming our country according to the vision in the manifesto is entirely in harmony with the core beliefs and tradition of the party.

The Leap Manifesto: A Call for a Canada Based on Caring for the Earth and One Another

We start from the premise that Canada is facing the deepest crisis in recent memory.

The Truth and Reconciliation Commission has acknowledged shocking details about the violence of Canada's near past. Deepening poverty and inequality are a scar on the country's present. And Canada's record on climate change is a crime against humanity's future.

These facts are all the more jarring because they depart so dramatically from our stated values: respect for Indigenous rights, internationalism, human rights, diversity, and environmental stewardship.

Canada is not this place today—but it could be.

We could live in a country powered entirely by renewable energy, woven together by accessible public transit, in which the jobs and opportunities of this transition are designed to systematically eliminate racial and gender inequality. Caring for one another and caring for the planet could be the economy's fastest growing sectors. Many more people could have higher wage jobs with fewer work hours, leaving us ample time to enjoy our loved ones and flourish in our communities.

We know that the time for this great transition is short. Climate scientists have told us that this is the decade to take decisive action to prevent catastrophic global warming. That means small steps will no longer get us where we need to go.

So we need to leap.

This leap must begin by respecting the inherent rights and title of the original caretakers of this land. Indigenous communities have been at the forefront of protecting rivers, coasts, forests and lands from out-of-control industrial activity. We can bolster this role, and reset our relationship, by fully implementing the United Nations Declaration on the Rights of Indigenous Peoples.

Moved by the treaties that form the legal basis of this country and bind us to share the land "for as long as the sun shines, the grass grows and the rivers flow," we want energy sources that will last for time immemorial and never run out or poison the land. Technological breakthroughs have brought this dream within reach. The latest research shows it is feasible for Canada to get 100% of its electricity from renewable resources within two decades; by 2050 we could have a 100% clean economy.

We demand that this shift begin now.

There is no longer an excuse for building new infrastructure projects that lock us into increased extraction decades into the future. The new iron law of energy development must be: if you wouldn't want it in your backyard, then it doesn't belong in anyone's backyard. That applies equally to oil and gas pipelines; fracking in New Brunswick, Quebec and British Columbia; increased tanker traffic off our coasts; and to Canadian-owned mining projects the world over.

The time for energy democracy has come: we believe not just in changes to our energy sources, but that wherever possible communities should collectively control these new energy systems.

As an alternative to the profit-gouging of private companies and the remote bureaucracy of some centralized state ones, we can create innovative ownership structures: democratically run, paying living wages and keeping much-needed revenue in communities. And Indigenous Peoples should be first to receive public support for their own clean energy projects. So should communities currently dealing with heavy health impacts of polluting industrial activity.

Power generated this way will not merely light our homes but redistribute wealth, deepen our democracy, strengthen our economy and start to heal the wounds that date back to this country's founding.

A leap to a non-polluting economy creates countless openings for similar multiple "wins." We want a universal program to build energy efficient homes, and retrofit existing housing, ensuring that the lowest income communities and neighbourhoods will benefit first and receive job training and opportunities that reduce poverty over the long term. We want training and other resources for workers in carbon-intensive jobs, ensuring they are fully able to take part in the clean energy economy. This transition should involve the democratic participation of workers themselves. High-speed rail powered by renewables and affordable public transit can unite every community in this country—in place of more cars, pipelines and exploding trains that endanger and divide us.

And since we know this leap is beginning late, we need to invest in our decaying public infrastructure so that it can withstand increasingly frequent extreme weather events.

Moving to a far more localized and ecologically based agricultural system would reduce reliance on fossil fuels, capture carbon in the soil, and absorb sudden shocks in the global supply—as well as produce healthier and more affordable food for everyone.

We call for an end to all trade deals that interfere with our attempts to rebuild local economies, regulate corporations and stop damaging extractive projects. Rebalancing the scales of justice, we should ensure immigration status and full protection for all workers. Recognizing Canada's contributions to military conflicts and climate change—primary drivers of the global refugee crisis—we must welcome refugees and migrants seeking safety and a better life.

Shifting to an economy in balance with the earth's limits also means expanding the sectors of our economy that are already low carbon: caregiving, teaching, social work, the arts and public-interest media. Following on Quebec's lead, a national childcare program is long past due. All this work, much of it performed by women, is the glue that builds humane, resilient communities—and we will need our communities to be as strong as possible in the face of the rocky future we have already locked in.

Since so much of the labour of caretaking—whether of people or the planet—is currently unpaid, we call for a vigorous debate about the introduction of a universal basic annual income. Pioneered in Manitoba in the 1970s, this sturdy safety net could help ensure that no one is forced to take work that threatens their children's tomorrow, just to feed those children today.

We declare that "austerity"—which has systematically attacked low-carbon sectors like education and healthcare, while starving public transit and forcing reckless energy privatizations—is a fossilized form of thinking that has become a threat to life on earth.

The money we need to pay for this great transformation is available—we just need the right policies to release it. Like an end to fossil fuel subsidies. Financial transaction taxes. Increased resource royalties. Higher income taxes on corporations and wealthy people. A progressive carbon tax. Cuts to military spending. All of these are based on a simple "polluter pays" principle and hold enormous promise.

One thing is clear: public scarcity in times of unprecedented private wealth is a manufactured crisis, designed to extinguish our dreams before they have a chance to be born.

Those dreams go well beyond this document. We call for town hall meetings across the country where residents can gather to democratically define what a genuine leap to the next economy means in their communities.

Inevitably, this bottom-up revival will lead to a renewal of democracy at every level of government, working swiftly towards a system in which every vote counts and corporate money is removed from political campaigns.

This is a great deal to take on all at once, but such are the times in which we live.

The drop in oil prices has temporarily relieved the pressure to dig up fossil fuels as rapidly as high-risk technologies will allow. This pause in frenetic expansion should not be viewed as a crisis, but as a gift.

It has given us a rare moment to look at what we have become—and decide to change.

And so, we call on all those seeking political office to seize this opportunity and embrace the urgent need for transformation. This is our sacred duty to those this country harmed in the past, to those suffering needlessly in the present, and to all who have a right to a bright and safe future.

Now is the time for boldness.

Now is the time to leap.

CONTRIBUTORS'
BIOGRAPHIES

Christo Aivalis is a Social Sciences and Humanities Research Council Postdoctoral Fellow in the history department at the University of Toronto. His first book, on Pierre Trudeau's relationship with labour and the left, was published by University of British Columbia Press in March 2018.

Stephanie Bangarth is an associate professor of history at King's University College at Western University. She researches and teaches the role of human rights, social movements, and migration in twentieth-century Canadian history.

Karl Bélanger is the president of Traxxion Strategies. A former national director of the New Democratic Party of Canada, he served as a senior advisor to four NDP leaders over the span of nineteen years on Parliament Hill. He has been president of the Douglas-Coldwell Foundation since 2016.

Bill Blaikie, a United Church minister, was a Winnipeg NDP MP from 1979 to 2008. From 2009 to 2011 he was a provincial MLA and served as Manitoba's minister of conservation. He is currently an adjunct professor of theology and politics at the University of Winnipeg.

David Blocker is a Ph.D. candidate at Western University. His dissertation examines the Waffle, the NDP, and Canada's New Left in the late 1960s and 1970s.

John Brewin is a life-long CCF/NDP activist, delegate to the NDP founding convention, former NDP Member of Parliament (Victoria, 1988 to 1993), labour lawyer, Master of Theological Studies (Vancouver School of Theology, 1997), political observer, and occasional political commentator.

Murray Cooke teaches in the politics department at York University. He is the co-author, with Dennis Pilon, of *Left Turn in Canada? The NDP Breakthrough and the Future of Canadian Politics* (Rosa Luxemburg Stiftung, 2012).

Erika Dyck is a professor and Canada Research Chair in Medical History at University of Saskatchewan. She is the author of *Psychedelic Psychiatry: LSD from Clinic to Campus* (Johns Hopkins, 2008; University of Manitoba Press, 2011); *Facing Eugenics: Reproduction, Sterilization, and the Politics of Choice* (University of Toronto, 2013); and *Managing Madness: The Weyburn Mental Hospital and the Transformation of Psychiatric Care in Canada* (University of Manitoba Press, 2017).

Matt Fodor is a Ph.D. candidate in political science at York University. His research interests include social democracy and Canadian politics, and he has written extensively on the NDP.

Peter Graham is an independent researcher and sessional instructor at McMaster University. His work examines municipal politics and the role of the left in Canada.

Jennifer Hassum is the head of the New Media & Information Technology Department for the United Steelworkers. She is also a lifelong NDP member and a fan of working-class history.

Avi Lewis is an award-winning documentary filmmaker and long-time television journalist. His films include *The Take* and *This Changes Everything*. He is a co-author of the Leap Manifesto and is the strategic director and co-founder of The Leap.

Roberta Lexier is an associate professor in the general education department at Mount Royal University. Her research examines social movements and social change, both past and present. Her current projects analyze the connections between social movements and left political parties to determine the benefits and limitations of combined action for social change.

Greg Marchildon is a professor and Ontario Research Chair in Health Policy and System Design at the University of Toronto. He is also a member of the board of the Broadbent Institute and was a deputy minister in the Saskatchewan government during the 1990s. He is the author of numerous articles on the history of Canadian medicare and two editions of *Health Systems in Transition: Canada,* co-published by the World Health Organization and the University of Toronto Press.

Robert McDonald, now retired, taught British Columbia history at the University of British Columbia for many years and is now writing *A Long Way to Paradise: A History of British Columbia Politics, 1870s to 1970s.*

Ian McKay is director of the Wilson Institute for Canadian History at McMaster University. He is the foremost expert on the left in Canada and is working on a study of the Canadian left from 1921 to 1948.

James Naylor is a professor of history at Brandon University and author of *The Fate of Labour Socialism: The Co-operative Commonwealth Federation and the Dream of a Working-Class Future* (Toronto: University of Toronto Press, 2016). He is currently researching the transformation of class and ethnicity in Winnipeg after World War II.

Jillian Ratti is a family physician in downtown Calgary and a clinical lecturer with the Faculty of Medicine at the University of Calgary. She was the NDP candidate for Calgary Centre in the 2015 federal election and continues to organize locally for the NDP at provincial and federal levels.

Jonathan Sas is the former policy and research director at the Broadbent Institute. He currently works in Victoria, BC, as the senior ministerial assistant to the Minister of Indigenous Relations and Reconciliation.

Corey Slumkoski is the author of *Inventing Atlantic Canada: Regionalism and the Maritime Reaction to Newfoundland's Entry into Canadian Confederation.* He teaches at Mount Saint Vincent University.

Jon Weier is an historian of war and society, writing on the history of the YMCA during the First World War. He also writes and lectures on Canadian identity and the politics of history, on commemoration and memory, on public and active history, and on the history of the left in Canada.

NOTES

Introduction

1   Regina Manifesto (1933), www.socialisthistory.ca/Docs/CCF/ReginaManifesto.htm.
2   Regina Manifesto.
3   Walter D. Young, *The Anatomy of a Party: The National CCF, 1932-1961* (Toronto: University of Toronto Press, 1969).
4   Desmond Morton, *NDP: The Dream of Power* (Toronto: A. M. Hakkert, 1974); Desmond Morton, *The New Democrats 1961-1986: The Politics of Change* (Toronto: Copp Clark Pitman, 1986); Ivan Avakumovic, *Socialism in Canada: A Study of the CCF-NDP in Federal and Provincial Politics* (Toronto: McClelland & Stewart, 1978); Norman Penner, *From Protest to Power: Social Democracy in Canada 1900* (Toronto: James Lorimer, 1992); Alan Whitehorn, *Canadian Socialism: Essays on the CCF-NDP* (Toronto: Oxford University Press, 1992).
5   See, Kenneth McNaught, *A Prophet in Politics: A Biography of J.S. Woodsworth,* (Toronto: University of Toronto Press, 1959); David Lewis, *The Good Fight: Political Memoirs 1909–1958* (Toronto: Macmillan, 1981); Allen Mills, *Fool for Christ: The Intellectual Politics of J.S. Woodsworth,* (Toronto: University of Toronto Press, 1991); Donald C. MacDonald, *The Happy Warrior: Political Memoirs,* 2nd ed. (Toronto: Dundurn Press, 1998); Doris French Shackleton, *Tommy Douglas* (Toronto: McClelland & Stewart, 1975); and Cameron Smith, *Unfinished Journey: The Lewis Family* (Toronto: Summerhill Press, 1989).
6   Walter Stewart, *Tommy: The Life and Politics of Tommy Douglas* (Toronto: McArthur & Company, 2003).
7   David McGrane, *Remaining Loyal: Social Democracy in Quebec and Saskatchewan* (Montreal and Kingston: McGill-Queen's University Press, 2014).
8   David Laycock and Lynda Erickson, eds., *Reviving Social Democracy: The Near Death and Surprising Rise of the Federal NDP* (Vancouver: University of British Columbia Press, 2015).

Chapter 1: The Co-operative Commonwealth Federation in the 1930s

1   From Stanley Knowles' acceptance speech for nomination in Winnipeg South Centre federal riding, *Manitoba Commonwealth*, February 1,1935.
2   There is much literature, mostly quite dated, on the foundation of the CCF. Most important are Walter D. Young, *The Anatomy of a Party: The National CCF, 1932–61* (Toronto: University of Toronto Press, 1969); Leo Zakuta, *A Protest Movement Becalmed* (Toronto: University of Toronto Press, 1964); Ivan Avakumovic, *Socialism in Canada: A Study of the CCF-NDP in Federal and Provincial Politics* (Toronto: McClelland & Stewart, 1978); Kenneth McNaught, *A Prophet in Politics: A Biography of J.S. Woodsworth* (Toronto: University of Toronto Press, 1959); Alan Whitehorn, *Canadian Socialism: Essays on the CCF-NDP* (Toronto: Oxford University Press, 1992); Norman Penner, *The Canadian Left: A Critical Analysis,* (Toronto: Prentice-Hall, 1977).

3   Literature on the CCF and Cold War largely focuses on the role of communist unions: Irving M. Abella, *Nationalism, Communism, and Canadian Labour* (Toronto: University of Toronto Press, 1973) and Gad Horowitz, *Canadian Labour in Politics* (Toronto: University of Toronto Press, 1968). For the broader effect of Cold War influences, see Benjamin Isitt's glimpse of the party at the outbreak of the Korean War: "Confronting the Cold War: The 1950 Vancouver Convention of the Co-operative Commonwealth Federation" in *Canadian Historical Review* 91, 3 (September 2010), 465–501. Although he reaches quite different conclusions than I do about the continuity of the CCF/NDP's "social democratic" core, David McGrane's *Remaining Loyal: Social Democracy in Quebec and Saskatchewan* (Montréal and Kingston: McGill-Queen's University Press, 2014) documents well the programmatic evolution of the NDP over the neoliberal decades.

4   Notably, even though the term was in wide use in the period, CCFers very rarely used it to describe their movement.

5   Repression occurred on many levels in the 1930s but is most associated with Prime Minister R. B. Bennett who promised to, and did, apply "the iron heel ruthlessly," cited in John Herd Thompson with Allan Seager, *Canada 1922–1930: Decades of Discord* (Toronto: McClelland & Stewart, 1985), 226.

6   On the labour revolt see Gregory S. Kealey, "1919: The Canadian Labour Revolt," *Labour/Le Travail*, 13 (Spring, 1984), 11–44; Craig Heron, ed. *The Workers' Revolt in Canada, 1917–1925*, (Toronto: University of Toronto Press, 1998).

7   David Jay Bercuson, *Confrontation at Winnipeg: Labour, Industrial Relations, and the General Strike*, rev. ed. (Montréal and Kingston: McGill-Queen's University Press, 1990), 133–35.

8   On the Winnipeg General Strike, see D. C. Masters, *The Winnipeg General Strike* (Toronto: University of Toronto Press, 1950); Bercuson, *Confrontation at Winnipeg*, rev. ed.; Reinhold Kramer and Tom Mitchell, *When the State Trembled: How A.J. Andrews and the Citizens' Committee Broke the Winnipeg General Strike* (Toronto: University of Toronto Press, 2010).

9   The strikers' defense committee took just such a tone: Norman Penner, ed. *Winnipeg 1919: The Strikers' Own History of the Winnipeg General Strike*, 2nd ed. (Toronto: James Lorimer, 1975).

10   Bercuson, *Confrontation at Winnipeg*, 178.

11   On labourism, see Craig Heron, "Labourism and the Canadian Working Class," *Labour/Le Travail, 13* (Spring 1984), 45–76. For the beginnings of this evolution in Ontario, see James Naylor, *The New Democracy: Challenging the Social Order in Industrial Ontario, 1914–25* (Toronto: University of Toronto Press, 1991), 245–253.

12   Although the role of farmers has, in the CCF, generally been overstated. Outside of Saskatchewan, this was quite rare, as the provincial farmers' organizations only affiliated to the CCF temporarily, if at all. The United Farmers of Ontario was, in the words of J. S. Woodsworth, "conditional," and they left in early 1934. Library and Archives Canada (LAC), CCF Records, RG 28 IV 4, (CCF) vol. 107, file J.S. Woodsworth 1933–42 (1 of 3), "Statement to Ontario C.C.F. Provincial Council." Only the Alberta farmers' organization remained affiliated; their connection was quite loose, and they left in 1937.

13   This was a common theme in CCF newspapers. An example is a letter to the *Commonwealth* (Vancouver), February 1, 1935: "The finest breeding ground for Fascism is found in the middle class." This sentiment was not confined to the left wing of the labour movement. For such statements from the British Labour Party, see Nigel Copsey, "'Every Time They Made a Communist, They Made a Fascist': The Labour Party and Popular Anti-Fascism in the 1930s," in Nigel Copsey and Andrzej Olechnowicz, eds. *Varieties of Anti-Fascism in Britain in the Inter-War Period* (London: Palgrave Macmillan, 2011), 60.

14   "Labor Party Would Muzzle C.C.F. Clubs: 'No Voting Power Unless Radically Affiliated' is Condition Set," *Toronto Daily Star*, February 20, 1933.

15   Provincial CCFs established "CCF Clubs" as a way for unaffiliated "middle-class" recruits to the movement to join the CCF. There was often conflict between the clubs and the labour affiliates. See James Naylor, *The Fate of Labour Socialism: The Co-operative Commonwealth Federation and the Dream of a Working-Class Future* (Toronto: University of Toronto Press, 2016), 112–167.

16 Winch is cited in Dorothy G. Steeves, *The Compassionate Rebel: Ernest Winch and the Growth of Socialism in Western Canada* (Vancouver: J. J. Douglas, 1960), 108.

17 University of British Columbia (UBC), Angus MacInnis Memorial Collection (AMMC), box 45, file 45–9 CCF (Provincial Party), minutes, Provincial Executive Council, C.C.F. (B.C.), 11 July 1933, Report by Angus MacInnis.

18 Hedrick J. Peddie, "ILP Divides Labor Forces: Special Convention of Party Voted 19 to 30 to Leave CCF," *Manitoba Commonwealth*, February 11, 1938.

19 The use of "comrade" was common in the labour sections but raised the hackles of the farmers (such as United Farmers of Ontario leader Agnes Macphail) and LSR members like Graham Spry. Gerald L. Caplan, *The Dilemma of Canadian Socialism: The CCF in Ontario* (Toronto: McClelland & Stewart, 1973), 28; Terry Crowley, *Agnes Macphail and the Politics of Equality* (Toronto: James Lorimer, 1990), 121. An example of such labour iconography was the widely representative Labour Party of Ontario, which defended the singing of "The Red Flag" and "The Internationale" at its convention, "The Bradford Convention," *Labor News* (Toronto), April 29, 1933. On May Day disputes within the CCF, see Naylor, *The Fate of Labour Socialism*, 195–203.

20 "Spirit of Unity Marks Great CCF Convention," *New Commonwealth* (Toronto), April 27, 1935.

21 Michiel Horn, *The League for Social Reconstruction: Intellectual Origins of the Democratic Left in Canada, 1930–1942* (Toronto: University of Toronto Press, 1980), 46, and Horn, "Frank Underhill's Early Drafts of the Regina Manifesto 1933," *Canadian Historical Review*, 54, 4 (December 1973), 398.

22 LAC, F.R. Scott Papers, MG 30 D 211, vol. 12, file: C.C.F., General, 1932–34, 1951, newspaper clipping, "New Political Party Adopts Fourteen Point Manifesto."

23 Horowitz, *Canadian Labour in Politics*, 26.

24 Norman Penner, *The Canadian Left: A Critical Analysis* (Toronto: Prentice-Hall, 1977), 45.

25 "World Socialist Unity Exemplified by Speeches of Cripps, Thomas, Irving: Not Nationalism, But a World Commonwealth of Socialist Peoples," *New Commonwealth* (Toronto), April 27, 1935.

26 Cameron Smith, *Unfinished Journey: The Lewis Family* (Toronto: Summerhill Press, 1989), 184 and David Lewis, *The Good Fight: Political Memoirs, 1909–1958* (Toronto: Macmillan, 1981), 75.

27 *Canadian Forum*, 16 (January 1937) 27–28 and 13 (October 1936), 24–25.

28 On the exodus from the Communist Party in this period, see Ian Angus, *Canadian Bolsheviks: The Early Years of the Communist Party of Canada* (Montréal: Vanguard, 1981), 199–200.

29 "Let Us Take Communism from the Communists," *Challenge* (Vancouver), March 1931.

30 UBC, AMMC, box 45, file 45–5, Socialist Party of Canada, Annual Convention, January 20 and 21, 1934, President's Report; "Brilliant Speech by King Gordon at City Meeting, *Commonwealth* (Vancouver), May 3, 1935.

31 Notably, George Weaver, a British Columbia CCF leader, felt that the LSR's *Social Planning for Canada* was guilty of just this kind of reformism leading to "state capitalism." He described the authors as "obviously outside the workers' movement," and the book itself as "not even Social-Democratic." LAC, CCF Records, vol. 105, file: George W. Weaver, Weaver to David Lewis, April 11, 1938.

32 This was the focus of the CCF's critique of the Communist Party after 1935. See Naylor, *The Fate of Labour Socialism*, 204–252.

33 LAC, CCF Records, vol., 48, file: Ontario Conventions, 1935–1945, minutes, Annual Convention of the C.C.F. (Ontario Section), April 20, 1935.

34 James Naylor, "Socialism for a New Generation: CCF Youth in the Popular Front Era, *Canadian Historical Review*, 94, 1 (March 2013), 55–79.

35 J. William Brennan, "'The common people have spoken with a mighty voice': Regina's Labour city Councils, 1936–1936," *Labour/Le Travail*, 71 (Spring 2013), 49–86.

36 This was particularly apparent in the debate over the popular front between Gerald Van, a leader of the CCF youth, and A. M. Stephen, among others, in the pages of *The Federationist* (Vancouver), over the winter of 1936–1937.

37   LAC, CCF Records, vol. 344, file "CCYM General 1935–1950, David Lewis to Eamon Park, Vice-President, CCYM, Ontario Section, May 18, 1938 and Volume 88, file "J. Stanley Allen, 1937–51," David Lewis to Stanley Allen, May 17, 1938.

38   Gerd-Rainer Horn, *European Socialists Respond to Fascism: Ideology, Activism and Contingency in the 1930s* (New York: Oxford University Press, 1996), 10.

39   Leon Trotsky, *Wither France?* (New York: Merit Publishers, 1938), 105.

40   Trotsky, *Wither France?* 115. On the London Bureau, see also Trotsky, "Centrism and the 4th International," *The Militant*, February 23, 1934, www.marxists.org/archive/trotsky/1934/02/centrism-tm.htm.

41   As an interesting example of searching for a political place in this context, long-time British Columbia CCF MLA Ernest Winch posed a motion to the Socialist Party (the labour affiliate and dominant partner in the BC CCF) that they investigate affiliation with the Trotskyist Fourth International. LAC, MG 10 K 3 Communist International fonds, file 180, "Report from District 9, (CAN), For A.A. Sec.," April 20, 1935.

Chapter 3: The Labour-Academic "Brain Trust" of the Early CCF, 1930–1950

1   Alan Sears, *The Next New Left: A History of the Future* (Fernwood Publishing: Toronto, 2014).

2   Michiel Horn, *The League for Social Reconstruction: Intellectual Origins of the Democratic Left in Canada, 1930–1942* (Toronto: University of Toronto Press, 1980). Horn set the tone for how many see LSR and the CCF as indistinguishable. He describes the LSR explicitly as the "CCF Brain Trust" (46) and describes the LSR as primarily remembered as a group of intellectuals who enunciated the Canadian socialism for the CCF (15).

3   James Naylor, *The Fate of Labour Socialism* (Toronto: University of Toronto Press, 2016).

4   Naylor, *The Fate of Labour Socialism*, 6.

5   David Lewis called building the CCF a "slow progress" in his memoirs, which document all the difficulties faced in building an electoral alternative. David Lewis, *The Good Fight: Political Memoirs 1909-1958* (Toronto: Macmillan of Canada, 1981).

6   The only two academic publications mentioning Millard are found in focus on his role in CIO organizing. Irving Abella, "Oshawa 1937," in Irving Abella, *On Strike: Six Key Labour Struggles in Canada 1919–1949* (Toronto: Lorimer, 1974), 93–128, and Laurel Sefton MacDowell, "The Career of a Canadian Trade Union Leader: C.H. Millard, 1937--1946," *Industrial Relations/Relations industrielles* 43 (1988), 609–31.

7   Lewis, *The Good Fight*, 80.

8   William Lyon Mackenzie King. Library and Archives Canada, Diaries of William Lyon Mackenzie King. August 27, 1942, www.bac-lac.gc.ca/eng/discover/politics-government/prime-ministers/william-lyon-mackenzie-king/Pages/item.aspx?IdNumber=24480&.

9   Felix Lazarus, "The Oshawa Strike," *Canadian Forum*, January 1937.

10   MacDowell, "Career of a Canadian Trade Union Leader," 9.

11   MacDowell, "Career of a Canadian Trade Union Leader," 12.

12   MacDowell, "Career of a Canadian Trade Union Leader," 17.

13   MacDowell, "Career of a Canadian Trade Union Leader," 20.

14   Eugene Forsey, "The Canadian Congress of Labour," *Bulletin des Relations Industrielles*, Vol. 4, No. 1 (September 1948), 5–9. www.jstor.org/stable/23066262.

15   Constitution of the CCL, 1941, http://socserv.mcmaster.ca/oldlabourstudies/onlinelearning/article.php?id=121.

16   Jeffrey Wilson, *Charles H. Millard, Architect of Industrial Unionism in Canada* (Wilfrid Laurier, MA Thesis, 1989), 18.

17   Lewis, *The Good Fight*, 147.

18   NAC, USWA, M628, I268, Vol. 129, Charles Millard interview with Morden and Margaret Lazaurus, Toronto, 1975.

19   Gerald Harrop, *Clarie: Clarence Gillis MP 1940–1957* (Hantsport, NS: Lancelot Press, 1987), 42.

20   Lewis, *The Good Fight*, 158.

21   Harrop, *Clarie*, 71.

22   Clarence Gillis, *Letter from Home* (Toronto: Canadian Forum Limited, 1943).

23   Lewis, *The Good Fight*, 153–57.

24   Harrop, *Clarie*, 19.

Chapter 4: The Rhetoric of Region

1   The history of the CCF in Atlantic Canada has been addressed in only a few arti-
cle-length studies. Ian McKay provides an overview of the party in the Maritimes, focused
primarily on Nova Scotia and New Brunswick, in Ian McKay, "The Maritime CCF:
Reflections on a Tradition," in *Toward a New Maritimes,* eds. Ian McKay and Scott Mil-
som (Charlottetown, PEI: Ragweed Press, 1982), 67–83. Terrence MacLean has provided
an overview of the CCF in Nova Scotia, see Terrence D. MacLean, "The Co-operative
Commonwealth Federation in Nova Scotia, 1938–56," in *More Essays in Cape Breton
History,* ed. R. J. Morgan (Windsor, NS: Lancelot Press, 1977), 21–41. New Brunswick's
experience with the CCF during the 1940s is detailed in Laurel Lewey, "A Near Golden
Age: The Co-operative Commonwealth Federation (CCF) in New Brunswick, 1940–
1949," *Journal of New Brunswick Studies,* 3 (2012), electronic edition, available at: https://
journals.lib.unb.ca/index.php/JNBS/article/view/20086. The history of the CCF on both
Prince Edward Island and in Newfoundland and Labrador remains to be told. Michael
Earle and H. Gamberg have explored the early years of the CCF in Nova Scotia in "The
United Mine Workers and the Coming of the CCF to Cape Breton," *Acadiensis* 19, 1
(Fall/Automne 1989), 3–26. The role of the CCF in Atlantic Canadian labour actions has
been detailed in Michael Earle, "'Down with Hitler and Silby Barrett': The Cape Breton
Miners' Slowdown Strike of 1941," *Acadiensis* 18, 1 (Fall/Automne 1988), 56–90, and in
Paul MacEwan, *Miners and Steelworkers: Labour in Cape Breton* (Toronto: Samuel Stevens
Hakkert & Company, 1976). Gregory Baum has a chapter that examines the relationship
between the Catholic Church and, in particular, St. Francis Xavier University's Antigonish
Movement and the CCF in Gregory Baum, *Catholics and Canadian Socialism: Political
Thought in the Thirties and Forties* (Toronto: Lorimer, 1980).

2   Terence MacLean, in his overview of the Nova Scotia CCF, charitably describes the
party's record outside of Cape Breton as "unimpressive." See MacLean, "The Co-operative
Commonwealth Federation in Nova Scotia, 1938–56," 36. During the 1940s, the CCF
held three Cape Breton seats in Nova Scotia's provincial legislature, along the Gillis' Cape
Breton South federal riding. Ian McKay makes the important point that in absolute numbers, support for the CCF was greater on the Maritime mainland than on Cape Breton,
but only in Cape Breton was support sufficiently concentrated to translate into electoral
success. See McKay, "The Maritime CCF," 74.

3   Clarence Gillis has received some scholarly attention. Gerry Harrop provides a relatively
brief overview of Clarence Gillis' time in Parliament in his *Clarie: Clarence Gillis MP,
1940–1957* (Hantsport, NS: Lancelot Press, 1987), while Paul MacEwan has a chapter on
"The C.C.F. and Clarence Gillis" in *Miners and Steelworkers.*

4   Gillis was also noted as a staunch supporter of both military veterans and labour, with the
CCF having used Gillis in 1942 to help organize and recruit Ontario union members to
the CCF. See "Clarie Gillis: Cape Breton's Miner M.P.," *Cape Breton Mirror,* 19. As Gerry
Harrop suggests with regard to labour, "There was no one in the House, of any party, who
could speak with the same authority [on labour issues as Gillis]. Gerry Harrop, *Clarie:
Clarence Gillis MP, 1940–1957*, 29.

5   Ian McKay, "The Maritime CCF: Reflections on a Tradition," 79. This is largely in keeping with a similar initiative proposed among the provincial premiers during the 1940s,
wherein it was put forth that they join forces as a *de facto* regional front in negotiating with
the federal government. As at the federal level, the provincial initiative proved short-lived
for provincial loyalties superseded regional ties. For more on this see Corey Slumkoski,
*Inventing Atlantic Canada: Regionalism and the Maritime Reaction to Newfoundland's Entry
into Canadian Confederation* (Toronto: University of Toronto Press, 2011), 108–124.

6   This argument is made throughout Slumkoski, *Inventing Atlantic Canada.*

7   See "Clarie Gillis: Cape Breton's Miner M.P.," *Cape Breton Mirror,* 2. Gillis' entry into
mining was delayed by his five-year service in World War One, by his having worked from
1920 to 1925 for District 26 of the UMWA, and by his five years studying economics at
St. Francis Xavier University's Extension Department.

8   As the *Cape Breton Post* wrote upon his 1960 passing, "Clarence, who cares more for the
working classes than any political party . . . made a mark in Parliament and in Canada's

public life equaled by few of his confreres and certainly by no private member during his 17 year tenure as CCF representative from Cape Breton South .... From the beginning of his term ... he was an outspoken and fearless proponent of the laboring class and the under-privileged. Cape Breton may well be proud to remember Clarence Gillis as one of the outstanding maritime Members in Canada's political history." *Cape Breton Post*, September 21, 1960, as cited in MacLean, "The Co-operative Commonwealth Federation in Nova Scotia, 1938–56," 35–36.

9   House of Commons, *Debates*, 1948, 5019–020. Black slightly overstates the degree of support for a crossing, as those employed by the ferry in the Mulgrave-Port Tupper region were largely against a fixed crossing. See Gerry Harrop, *Clarie: Clarence Gillis, MP 1940–1957*, 43–44.

10   Harrop, *Clarie*, 48.

11   House of Commons, *Debates*, 1949, 5492.

12   Clarence Gillis, "Broadcast to be made over CJCB – Thursday, March 31st [1949]– C. Gillis, M.P.," Eachdraidh Archives, Beaton Institute, Cape Breton University, MS/9 B1.

13   House of Commons, *Debates*, 1949, 610. See also Halifax *Chronicle-Herald*, February 17, 1949.

14   On March 22, 1949, it was announced that rates for goods shipped from Port-aux-Basques to St. John's on the Newfoundland Railway would drop and be essentially on par with seaborne shipping rates from Halifax to the Newfoundland capital. Some goods, such as feed, onions, and carrots, would be cheaper if shipped by rail (although flour would be more expensive). With goods shipped by rail covered by the MFRA, there would seemingly be no reason for Canadian exporters or Newfoundland importers to ship through Halifax. See Halifax *Chronicle-Herald*, March 23, 1949.

15   For more on the creation of Unemployment Insurance, see James Struthers, *No Fault of Their Own: Unemployment and the Canadian Welfare State, 1914–1941* (Toronto: University of Toronto Press, 1983).

16   House of Commons, *Debates*, 1955, 4628.

17   House of Commons, *Debates*, 1955, 4628.

18   House of Commons, *Debates*, 1955, 4758.

19   For more on the conflict over the Louisburg fish plant, see Slumkoski, *Inventing Atlantic Canada*, 52–60.

20   Clarence Gillis, "Broadcast to be Made over CJCB – Thursday, March 17th [1945] – C. Gillis M.P.," Eachdraidh Archives, Beaton Institute, Cape Breton University, MS 9/9 B1.

21   Clarence Gillis, "Radio Broadcast – Radio Station CJCB, Sydney, N.S., Saturday, March 25th [1950]," Eachdraidh Archives, Beaton Institute, Cape Breton University, MS 9/9 B1.

22   House of Commons, *Debates*, 1954, 2822–824.

23   House of Commons, *Debates*, 1954, 2949.

24   House of Commons, *Debates*, 1954, 2948.

25   House of Commons, *Debates*, 1954, 2949.

26   British Columbian opposition to the project is revealed by the fact that a "Vancouver member" seconded a proposal by Gillis to send the bill authorizing the Trans-Canada Pipeline back to committee for further study, a diversionary tactic that only succeeded in having the bill held up for "a couple of days." See Clarence Gillis, "Broadcast: Radio Station CJBC, Sydney, N.S." June 12, 1956, Broadcast Date June 16, 1956, Eachdraidh Archives, Beaton Institute, Cape Breton University, MS 9/9, B4.

27   Clarence Gillis, "Broadcast: Radio Station CJBC, Sydney, N.S." June 12, 1956, Broadcast Date June 16, 1956, Eachdraidh Archives, Beaton Institute, Cape Breton University, MS 9/9, B4.

28   Margaret Conrad, "The 1950s: The Decade of Development," in *The Atlantic Provinces in Confederation*, eds. E. R. Forbes and D. A. Muise (Toronto: University of Toronto Press, 1993), 390.

29   Clarence Gillis, "Radio Broadcast CJBC, Sydney, N.S., C. Gillis, M.P.," June 1, 1954, Eachdraidh Archives, Beaton Institute, Cape Breton University, MS 9/9, B3. Gillis would later change his tactics and begin to lobby for the maintenance of the Cape Breton coal industry as being necessary to support the Canadian steel industry, and, in particular, the shipbuilding industry. In this fashion, he was able to link three important Maritime industries to the continued viability of Cape Breton coal. See Clarence Gillis, "Radio Broadcast

Station C, Sydney, N.S., C. Gillis, M.P.," March 8, 1955, Eachdraidh Archives, Beaton Institute, Cape Breton University, MS 9/9, B4.

30 For more on this see David Lewis, *The Good Fight: Political Memoirs, 1909–1958* (MacMillan of Canada: Toronto: 1981), 157.

31 An argument made in bell hooks, *Feminist Theory: From Margin to Center* (Cambridge, MA: South End Press, 2000).

32 Lewis, *The Good Fight*, 159.

Chapter 5: The Left at Home and Abroad

1 Frank R. Scott, "Expanding Concepts of Human Rights," in *Essays on the Constitution: Aspects of Canadian Law and Politics* (Toronto: University of Toronto Press, 1977), 353.

2 Eric Adams asserts that Brewin was the first to use this phrase in his *Switzman* case comment: F. Andrew Brewin Case Comment on *Switzman v. Elbling*, (1957), *Canadian Bar Review*, vol. 35, no. 5 (May 1957), 557. Eric Adams, "Building a Law of Human Rights: *Roncarelli v. Duplessis* in Canadian Constitutional Culture," *McGill Law Journal*, 55, 3 (2010), 440.

3 Quoted from a January 27, 1947 speech delivered by Brewin to the Civil Liberties Association of Toronto, enclosed in a letter, Brewin to Roger Baldwin (ACLU president), February 3, 1947, Princeton University, Mudd Library, ACLU Papers, box 1055, folder 6.

4 LAC, MG30 D211, vol. 10, reel H-1222, file "Civil Liberties, National Council 1946–1951"; Brewin to Scott, March 24, 1947; "A Bill of Rights for Canada," *Toronto Star*, January 31, 1947.

5 "Submission of Committee for a Bill of Rights in Support of Statement for a Bill of Rights to the Special Joint Committee of the Senate and the House of Commons on Human Rights and Fundamental Freedoms," Special Joint Committee on Human Rights and Fundamental Freedoms (1947, 1948), vol. 51.

6 Carmela Patrias, "Socialists, Jews, and the 1947 Saskatchewan Bill of Rights," *Canadian Historical Review*, 87, 2 (June 2006), 269.

7 For more on the political movement to obtain a constitutionally entrenched bill of rights, see Christopher MacLennan, *Toward the Charter: Canadians and the Demand for a National Bill of Rights, 1929–1960* (Kingston and Montreal: McGill-Queen's University Press, 2003); Ross Lambertson, *Repression and Resistance: Canadian Human Rights Activists, 1930–1960* (Toronto: University of Toronto Press, 2005), 370.

8 Paul Evans, "Harper in China," *Toronto Star*, December 11, 2009. On the process of China's increasing "soft power" over Canada and Stephen Harper's visit to China, see Sonny Shiu-Ling Lo, "The Politics of Soft Power in Sino-Canadian Relations: Stephen Harper's Visit to China and the Neglected Hong Kong Factor," in Huhua Cao and Vivienne Poy, eds. *The China Challenge: Sino-Canadian Relations in the 21st Century* (Ottawa: University of Ottawa Press, 2011).

9 See Andrew Brewin, *Stand on Guard: The Search for a Canadian Defense Policy* (Toronto: McClelland & Stewart, 1965).

10 See an interesting exchange between Brewin and Philip Resnick on anti-Americanism in file 10–10, vol. 10, MG32 C26, Library and Archives Canada (LAC), Ottawa, Ontario.

11 Don Page, "The Representations of China in the United Nations: Canadian Perspectives and Initiatives, 1949-1971," in Paul Evans and B. Michael Frolic, eds. *Reluctant Adversaries: Canada and the People's Republic of China, 1949–1970* (Toronto: University of Toronto Press, 1991): 86–89.

12 J. L. Granatstein and Norman Hillmer, *Empire to Umpire: Canada and the World to the 1990s* (Toronto: Copp Clark Longman, 1994), 293.

13 House of Commons, *Debates*, November 17, 1966, 9999-10000; November 24, 1966, 10287–288.

14 Untitled statement sent to newspapers, 14 July 1953, file 7–30, vol. 7, MG32 C26, LAC.

15 House of Commons, *Debates*, November 24, 1966, 10286–90.

16 House of Commons, *Debates*, November 24, 1966, 10286–287; untitled notes, n.d., file 80–1, vol. 80, MG32 C26, LAC.

17   Many people I have interviewed expressed as much to me, including Gerry Caplan and
     Stephen Lewis.
18   John English, *Just Watch Me: The Life of Pierre Elliott Trudeau, 1968–2000* (Toronto: Knopf
     Canada, 2009): 65–66.
19   Andrew Brewin and David MacDonald, *Canada and the Biafran Tragedy* (Toronto: James
     Lorimer, 1970); see also Stephen Lewis, *Journey to Biafra* (Don Mills, ON: Thistle Print-
     ing, 1968).
20   House of Commons, *Minutes of Proceedings and Evidence*, Standing Committee on Exter-
     nal Affairs and National Defence, October 10, 1968, 144.
21   This line was indicated independently to me by both Rev. McLean and Rev. David
     MacDonald. Interview, Stephanie Bangarth with Rev. Walter McLean, January 5, 2012;
     Interview, Stephanie Bangarth with Rev. David MacDonald, August 4, 2011.
22   Lewis, *Journey to Biafra*, 35–36; Brewin and MacDonald, *Canada and the Biafran Tragedy*,
     118–120.
23   Rev. McLean, John Brewin, and David MacDonald expressed as much during their inter-
     views with me.
24   Paul Dewar, "Leftist policies should not simply critique, they must propose solutions,"
     in *The State of Leftist Foreign Policy*, OpenCanada.org, www.opencanada.org/features/
     state-leftist-foreign-policy/.
25   M. J. Coldwell, *Am I My Brother's Keeper?* (Ottawa: CCF National Office, 1948), 13.

Chapter 6: Fabianism and the Progressive Left in British Columbia

1   James Naylor, *The Fate of Labour Socialism: The Co-operative Commonwealth Federation and
     the Dream of a Working-Class Future* (Toronto: University of Toronto Press, 2016), 7–8, 14,
     and 315.
2   Chris Renwick, *Bread for All: The Origins of the Welfare State* (United Kingdom: Allen
     Lane, 2017), 50. Other analyses of Fabian thought include Rodney Barker, "Fabianism,"
     in William Outhwaite and Tom Bottomore, eds. *The Blackwell Dictionary of Twenti-
     eth-Century Social Thought* (Oxford: Oxford University Press, 1993), 220–221; and John
     Callaghan, *Socialism in Britain Since 1884* (Oxford: Oxford University Press, 1990), chap-
     ter 3, "Fabianism."
3   Quotations from Sean Mills, "When Democratic Socialists Discovered Democracy: The
     League for Social Reconstruction Confronts the 'Quebec Problem'," *Canadian Historical
     Review*, 86, 1 (March 2005) 53 and 57–58. Also, for the League for Social Reconstruction
     and the Fabian influence in Canada, see Michiel Horn, *The League for Social Reconstruction:
     Intellectual Origins of the Democratic Left 1930–1942* (Toronto: University of Toronto Press,
     1980) and Naylor, *The Fate of Labour Socialism*, 113–119.
4   *Vancouver Sun*, October 26, 1945, 6.
5   Desmond Morton, *The New Democrats 1961–1986: The Politics of Change* (Toronto: Copp
     Clark Pitman, 1986), 17–21.
6   Carolyn Swayze, *Hard Choices: A Life of Tom Berger* (Vancouver: Douglas and McIntyre,
     1987), 89 and chapter 2. For a biography of Thomas Berger see University of British
     Columbia, Rare Books and Special Collections (hereafter UBCRBSC), "Berger Biogra-
     phy" in the Thomas Berger Fonds (hereafter Berger Papers), Box 1, File 4 and *Vancouver
     Sun*, March 1, 1969, 29 (Allan Fotheringham).
7   "Speeches Misc." in the Berger Papers, Box 3, File 3–1 and Swayze, *Hard Choices*, 88.
     For the history of the formation of the New Democratic Party see Morton, *The New
     Democrats*, 18–32, and Gad Horowitz, *Canadian Labour in Politics* (Toronto: University of
     Toronto Press, 1968), chapter 6.
8   Tom Berger interview with Robert McDonald, July 21, 2014.
9   For Strachan see the *Globe and Mail*, July 22, 1981, 12; *Vancouver Sun*, May 10, 1967,
     14c, and July 22, 1981, A3; and letters between Robert Strachan and John Laxton in the
     British Columbia Archives (hereafter BCA), Robert Strachan Fonds (hereafter Strachan
     Papers), Ms.1291, Box 12, File 7, two letters between John Laxton and Strachan originally
     published in the *Clarion Call*, January 1969. Strachan's identity as a socialist is expressed

in Robert Strachan to Mrs. Rita Phelps, April 24, 1967, Strachan Papers, Box 12, File 2.

10 Dr. Raymond Parkinson interview with Robert McDonald, March 26, 2011.

11 Walter D. Young, *The Anatomy of a Party: The National CCF 1932–61* (Toronto: University of Toronto Press, 1969) and Alan Whitehorn, *Canadian Socialism: Essays on the CCF-NDP* (Toronto: Oxford University Press, 1992), chapter 2, quotation from 18–19. Young's thesis is sharply contested by James Naylor, who argues that the early CCF was in fact not a movement but a labour socialist party.

12 In one newspaper story, Walter Young was described as "the Grey Eminence or Power Behind the Throne . . . in lawyer Tom Berger's dynamic thrust to become head of the B.C NDP party." See newspaper clipping, n.p, n.d, in Berger Papers, Box 2, File 6. For Young's role as Chair of the Policy Research Committee, see Tom Berger, Chairman of the (1963) Provincial Election Campaign Committee, "Campaign Chairman's Report," n.d., in UBCRBSC, Walter Young Fonds (hereafter Young Papers), Box 8, File 25, and Arthur J. Turner to Walter Young, February 21, 1964, in Young Papers, Box 8, File 14.

13 Trevor Lloyd to Walter Young, November 6, 1962 and Walter Young to Trevor Lloyd, November 21, 1962, in Young Papers, Box 2, File 2.

14 Des Sparham to Walter Young, November 16, 1963; Marion Bryden to Walter Young, January 19, 1964; Marion Bryden to "All Members and Prospective Members of Exchange or ERIC," February 6, 1964; Walter Young to Marion Bryden, February 7, 1964; John Rich to Walter Young, June 9, 1964; and Walter Young to John Rich, June 15, 1964, in Young Papers, Box 2, File 2; and Morton, *The New Democrats*, 50–51.

15 Des Sparham to Walter Young, December 1, 1962 and Des Sparham to Walter Young, June 25, 1964, Young Papers, Box 2, File 2, and Walter D. Young, "Old-Left, New-Left in the New Democratic Party," *Canadian Dimension*, 5, 1 (November-December 1967), p.8 in Strachan Papers, Box 12, File 6.

16 Walter Young to Des Sparham, January 4, 1963, in Young Papers, Box 2, File 2. Young was also impatient with the traditional farm base of the social democratic left and was quoted in the farm magazine *Star Weekly* on January 8, 1966 as saying, "The N.D.P is going to be a labor party and to hell with the farmers. They're a declining force anyway . . . Most of the people we get elected are relics." On February 9 the caucus of British Columbia MLA's wrote to Woodrow Lloyd, Saskatchewan's Opposition Leader, "completely repudiating Walter Young's statements." Strachan Papers, "The Leadership Challenge," 8–9.

17 Parkinson interview, March 26, 2011. Also, see M. K. Oliver to Walter Young, October 18, 1961, Young Papers, Box 1, File 41. On Young's early support for Tom Berger, see Walter Young to Des Sparham, July 22, 1963, in Young Papers, Box 2, File 2.

18 On Fabianism, see n. 2.

19 "The NPD Leadership Race," *The Voice* [Spring 1967] and "The Berger Booster" [January 1969], Berger Papers, Box 1, File 1–6; and Tom Berger to the Provincial Executive, New Democratic Party, October 15, 1963, Strachan Papers, Box 5, File 2.

20 *The Labour Statesman*, April 1967, 10.

21 Tom Berger interviewed by Doug Collins, CBC, April 17, 1967, transcript, in Strachan Papers, Box 12, File 4, 1–4.

22 John Tupper Saywell, ed. *Canadian Annual Review for 1969* [hereafter, *CAR for 1969*] (Toronto: University of Toronto Press, 1970), 142–143; *Vancouver Province*, April 22, 1967, 4; and Robert Strachan to the Editor, *Canadian Dimension*, January 12, 1968, Strachan Papers, Box 12, File 6.

23 Tom Berger to Provincial Executive, New Democratic Party, October 15, 1963, Strachan Papers, Box 5, File 2.

24 Strachan, "Leadership Challenge", Strachan Papers, Box 12, File 2, 2–5.

25 Morton, *The New Democrats*, 49–50.

26 Thomas Berger, "Speeches Misc.," n.d., Berger Papers, Box 3, File 3–1.

27 Peter S. McInnis, *Harnessing Labour Confrontation: Shaping the Postwar Settlement in Canada, 1943-1950* (Toronto: University of Toronto Press, 2002), 2.

28 Andrew Neufeld and Andrew Parnaby, *The IWA in Canada: The Life and Times of an Industrial Union* (Vancouver: IWA Canada/New Star Books, 2000), 133–134 and 195.

29 Horowitz, *Canadian Labour in Politics*, 190; Morton, *The New Democrats*, 21–22; Ben Isitt, *Militant Minority: British Columbia Workers and the Rise of a New Left, 1948–1972*

(Toronto: University of Toronto Press, 2011), 168–172; and Peter Zudak's unfinished manuscript, "Factionalism in the British Columbia New Democratic Party 1962 to 1972," n.d., Chapter III, UBCRBSC, Barrett Papers, Box 15, File 3. Peter Zudak's insights derived from his work as an NDP organizer in Vancouver Centre in the 1972 provincial election and from the research that he carried out for an Honours B.A. thesis in the political science department at the University of Guelph in the mid-1970s.

30 Grace MacInnis to Carl Hamilton, CCF National Secretary, May 3, 1958, Library and Archives Canada (hereafter LAC), CCF/NDP Fonds, MG28-IV-I, Box 102 (Grace MacInnis).

31 *CCF News*, 25, 4 (April 26, 1961), 6 and *Vancouver* Sun, April 23, 1960, 17.

32 Pat Carney, "Tight-Rope on a Wire," based on an interview by Carney with Robert Strachan, *Vancouver Province*, April 27, 1963, in Strachan Papers, Box 2, File 10. Many trade unionists were also ambivalent about the value to them of the NDP connection. See Grant MacNeill, "Submission to Joint Conference re: Trade Union Relations," April 19, 1965, in Strachan Papers, Box 11, File 13 and *Daily Colonist*, April 13, 1969, 1 (Ian Street).

33 *Daily Colonist*, May 11, 1969, 5 (Ian Street).

34 In addition to Calder, supporting MLAs were Dr. Ray Parkinson, a psychiatrist; Surrey's Ernest Hall, like Berger a new member; and Randolph Harding, the dean of the NDP caucus.

35 *Vancouver* Sun, October 15, 1968, 61; *Vancouver Province*, November 14, 1968, 5; and John Laxton, "What Value a Leadership Contest?' in *The Clarion Call*, January 1969, and John Laxton to R. M. Strachan, February 11, 1969, Strachan Papers, Box 12, File 7. Also, see Paul Litt, *Trudeaumania* (Vancouver: University of British Columbia Press, 2016).

36 Robert Strachan to John Laxton, February 7, 1969, Strachan Papers, MS 1291, Box 12, File 7.

37 *Vancouver Sun*, May 5, 1967, 65. Also see Tom Hazlitt, "NDP's Pros at the Helm," *Vancouver Province*, May 25, 1965, 1, 2.

38 *Victoria Daily Times*, June 9, 1967, 2 (John Mika). Also see Isitt, *Militant Minority*, 178–79. One story claimed that Strachan had the support of eight caucus members and Berger six (*Vancouver Province*, March 29, 1968, 16).

39 *Victoria Times*, June 2, 1967, 3.

40 Geoff Meggs and Rod Mickleburgh, *The Art of the Impossible: Dave Barrett and the NDP in Power 1972–1975* (Madiera Park, BC: Harbour Publishing, 2012), 33. Also see a similar comment by Colin Cameron, MP, in the *Vancouver Sun*, May 26, 1967, 16.

41 Patrick L. McGeer, *Politics in Paradise* (Toronto: Peter Martin Associates, 1972), 22; Isitt, *Militant Minority*, 178; and *Vancouver Province*, April 30, 1969, 17 (Jack Clarke). The other two candidates, who withdrew after the first ballot in favour of Barrett, were Bob Williams, a community planner, and J.F. Conway, a radical student from Simon Fraser University.

42 Isitt, *Militant Minority*, 178.

43 *Vancouver Province*, April 11, 1969, 31. Also, see *Vancouver Sun*, April 12, 1969, 8 (George Dobie).

44 *CAR for 1969*, 146.

45 Tom Berger to Lance Randle, October 1, 1969, Berger Papers, Box 4, File 4–4; B. H. Emerson to C. L. Dennis, August 28, 1869 (*sic 1969)*, Berger Papers, Box 4, File 4–5; *Vancouver Province*, August 29, 1969, 4; and Karen Jackson, *Ideology of the NDP in B.C.: Manifest Socialism, 1966, 1969 and 1972 Election Campaigns* (Victoria: University of Victoria, 1983), 43.

46 Jackson, *Ideology of the NDP in B.C.*, 25–51. On the rise of social movement politics, see Nelson Wiseman and Benjamin Isitt, "Social Democracy in Twentieth Century Canada: An Interpretive Framework, *Canadian Journal of Political Science*, 40:3 (September 2007): 581–586.

47 *Vancouver Sun*, August 9, 1969, 8 (Dave Ablett), and BCA, Aural History, Accession No. 3224, Nimsick Interview, Transcripts, Tape 13–2, 12.

48 *Vancouver Sun*, August 9, 1969, 6 and 15; David J. Mitchell, *W.A.C.: Bennett and the Rise of British Columbia* (Vancouver: Douglas and McIntyre, 1983), 387–389; and Martin Robin, *Pillars of Profit: The Company Province, 1934–1972* (Toronto: McClelland & Stewart, 1973), 273.

49 Historian Robin Fisher makes clear that Pattullo's ideas were informed by his family's association with the Liberal government of Oliver Mowat in late nineteenth-century Ontario and nurtured by his business and political experience in the resource towns of the northern frontier. Thus, his belief that "a thorough-going reform of capitalism" could be achieved through state initiative appears to have emerged from influences different from those of Weir and Cassidy. As Fisher says, Pattullo's ideas "were his own." Yet his commitment to liberal reform opened his government to the hiring of Weir and the influence of Fabianism in the social policy field. See *Duff Pattullo of British Columbia* (Toronto: University of Toronto Press, 1991), 213–215.

50 Megan Davies, "Competent Professionals and Modern Methods: State Medicine in British Columbia during the 1930s," *Bulletin of the History of Medicine*, 76, 1 (2002): 63. Also, see the *Vancouver News-Herald*, December 6, 1949, 4.

51 Jean Mann, "G.M. Weir and H.B. King: Progressive Education for the Progressive State," in J. Donald Wilson and David C. Jones, eds. *Schooling and Society in Twentieth Century British Columbia* (Calgary: Detselig, 1980), 92–104, and John Farley, *To Cast Out Disease: A History of the International Health Division of the Rockefeller Foundation (1913–1951)* (Oxford: Oxford University Press, 2004), 224.

52 Mann, "G.M. Weir and H.B. King," 104; Weir, *Survey of Nursing Education in Canada* (Toronto: University of Toronto Press, 1932), 302–314; and *Vancouver Sun*, April 14, 1936, 1 and 4.

53 Davies, "Competent Professionals and Modern Methods," 57–58.

54 BCA, Thomas Dufferin Pattullo Papers, Add. Mss. 3, vol.76, file 6 (micro A 01810), 10.

55 *Vancouver Province*, June 20, 1934, 1, and H. M. Cassidy, "Planning the Health and Welfare Programme: Notes for Address, Departmental Conference, Vancouver, January 5, 1937," in University of Toronto Archives, Harry Cassidy Papers, B70022 (hereafter Cassidy Papers), Box 51, File 02.

56 Horn, *The League for Social Reconstruction*, 183.

57 Allan Irving, "Canadian Fabians: The Work and Thought of Harry Cassidy and Leonard Marsh, 1930–1945," *Canadian Journal of Social Work and Education*, 7, 1 (1981): 15–18, and Naylor, *The Fate of Labour* Socialism, 119–124 and 311.

58 For League connections, see Keith Walden, ed. *The Papers of Harry Cassidy and Beatrice Pearse: The Courtship Years, 1917–1925* (Toronto: The Champlain Society, 2009), Introduction; Irving, "Canadian Fabians," 7–28; Horn, *The League for Social Reconstruction*, 36–53, 66–68, 84–93, and 101–103; and Katz, "The Last Days of Harry Cassidy," 7–49. Quotation from Davies, "Competent Professionals and Modern Methods," 59. For McGill University's program to advance social science research in the interwar years, see Marlene Shore, *The Science of Social Redemption: McGill, the Chicago School, and the Origins of Social Research in Canada* (Toronto: University of Toronto Press, 1987), chapter 6 and *passim*.

59 H. M. Cassidy to Prof. H. S. Slichter, Harvard University, December 4, 1934, Cassidy Papers, Box 17, File. 01.

60 An exception is Fisher, *Duff Pattullo of British Columbia*, 274–75 and 294–95.

61 Walden, *The Papers of Harry Cassidy*, 8. One suspects that Harry Cassidy would have agreed with John Maynard Keynes' observation that the "class war will find me on the side of the educated *bourgeoisie*." Cited in Renwick, *Bread for All*, 193.

62 Walden, *The Papers of Harry Cassidy*, 9 and 22–26. Walden also cites evidence that Cassidy, upon return from the war, expressed contempt "for the 'uneducated, radical lout' who ran the One big Union local in Rock Bay [Victoria]," a view that supports Naylor's contention that "Fabian ideology was prejudicial to independent working-class activity." See Walden, *The Papers of Harry Cassidy*, 25, and Naylor, *The Fate of Labour Socialism*, 117.

63 Morton, *The New Democrats*, 49.

64 *Vancouver Sun*, November 5, 1970, 12, the observation of labour reporter George Dobie.

65 Barrett interview with Ben Isitt, April 24, 2006, cited in Isitt, *Militant Minority*, 190 and n.165, 359. Also, see Robin, *Pillars of Profit*, 309–310, and the *Daily Colonist*, October 12, 1969, 5.

66 Robin, *Pillars of Profit*, 308–309.

67 Private correspondence, Peter Zudak to Robert McDonald, April 18, 2011.

68 Horn, *The League for Social Reconstruction*, 49.

69   For instance, in *Bread for All*, historian Chris Renwick argues that the welfare state in Britain was "an intergenerational project, built by a variety of different and sometimes conflicting individuals and groups, not all of whom fit neatly within the 'progressive' or 'radical' tradition." See 6, 50, and 264, quotation on 6.

Chapter 7: Waffling in Winnipeg and London

1   For a detailed discussion of the Waffle in Ontario, see John Bullen, "The Ontario Waffle and the Struggle for an Independent Socialist Canada: Conflict within the NDP," *Canadian Historical Review*, 64 (June 1983): 188–215; Robert Hackett, "Pie in the Sky: A History of the Ontario Waffle," *Canadian Dimension*, special edition (October-November 1980); for the Waffle in Saskatchewan, see Peter Borch, "The Rise and Fall of the Saskatchewan Waffle, 1966–73," M.A. thesis, University of Regina, 2005; for the Waffle in New Brunswick, see Patrick Webber, "'For a Socialist New Brunswick': The New Brunswick Waffle, 1967–1972," *Acadiensis* 38, 1 (Winter-Spring 2009): 75–103; for a collection of articles by former Wafflers, see *Studies in Political Economy* 32 and 33 (1990).

2   Dan Heap, "The Waffle – the Recipe?" *Canadian Dimension* (December 1981), 43.

3   Bullen, "The Ontario Waffle"; Hackett, "Pie in the Sky."

4   "Left of Central Canada," *Waffle News*, January 1970, 2008—017/001 (01), Kim Malcomson and Paul Barber fonds, Clara Thomas Archives and Special Collections (CTASC), York University, Toronto, Ontario, Canada.

5   Meyer Brownstone and T. J. Plunkett, *Metropolitan Winnipeg: Politics and Reform of Local Government* (Berkeley: University of California Press, 1983), 17; Alan F. J. Artibise, *Winnipeg: An Illustrated History* (Toronto: J. Lorimer, 1977), 170.

6   Brownstone, *Metropolitan Winnipeg* (Berkeley: University of California Press, 1983), 15.

7   A. Gerald Bedford, *The University of Winnipeg: A History of the Founding Colleges* (Toronto: University of Toronto Press, 1976).

8   Brownstone, *Metropolitan Winnipeg*, 17.

9   See Nelson Wiseman, *Social Democracy in Manitoba: A History of the CCF-NDP* (Winnipeg: University of Manitoba Press, 1983) for background on the party's electoral record in Winnipeg.

10   "On the Move in Manitoba," *Waffle News*, May 1970, 2008017/001 (01), Kim Malcomson and Paul Barber fonds, CTASC.

11   Cy Gonick, "Manitoba being colonized," *Waffle News*, December 1970, 2008–017/001 (01), Kim Malcomson and Paul Barber fonds, CTASC.

12   "41 Resolutions Dealt With by NDP," *Winnipeg Free Press*, November 2, 1970.

13   Correspondence from Sheila Kuziak to Kim Malcomson, November 15, 1970, 2008–017/001 (05), Kim Malcomson and Paul Barber fonds, CTASC; Correspondence from Sheila Kuziak to Kim Malcomson, November 29, 1970, 2008–017/001 (05), Kim Malcomson and Paul Barber fonds, CTASC.

14   Paul Barber, "Ten Wafflers in Manitoba, Appendix I – A Short History of the Manitoba Waffle," 2008–017/001 (08), Kim Malcomson and Paul Barber fonds, CTASC.

15   "Waffle Policies Passed – Gonick," *Winnipeg Free Press*, November 22, 1971. Among the Waffle-supported policy resolutions passed by the convention were a commitment to the provincial government takeover of the Greater Winnipeg Gas Company and to holding a large-scale conference on unemployment and American economic policies. The Waffle was disappointed, however, that the provincial convention defeated a resolution calling for abortion to be removed from the Criminal Code. Transportation Minister Joe Borowski's outspoken opposition to abortion divided the Manitoba NDP in the early 1970s.

16   "NDP Returns Bell," *Winnipeg Free Press*, November 22, 1971.

17   Paul Barber, "Ten Wafflers in Manitoba, Appendix I – A Short History of the Manitoba Waffle," 2008–017/001 (08) Kim Malcomson and Paul Barber fonds, CTASC; Minutes of National Waffle Meeting held at Regina, Sask. May 5 and 6, 1973, 2008–017/001 (07), Kim Malcomson and Paul Barber fonds, CTASC.

18   Orlo Miller, *London 200: An Illustrated History* (London, ON: London Chamber of Commerce, 1992), 216.

19   Miller, *London 200*, 221.

20 Nancy Geddes Poole, *The Art of London 1830-1980* (London, ON: Blackpool Press, 1984), 125.

21 Miller, *London 200*, 223–4.

22 Roberta McClelland, "Mary Campbell," in eds. Michael Baker and Hilary Bates Neary, *100 Fascinating Londoners* (Toronto: James Lorimer & Company, 2005).

23 Hilary Bates Neary, personal interview, December 8, 2009.

24 James King, *The Way It Is: The Life of Greg Curnoe* (Toronto: Dundurn, 2017).

25 Poole, *The Art of London*, 140–41. The mural, titled *Homage to the R 34*, included texts referencing draft-dodger Muhammad Ali, and a page from Curnoe's journal deemed anti-American. Moreover, Curnoe's depiction of a man falling out of the second gondola with his hand severed by the propeller bore an uncanny likeness to US president Lyndon Johnson, although Curnoe claimed it was of a neighbour.

26 Letter, Mary Campbell to Mel Watkins and Kelly Crichton, July 20, 1972, personal files; "Jane Bigelow re-elected," *London Free Press*, October 5, 1970.

27 Paddy Musson, personal interview, December 7, 2009.

28 Interestingly, Campbell chose to run in Middlesex-Lambton-London out of concern for the NDP candidate's prospects in the other, more traditionally left-wing London ridings. "London Election Report," *Advance*, September 23, 1973, Box 1, File 8, New Democratic Party Waffle Collection, William Ready Division of Archives and Research Collections at McMaster University, Hamilton, Ontario, Canada.

29 James Laxer portrayed the election of Joan Newman, representing the Association for Tenants' Action, Kingston, to city council in Kingston as representing "the beginnings of a new coalition of poor tenants, labour and students" in James Laxer, "The Student Movement and Canadian Independence," *Canadian Dimension* (August-September 1969), 29.

30 *Manitoba Waffle News* n.d. [1971], File 446–21, CCF-NDP fonds, Library and Archives Canada (LAC), Ottawa, Ontario, Canada.

31 *Manitoba Waffle News* n.d. [1971], File 446–21, CCF-NDP fonds, LAC.

32 Paul Barber, "Ten Wafflers in Manitoba, Appendix I – A Short History of the Manitoba Waffle," 2008–017/001 (08), Kim Malcomson and Paul Barber fonds, CTASC.

33 Douglas MacKay, "NDP Adopts Civic Election Platform", *Winnipeg Free Press*, August 23, 1971.

34 Alvin Finkel, "Why the NDP lost the North End," and Paul Barber, "Unicity Elections – South End," *Waffle News*, 1971–72, File Manitoba Waffle, R-1217 Saskatchewan Waffle Records, Saskatchewan Archives Board, Regina, Saskatchewan, Canada.

35 "ICEC Will Control New Central Council," *Winnipeg Free Press*, October 7, 1971; John Gillespie, "11 School Boards Elected; NDP In Control of Winnipeg's," *Winnipeg Free Press*, October 7, 1971.

36 Jason Russell, "The Union Local in Post-Second World War Canada: A Case Study of UAW/CAW Local 27 from 1950 to 1990," Ph.D. diss., York University, Toronto, 2010, 77–8.

37 Russell, "The Union Local," 80.

38 Russell, "The Union Local," 44.

39 Cy Gonick, *A Very Red Life: The Story of Bill Walsh* (St. John's: Canadian Committee on Labour History, 2001), 252; One of the Eaton Automotive workers told a local reporter that he did not want the plant closure to be "used as a political platform for groups such as Militant Co-Op or the NDP Waffles." Quotation from Russell, "The Union Local," 44.

40 For a detailed discussion of the Texpack strike, see Joan Sangster, "Remembering Texpack: Nationalism, Internationalism, and Militancy in Canadian Unions in the 1970s," *Studies in Political Economy* 78 (2006): 41–66.

41 Marc Zwelling, "The Strike at Texpack's Vanishing Plant," *Canadian Dimension* (November 1971): 8–11.

42 "Striking Union Says Rival Aids Texpack," *Toronto Star*, October 12, 1971.

43 Craig Simpson, personal interview, December 8, 2009.

44 "Watkins, 13 Others Arrested at Texpack During Demonstration by Waffle Members," *Globe and Mail*, September 10, 1971.

45 In 1969, the government of Pierre Trudeau amended the *Criminal Code*, allowing doctors to perform abortions in hospitals if a pregnancy threatened the health or life of a woman,

a decision made only by a committee of doctors. Otherwise, abortion remained illegal in Canada. Vancouver Wafflers D. J. O'Donnell and Dawn Carrell were among the key organizers of the Abortion Caravan in the Vancouver Women's Caucus. For further information on the Abortion Caravan, see Christabelle Sethna and Steve Hewitt, "Clandestine Operations: The Vancouver Women's Caucus, the Abortion Caravan, and the RCMP," *Canadian Historical Review* 90, 3 (September 2009): 463–96; Shannon Stettner, "'We Are Forced to Declare War': Linkages between Women's Anti-War Protests and the 1970 Abortion Caravan," *Social History/Histoire Sociale* 46, 92 (November 2013): 159–78.

46   Barbara Vedan, "Abortion Campaign Not Whole Story," *Winnipeg Free Press*, May 4, 1970.

47   Dr. C. C. Merry, "Letter – New York Abortions," *Winnipeg Free Press*, August 28, 1971; "Clinic Grant Endorsed," *Winnipeg Free Press*, August 19, 1971; Ron Campbell, "Anti-Abortion Stand Supported," *Winnipeg Free Press*, September 8, 1971.

48   Barbara Vedan, "Winnipeg Leader of NDP Quintet Will Change Tactics Next Time," *Winnipeg Free Press*, February 5, 1970.

49   Anonymous, quotation from Paul Barber, "Ten Wafflers in Manitoba," 2008–017/001 (08), Kim Malcomson and Paul Barber fonds, CTASC.

50   Anonymous, quotation from Paul Barber, "Ten Wafflers in Manitoba," 2008–017/001 (08), Kim Malcomson and Paul Barber fonds, CTASC.

51   Anonymous, quotation from Paul Barber, "Ten Wafflers in Manitoba," 2008–017/001 (08), Kim Malcomson and Paul Barber fonds, CTASC.

52   Anonymous, quotation from Paul Barber, "Ten Wafflers in Manitoba," 2008–017/001 (08), Kim Malcomson and Paul Barber fonds, CTASC.

53   Paul Barber, "Ten Wafflers in Manitoba," 2008–017/001 (08), Kim Malcomson and Paul Barber fonds, CTASC.

54   Paddy Musson, personal interview, December 7, 2009.

55   Margaret Simpson, personal interview, December 8, 2009.

56   Paddy Musson, personal interview, December 7, 2009.

57   Desmond Morton, *The New Democrats, 1961–1986: The Politics of Change* (Toronto: Copp Clark Pitman, 1986). Morton, a contemporary of the Waffle, criticizes their activities within the NDP.

Chapter 8: New Leftists, "Party-liners," and Municipal Politics in Toronto

1   A youthful Jack Layton was hardly alone in suggesting that community was incompatible with liberal ideology. See Jack Layton, "Urban Government & Politics: Delivery of Services: 'Transportation Policy'" (March 7, 1972), Jack Layton fonds, Ryerson University Archives and Special Collections, 404.04.

2   David Harvey, "The Right to the City," *New Left Review* 53 (September-October 2008), 28; Timothy Lloyd Thomas, *A City with a Difference: The Rise and Fall of the Montreal Citizen's Movement* (Montreal: Vehicule Press, 1997); Donna Vogel, "The Coalition of Progressive Electors: A Case Study in Post-Fordist Counter-Hegemonic Politics" (Ph.D. Thesis, University of British Columbia, 1999).

3   Kevin T. Brushett, "Blots on the Face of the City: The Politics of Slum Housing and Urban Renewal in Toronto, 1940–1970" (Ph.D. Thesis, Queen's University, 2001), 253, 262, 480, 615, 627.

4   John Sewell, *Up Against City Hall* (Toronto: James Lewis & Samuel, 1972), 10–19, 42–44, 47–51. In typical New Left fashion, Sewell also rejected the ward's NDP association for being too middle class, despite his own middle-class status.

5   N.D.P., Municipal Program (Toronto: Craftsmen Printers, 1969). A mere five years prior, Communist Party delegates had decided not to include the long-term goal of free public transit in their municipal platform, fearing it would appear too unrealistic. See "Red Tells Colleagues to Keep Open Mind," *Globe and Mail*, 5 October 1964.

6   "The Fretful Candidate," *Globe and Mail*, October 19, 1966; "Dennison Lacks Courage to Admit Tax Truths, Givens says," *Globe and Mail*, November 25, 1966; "Two Candidates Back Sunday Liquor Serving," *Globe and Mail*, November 26, 1966; "Clarkson Sees Priority Need for Transit," *Toronto Telegram*, October 14, 1969; Graham Fraser, *Fighting Back: Urban Renewal in Trefann Court* (Toronto, Hakkert, 1972), 175–77.

7   Sewell, 74–75; "Radical Aldermen Criticize City Hall 'Reformers'," *Toronto Star*, December 13, 1969; "4 Aldermen Break with Council, Ask Power for Poor, *Toronto Star*, March 11, 1970.

8   "Chess Game 'Climax of Degeneration'," *Toronto Telegram*, February 11, 1971; "City Throws Out Jest Motion on Agitators," *Toronto Telegram*, April 1, 1971.

9   "New Democrat Fears Labor-ruled Party," *Globe and Mail*, March 4, 1965; "Action Canada Plans Nation-wide Campaign to Sign Up Members," *Globe and Mail*, May 26, 1971; "Report of the Extra-Parliamentary Activities Committee to the Federal Council of the New Democratic Party," Jaffary fonds, Toronto Archives, 145495-NDP-EPA Committee, 1970–1971 folder; "Alderman Gives 16 Union Leaders Course in Confrontation Politics," *Globe and Mail*, July 1, 1971; Editorial, "'Reform' City Council Not Enough," *Varsity*, December 1, 1972; Boyce Richardson, *The Future of Canadian Cities* (Toronto: New Press, 1972), 10–15, 93, 140.

10   Jon Caulfield, *The Tiny Perfect Mayor* (Toronto: James Lorimer & Company, 1974): 11–14.

11   "Indignant Alderman Calls Leaflet Sexist," *Globe and Mail*, February 14, 1974.

12   Though Heap's ward had substantial working-class and post-secondary student populations, election rules had tended to work against left-wing candidates. Non-citizens, and many rooming house residents, were barred from voting, which was a big factor, considering the ward's substantial number of recent immigrants and people living in poverty. Business owners, on the other hand, were able to vote even if they did not live in the ward. But left-wing candidates were aided by the decline of so-called "strip" ridings, which attached working-class neighbourhoods south of Bloor to more affluent areas in the north. A key reason for Sewell and Jaffary's victory was that their ward had been severed from Rosedale, whose residents used to dominate elections because of their higher turnouts. See Jerry F. Hough, "Voters' Turnout and the Responsiveness of Local Government: The Case of Toronto, 1969," Karl Jaffary fonds, Toronto Archives, 145488-18.

13   "Chinese View Spadina as Racism, Woman Tells Metro Road Hearing," *Globe and Mail*, April 11, 1970. One of the many young activists who helped with Heap's campaign was ecstatic that the new alderman had won 263 of the 275 ballots cast by Rochdalians. See "Marks, Brown Lose to Radical Priest 'I had the people'," *Toronto Star*, December 3, 1972; "Ward Six Residents Confront Problems of Starting Council," *Toronto Citizen*, January 11, 1973; "Objectives of the Ward Six Council," Dan Heap fonds, Toronto Archive, 138439–14; "The Ward Six Council," Dan Heap fonds, Toronto Archive, 138439–14; "Next Ward Six Council Meeting," Dan Heap fonds, Toronto Archive, 138439–14; "Next Meeting," Dan Heap fonds, Toronto Archive, 138439–14; "Ward 6 Council," Dan Heap fonds, Toronto Archive, 138439–14.

14   "Platform of the Ward 6 Community Organization," Dan Heap fonds, Toronto Archive, 138439–11.

15   J. Doiron, "Organizing – Ideas for Consideration by the Reform Caucus" (January 15, 1974), Karl Jaffary fonds, Toronto Archives, 145460–18.

16   "'Trouble Started When Police Began Crowding Protesters'," *Toronto Star*, May 13, 1970; "'Toronto Press Derelict on Bookstore Raids'," *Toronto Star*, July 6, 1971. Heap thought W6CO's successful drive to remove business owners who also voted in their home ridings from the ward's elector's list aided in this victory. As an example of the real difference this made, Heap received only two votes at the Toronto Dominion Centre in 1972, while his Progressive Conservative opponent won 268. There was a similarly lopsided result in 1974, but its effect was blunted because only forty ballots were cast. See "Voters Reject Aldermen Archer and Chisholm," *Toronto Star*, December 3, 1974.

17   "Post-Election Meeting Agrees to Structure Reform Citizens Movement," 145460–18; John Sewell, Untitled proposal (December 5, 1974), Karl Jaffary fonds, Toronto Archives, 145460–18; "Citizens Reform Movement," Karl Jaffary fonds, Toronto Archives, 145460–18; "An announcement to all reform citizens...," Nelson and Phyllis Clarke fonds, Toronto Public Library, Marilyn and Charles Baillie Special Collections Centre, 27 Papers of Reform Metro (movement for municipal reform); "Citizens' Federation Formed in Toronto," *Canadian Tribune*, June 11, 1975.

18   "New Reform Movement Woos Suburban Voters," *Toronto Star*, November 25, 1975; "Reid Scott Sheds 20 Years of Politics for Bench Career," *Globe and Mail*, August 7, 1976.

19 "What Strategy for Workers in Civic Politics?" *Labour Challenge*, November 22, 1976.

20 "Mrs. Thomas Resigns from Reform Caucus," *Globe and Mail*, January 30, 1976; "Reform Defector in Limbo," *Globe and Mail*, February 11, 1976; "Privileged Class and Radicals," *Toronto Sun*, June 13, 1974.

21 "NDP Must Run Full Slate in Toronto," *Labour Challenge*, December 6, 1971; "Toronto NDP Should Fight for Civic Power," *Labour Challenge*, April 25, 1977.

22 "Toronto NDPers Field Aldermanic Candidate," *Labour Challenge*, August 30, 1976; "Join Us in Working for a Radical, Revitalized New Democratic Party," 203792–4; Many of the NDP association's strongest supporters of a party slate belonged to a Marxist-oriented study group (and defacto invitation-only caucus). See Pantalone fonds, Toronto Archives, 138887–15.

23 "NDP Distrusts ReforMetro," *Toronto Clarion*, November 1978; "Press and NDP Off-base," *Toronto Clarion*, December 1978; "Minutes: Metro Toronto Area Council at Toronto City Hall, 27 February 1978,"; Untitled; "Election Organizing and Strategy," Pantalone fonds 138887–16; "Sparrow, Dorion, Nagle, Colle Endorsed," *Ward 6 News*, June 25, 1978. Labour Council had regularly endorsed most ReforMetro candidates and the occasional flare-up, which had marred relations between New Left-leaning aldermen and organized labour, appeared to have ceased. In one instance, a labour leader had supported a candidate promising "to get rid of the two Karls in City Hall – Karl Jaffary and Karl Marx." See "For Development, Not Developers," *Canadian Tribune*, November 22, 1972.

24 Alice and Dan Heap, "Why run an NDP candidate for alderman in ward six now?" Heap fonds, Toronto Archive, 140197–11; Irene Harris to Dan Heap, July 17, 1978, Dan Heap fonds Toronto Archive, 140197–11. W6CO used lengthy membership surveys and question and answer sessions to try to keep their elected representatives accountable. See "Evaluating our people in public office," Jaffary fonds, Toronto Archives, 145460–3.

25 "The Time, the Place, and the Person," *Body Politic*, November 1980; "Ward Healer," *Body Politic*, June-July 1980; "George Hislop, Alderman," *Ward 6 News*, April 1980; "Jack Layton, Alderman," *Ward 6 News*, April 1980.

26 "Joan Dorion, "Public School Trustee," *Ward 6 News*, April 1980; "Ward Healer," *Body Politic*, June-July 1980; "Hislop Gets Nod," *Ward 6 News*, May 1980.

27 "Sue Harris: Entering the Political Mainstream," *Body Politic*, February 1985; "'Reactionary' and 'obscene'," *Body Politic*, July-August 1974; "Vancouver Gays Hit Barrett Slanders," *Body Politic*, January-February 1975; "Gay Rights a 'Fad Issue': NDP Leader," *Body Politic*, February 1977; "Ward Healer," *Body Politic*, June-July 1980.

28 "Close, But Not Enough," *Body Politic*, December-January 1981.

29 Jack Layton, "A Typology of Democratic Theories," Jack Layton fonds, 404.04.19; Letter from Jack Layton to Charles Taylor, Jack Layton fonds, 404.04.12; Jeff Grant and Jack Layton, "The Politics of Pollution in Canada," Jack Layton fonds, 404.04.38. Layton's references to the New Left seem to reflect a popular mid-1960s understanding of this movement, which misses its evolution in the late 1960s and early 1970s. Like others attracted to New Left ideas, including Ed Broadbent before his leadership of the federal NDP, he was enthusiastic about Yugoslavian experiments in workers' self-management. Layton thought a concept he dubbed "Environmental Socialism" might be a solution to the disjuncture between the new and old lefts.

30 Jack Layton, *Speaking Out Louder: Ideas That Work for Canadians* (Toronto: Key Porter Books, 2006), 35–37; Jack Layton, "'The Community Power Debate': A Discussion Paper," Jack Layton fonds 404.04.03; Minutes, Wilson Heights NDP, Executive Meeting, February 4, 1979, 469565–1. Layton's folders of Waffle material, which include numerous internal bulletins, North York-specific newsletters and leaflets, as well as handwritten meeting notes, suggest he was a member. It is noteworthy that the documents were produced subsequent to the Waffle's expulsion from the NDP. See Jack Layton fonds, 404.04.29; 404.04.54.

31 "Platform," *Ward 6 News*, December 1979; "Jack Layton, Alderman," *Ward 6 News*, April 1980.

32 "City Politics Program #23," Ryerson University Archives, RG 7.05.03.

33 "City Politics Program #16," Ryerson University Archives, RG 7.05.03.

34 "City Politics Program #3," Ryerson University Archives, RG 7.05.03; "City Politics Program #24," Ryerson University Archives, RG 7.05.03.

35   "City Politics Program #45." Ryerson University Archives, RG 7.05.03.
36   Layton, *Speaking Out Louder*: 42; Dan Fast, "Ward Six Triumphant," *St. George NDP Newsletter*, November 1982. Layton's campaign manager notably avoided mentioning homophobia when musing about the reasons for the 1980 election defeat. Testifying to the ward's continued tendency to elect strongly left politicians, Layton's seatmate after the subsequent election was a tenant organizer who had resigned from the Communist Party and joined the NDP.
37   "Battles Seem All in the Past for Toronto's Citizen-activists," *Globe and Mail*, August 14, 1982; Joe Pantalone and George Comninel, "Draft Position: The Peace Movement, Working-Class Needs, and the NDP," Pantalone fonds, 138888–7; Jack Layton, "Re: 'The Peace Movement, Working Class Needs and the N.D.P,'" Jack Layton fonds, Toronto Archives, 140027–66.
38   "A New Vision for Toronto," Jack Layton fonds, Toronto Archives,140005–15.
39   "One Year After: Liberals and Reformers Divided," *Varsity*, December 7, 1973.

Chapter 9: Tommy Douglas, David Lewis, Ed Broadbent, and Democratic Socialism in the New Democratic Party, 1968–1984

1   *Constitution of the New Democratic Party of Canada*, April 1, 2013, http://xfer.ndp.ca/2013/constitution/2013_CONSTITUTION_E.pdf; *Constitution of the New Democratic Party of Canada*, June 3, 2011. http://xfer.ndp.ca/2011/2011-constitution/2011-06-CONSTITU-TION-ENG.pdf.
2   Alan Whitehorn, *Canadian Socialism: Essays on the CCF-NDP* (Toronto: Oxford University Press, 1992); Nelson Wiseman and Ben Isitt, "Social Democracy in Twentieth Century Canada: An Interpretive Framework," *Canadian Journal of Political Science* 40 (September 2007): 567–589; David McGrane, *Remaining Loyal: Social Democracy in Quebec and Saskatchewan* (Montreal and Kingston: McGill-Queen's University Press, 2014).
3   Leo Zakuta, *A Protest Movement Becalmed: A Study of Change in the CCF* (Toronto: University of Toronto Press, 1964); Walter Young, *The Anatomy of a Party: The National CCF, 1932–61* (Toronto: University of Toronto Press, 1969); James Naylor, *The Fate of Labour Socialism: The Co-operative Commonwealth Federation and the Dream of a Working-Class Future* (Toronto: University of Toronto Press, 2016).
4   Speech by Douglas to the 1971 NDP Convention, www.youtube.com/watch?v=MU-wRULlgMec#t=518.
5   Douglas Fonds, Vol. 148, File 19, "Can We Have Jobs without Inflation?"; Douglas Fonds, Vol. 150, Douglas, "Beyond Controls—What?" January 10, 1976.
6   Douglas Fonds, Vol. 147, File 7, "Excepts from an Address by T. C. Douglas," June 7, 1969; Douglas Fonds, Vol. 147, File 22, "Some Solutions Suggested by Watkins Commission"; Douglas Fonds, Vol. 28, File 14–9, Douglas to D. E. Macdonell, March 12, 1970; Douglas Fonds, Vol. 147, Douglas, "Radio Bureau," March 5, 1969; Douglas Fonds, Vol. 149, Douglas, "The Case for Nationalizing Canada's Oil and Gas Industries," November 28, 1975; CCF-NDP Fonds, Vol. 367, File 5, Douglas, "Notes for Report to Federal Council."
7   Douglas Fonds, Vol. 150, Douglas, "Beyond Controls—What?"
8   Douglas Fonds, Vol. 147, Douglas, "Radio Bureau," March 5, 1969; CCF-NDP Fonds, Vol. 421, File 3, "Partial Text of a Speech by Mr. T.C. Douglas," May 13, 1968. Emphasis in the original.
9   Douglas Fonds, Vol. 123, "Arguments in Favour of Public Ownership," November 4, 1974; Douglas Fonds, Vol. 123, Douglas, "Opening Statement: The Great Debate, Global Television," December 12, 1974.
10   Douglas Fonds, Vol. 123, Douglas, "The Syncrude Fiasco," February 11, 1975; CCF-NDP Fonds, 1993 accession, Vol. 35, Ron Campbell, "Control of Resources Urged: Former NDP Leader says Multinationals Milk Canada," *Winnipeg Free Press*.
11   Douglas Fonds, Douglas, "Notes for Speech, Federal Convention," October 28, 1969.
12   Lewis Fonds, Vol. 16, File 8–1, "Notes for a Speech by David Lewis," October 2, 1972; Lewis, "The Corporations. How They're Taking Over while You're Getting Taken," *CUPE Journal*, June-July 1974.

13   Lewis, "The Dishonesty of the 'Union Power' Myth," *Miners' Voice*, December 1976.
14   CCF-NDP Fonds, 1993 Accession, Vol. 41, File 16, "Notes for a Speech to be Delivered by David Lewis," August 11, 1972; CCF-NDP Fonds, Vol. 367, File 4, Lewis, "Report to the Federal Council of the NDP," November 14, 1971; Lewis Fonds, Vol. 95, "David Lewis Interviewed by Bruce Philips, Finlay MacDonald, Charles Lynch, and Douglas Fisher," June 15, 1973.
15   Lewis Fonds, Vol. 88, 1972 Speech by Lewis. See also Lewis, *Louder Voices: The Corporate Welfare Bums* (Toronto: James Lewis & Samuel, 1972); Lewis quoted in "Who Owns Canada?" *Canadian Transport*, September 15, 1969; Lewis, "The Dishonesty of the 'Union Power' Myth"; Mitchell C. Lynch, "Canada's Uneasy Power Broker," *The Wall Street Journal*, January 2, 1973.
16   Lewis Fonds, Vol. 128, "Speech by David Lewis to the OFL Political Education Conference," March 19–23, 1979; Lewis Fonds, Vol. 92, "David Lewis Interviewed by Bruce Phillips, Douglas Fisher, Charles Lynch, and Michael McCourt," November 23, 1973.
17   CCF-NDP Fonds, Vol. 367, File 4, Lewis, "Report to the Federal Council of the NDP."
18   V. I. Lenin, "What is to be Done? Burning Questions of our Movement," (1902).
19   Broadbent, "What is to be Done?" *Oshaworker*, March 6, 1969.
20   Broadbent Fonds, Vol. 1, File 50, Broadbent, "The White Paper on Tax Reform," July 22, 1970.
21   Broadbent Fonds, Vol. 3, File 26, "Broadbent Speech to Federal NDP Council," January 24, 1976; Broadbent Fonds, Vol. 1, File 17, Broadbent, "Socialist and Liberal Views on Man, Society, and Politics," January 1969.
22   CCF-NDP Fonds, 1993 Accession, Vol. 46, File 78, "Notes for Luncheon Address by Ed Broadbent," November 17, 1976.
23   J. K. Galbraith, *Economics and the Public Purpose* (Boston: Houghton, Mifflin Company, 1973).
24   Broadbent, "But Who Will Listen to this Fabian Song?" *Globe and Mail*, October 27, 1973.
25   Broadbent Fonds, Vol. 48, File 4, "New NDP Statement of Principles and Objectives: Draft #3," October 1982; CCF-NDP Fonds, 1993 Accession, Vol. 46, File 78, "Notes for Luncheon Address by Ed Broadbent."
26   "Broadbent Unveils Energy Scheme," *Winnipeg Free Press*, September 10, 1981.
27   For more on Trudeau's approach to the question of foreign energy control, see Christo Aivalis, *The Constant Liberal: Pierre Trudeau, Organized Labour, and the Canadian Social Democratic Left* (Vancouver: University of British Columbia Press, 2018), chapter 6.
28   CCF-NDP Fonds, 1993 Accession, Vol. 50, "Broadbent-Notley Joint Release on Energy," September 17, 1981.
29   CCF-NDP Fonds, 1993 Accession, Vol. 35, File 9, Broadbent and Ian Waddell, "A Program for Energy Security: An End to Oil Price Rip-Offs," March 6, 1981.
30   Douglas Fonds, Vol. 109, File 1–14, "Twenty Million Questions," May 6, 1969; Douglas Fonds, Vol. 147, Douglas, "A World in Revolt," June 5, 1969.
31   John Porter, *The Vertical Mosaic: An Analysis of Social Class and Power in Canada* (Toronto: University of Toronto Press, 1965); Douglas Fonds, Vol. 147, Douglas, "Notes for Speech, Federal Convention."
32   Douglas Fonds, Vol. 49, Douglas to Vincent J. MacLean, December 22, 1975.
33   Douglas Fonds, Vol. 148, Douglas, "Labour in a Free Society," January 6, 1970.
34   Lewis, "Labor in Canada: A Feeling of Being Under Siege," *Steel Labor Canada*, March 1972.
35   CCF-NDP Fonds, 1993 Accession, Vol. 40, File 46, "Comments by NDP Federal Leader David Lewis on Canada Labor Code Amendments," March 27, 1972.
36   Lewis Fonds, Vol. 102, Lewis quoted in "Don't Give in to the Anti-Labor Code Lobby, Lewis tells Government," January 31, 1972; CCF-NDP Fonds, 1993 Accession, Vol. 40, File 143, Lewis, "Towards Equality Before the Law," January 31, 1972; Lewis Fonds, Vol. 128, "Speech by David Lewis to the OFL Political Education Conference."
37   Broadbent Fonds, Vol. 1, File 17, Broadbent, "Socialist and Liberal Views on Man, Society, and Politics"; Broadbent, "What is to be Done?" *Oshaworker*, March 6, April 3, 1969.

38 Broadbent, "On Independence and Socialism," *Canadian Forum,* April 1972; Broadbent Fonds, Vol. 39, File 8, Broadbent, "Industrial Democracy: Where do we go from here"?

39 Broadbent Fonds, Vol. 39, File 8, Broadbent, "A Program to Improve Labour Relations," March 17, 1971.

40 Broadbent Fonds, Vol. 39, File 8, Broadbent, "Industrial Democracy: A Proposal for Action," June 1969.

41 Broadbent, *The Liberal Rip-Off: Trudeauism Vs. The Politics of Equality* (Toronto: New Press, 1970), 80–84.

42 Douglas Fonds, Vol. 147, Tommy Douglas, "Incomes Distribution, Poverty, and Politics," October 1969.

43 Douglas Fonds, Vol. 147, Douglas, "A World in Revolt."

44 Douglas Fonds, Vol. 149, Douglas, "The Christian Ethic and the Trade Union Movement," 1974; Douglas Fonds, Vol. 149, Douglas, "Christian Socialism in Canadian Politics," March 24, 1973.

45 Lewis Fonds, Vol. 47, "I am a Socialist," February 25, 1969.

46 Info according to the Bank of Canada Inflation Calculator; Lewis Fonds, Vol. 128, "Speech by David Lewis to the OFL Political Education Conference."

47 Lewis Fonds, Vol. 52, Lewis quoted by Pierre-C. O'Neil, "The Just Society is Impossible Outside a Socialist Society."

48 CCF-NDP Fonds, 1993 Accession, Vol. 40, File 143, Lewis, "Towards Equality Before the Law."

49 CCF-NDP Fonds, 1993 Accession, Vol. 40, File 143, Lewis, "Towards Equality Before the Law."

50 Karl Marx, *Critique of The Gotha Programme* (1875).

51 Broadbent Fonds, Vol. 1, File 17, Broadbent, "Socialist and Liberal Views on Man, Society, and Politics."

52 Broadbent, "Socialist and Liberal Views on Man, Society, and Politics."

53 Broadbent, "What is to be Done?" *Oshaworker,* February 20, 1969.

54 Despite this, Broadbent failed to champion economic and labour rights during the Charter debates. See Christo Aivalis, "Pierre Trudeau, Organized Labour, and the Canadian Social Democratic Left, 1945–2000," (Ph.D. Thesis, Queen's University, 2015), 332–41.

55 Broadbent Fonds, Vol. 1, File 32, Broadbent, "Socialism in the '70s: A Comment," *Canadian Dimension*; Broadbent Fonds, Vol. 1, File 44, Broadbent: "Private Member's Motion: Guaranteed Minimum Income," April 6, 1970; Broadbent Fonds, Vol. 16, File 14, Broadbent, "Notes for CLC Economic Conference," March 2, 1983.

56 "Tommy Douglas: Keeper of the Flame," 1986, www.youtube.com/watch?v=ZkCxEX-qiNxg.

57 Broadbent Fonds, Vol. 16, File 28, Broadbent, "Report to Federal Council," April 29, 1983.

58 Broadbent Fonds, Vol. 124, Broadbent, "What We Desire for Ourselves, We Wish for All," May 20, 1976; Lewis Fonds, Vol. 128, "Speech by David Lewis to the OFL Political Education Conference."

Chapter 10: Challenge from Within

1 Andrew Loewen, Dru Oja Jay, and Navjot Kaur, "What Will It Take to Embolden and Strengthen the Left," *briarpatch,* June 30, 2017.

2 www.couragecoalition.ca/en-unity/.

3 Dru Oja Jay, Interview with the author, October 31, 2017.

4 Loewen, et al, "What Will It Take to Embolden and Strengthen the Left."

5 Dru Oja Jay, Interview with the author, October 31, 2017.

6 Dru Oja Jay, Interview with the author, October 31, 2017.

7 Dru Oja Jay, Interview with the author, October 31, 2017.

8 Walter D. Young, *The Anatomy of a Party: The National CCF, 1932-1961* (Toronto: University of Toronto Press, 1969).

9 John Bullen, "The Ontario Waffle and the Struggle for an Independent Socialist Canada: Conflict within the NDP," *Canadian Historical Review,* 64:2 (1983), 188.

10 "Comment: A Discussion Paper on The New Politics Initiative," *Studies in Political Econ-*

omy Vol.66 (Autumn 2001), 143.

11   "The Leap Manifesto," https://leapmanifesto.org/en/the-leap-manifesto/.

12   See, for example, Bryan D. Palmer, *Canada's 1960s: The Ironies of Identity in a Rebellious Era* (Toronto: University of Toronto Press, 2008); Lara A. Campbell, Dominique Clement, and Gregory S. Kealey, eds. *Debating Dissent: Canada and the 1960s* (Toronto: University of Toronto Press, 2012); Sean Mills, *The Empire Within: Postcolonial Thought and Political Activism in Sixties Montreal* (Montreal and Kingston: McGill-Queens University Press, 2010); Doug Owram, *Born at the Right Time: A History of the Baby Boom Generation* (Toronto: University of Toronto Press, 1996); Todd Gitlin, *The Sixties: Years of Hope, Days of Rage* (New York: Bantam Books, 1987); Van Gosse, *Rethinking the New Left: An Interpretive History* (New York: Palgrave Macmillan, 2005); and Arthur Marwick, *The Sixties: Cultural Revolution in Britain, France, Italy, and the United States, c.1958–c.1974* (Oxford: Oxford University Press, 1998).

13   James Laxer, Interview with the author, May 29, 2012.

14   See, for example, Jim Harding, "SUPA: an ethical movement in search of an analysis," in *Our Generation Against Nuclear War*, ed. Dimitrios Roussopoulos, (Montreal: Black Rose Books, 1983), 335–343. See also Roberta Lexier, "'The Backdrop Against Which Everything Happened': English-Canadian Student Movements and Off-Campus Movements for Change," *History of Intellectual Culture* Vol.7, No.1 (2007).

15   James Laxer, Interview with the author, May 29, 2012.

16   Lorne Brown, Interview with the author, May 14, 2012.

17   Varda Burstyn, Interview with the author, January 14, 2013.

18   Lorne Brown, Interview with the author, May 14, 2012.

19   "For an Independent Socialist Canada," in Michael Cross, ed. *The Decline and Fall of a Good Idea: CCF-NDP Manifestoes 1932–1969* (Toronto: New Hogtown Press, 1974).

20   Bullen, "The Ontario Waffle and the Struggle for an Independent Socialist Canada," 188.

21   Bullen, "The Ontario Waffle and the Struggle for an Independent Socialist Canada," 196.

22   Bullen, "The Ontario Waffle and the Struggle for an Independent Socialist Canada," 197.

23   James Laxer, Interview with the author, May 29, 2012.

24   Mel Watkins, Interview with the author, June 28, 2012. See also LAC, MG28 IV-I Vol.446–3 "Waffle Publications, 1969–70." "For an Independent Socialist Canada: Resolutions Prepared by the Waffle Movement in the New Democratic Party for the consideration of Riding Associations, Affiliated Local Unions, and Youth Clubs for the Federal Convention of the New Democratic Party, Ottawa, April 1971" and LAC, MG28, Vol.446–3 "Waffle Publications, 1969–71." "James Laxer for NDP National Leader."

25   Bullen, "The Ontario Waffle and the Struggle for an Independent Socialist Canada," 197.

26   Bullen, "The Ontario Waffle and the Struggle for an Independent Socialist Canada," 210.

27   See Roberta Lexier, "Two Nations in Canada: The New Democratic Party, the Waffle Movement, and Nationalism in Quebec," *British Journal of Canadian Studies* Vol.30, No.1 (2017) and Roberta Lexier, "Waffling Towards Parity in the New Democratic Party," in eds. Roberta Lexier and Tamara A. Small, *Mind the Gaps: Canadian Perspectives on Gender and Politics* (Halifax: Fernwood Press, 2013).

28   Stephen Lewis, Interview with the author, April 21, 2013.

29   Michael Lewis, Interview with the author, October 3, 2017.

30   Stephen Lewis, "A report to the Provincial Council by Stephen Lewis MPP for Scarborough West and Leader of the New Democratic Party of Ontario," March 18, 1972, MG28 IV-I Vol.446 'Waffle Ontario Debate, 1971–2,' LAC. Also, Stephen Lewis, Interview with the author, April 21, 2013.

31   Stephen Lewis, "A report to the Provincial Council."

32   Stephen Lewis, Interview with the author, April 21, 2013.

33   Christopher Rootes and Nikos Sotirakopoulos, "Global Justice Movement," in eds. David A. Snow, Donatella Della Porta, Bert Klandermans, and Doug McAdam, *The Wiley-Blackwell Encyclopedia of Social and Political Movements* (New York: Wiley, 2013).

34   Donatella Porta, "Making the Polis: Social Forums and Democracy in The Global Justice Movement," *Mobilization: An International Quarterly* Vol.10, No.1 (2005), 73–94.

35   "Comment: A Discussion Paper on The New Politics Initiative."

36   Dave Meslin, "Four year campaign," Personal Archives.

37 Meslin, "Four year campaign."

38 "Comment: A Discussion Paper on The New Politics Initiative."

39 Nathan Rao, "Rise and Fall of the New Politics Initiative: Lessons for the Left," *New Socialist Magazine*, www.newsocialist.org/old_mag/magazine/47/article0.html. See David Meslin, Interview with the author, October 16, 2017.

40 Meslin, "Four year campaign."

41 Murray Dobbin, "Occupy, the New Politics Initiative and reclaiming the commons," *Rabble.ca*, November 30, 2011.

42 Jim Stanford, "The history of the New Politics Initiative: Movement and party, then and now," *Rabble.ca*, November 29, 2011. See also Jim Stanford, Interview with the author, September 25, 2017.

43 Meslin, "Four year campaign." See also Libby Davies, Interview with the author, September 19, 2017 and Judy Rebick, Interview with the author, October 16, 2017.

44 "Comment: A Discussion Paper on The New Politics Initiative," 145, and Jim Stanford, Interview with the author, September 25, 2017.

45 Judy Rebick, "The New Politics Initiative: Ahead of its time?" *Rabble.ca*, November 29, 2011.

46 Judy Rebick, Interview with the author, October 16, 2017.

47 "New Politics Initiative Newsletter #4," November 7, 2001, https://web.archive.org/web/20031231030322/http://www.newpolitics.ca:80/newsletter.php?ID=6.

48 According to Judy Rebick, anti-globalization activists opposed the term manifesto because it implied a hierarchical process that they did not support. Judy Rebick, Interview with the author, October 16, 2017.

49 Judy Rebick, Interview with the author, October 16, 2017.

50 Morna Ballantyne, Dave Meslin, Judy Rebick, Svend Robinson, and Jim Stanford, "The Left Needs New Voices," *Globe and Mail*, June 7, 2001, A15.

51 Ballantyne, et al., "The Left Needs New Voices."

52 Ballantyne, et al., "The Left Needs New Voices."

53 Jim Stanford, Interview with the author, September 25, 2017; Libby Davies, Interview with the author, September 19, 2017; Judy Rebick, Interview with the author, October 16, 2017

54 Libby Davies, Interview with the author, September 19, 2017, David Meslin, Interview with the author, October 16, 2017; and Buzz Hargrove, Interview with the author, September 15, 2017.

55 "New Politics Initiative Newsletter #4."

56 Stanford, "The history of the New Politics Initiative," and Rao, "Rise and Fall of the New Politics Initiative."

57 See Jon Weier, Interview with the author, October 18, 2017 and Bill Blaikie, Interview with the author, October 5, 2017. See also Rao, "Rise and Fall of the New Politics Initiative."

58 See Jon Weier, Interview with the author, October 18, 2017, and Rao, "Rise and Fall of the New Politic Initiative."

59 Rao, "Rise and Fall of the New Politics Initiative."

60 Marc Lee, "The New Politics Initiative: Reflections on the 10th anniversary," *Rabble.ca*, November 29, 2011. See also Libby Davies, Interview with the author, September 19, 2017; David Meslin, Interview with the author, October 16, 2017; Buzz Hargrove, Interview with the author, September 15, 2017; Jon Weier, Interview with the author, October 18, 2017; Judy Rebick, Interview with the author, October 16, 2017; and Jim Stanford, Interview with the author, September 25, 2017.

61 Libby Davies, Interview with the author, 19 September 2017; David Meslin, Interview with the author, October 16, 2017; Buzz Hargrove, Interview with the author, September 15, 2017; Judy Rebick, Interview with the author, October 16, 2017; and Jim Stanford, Interview with the author, September 25, 2017.

62 Bill Blaikie, Interview with the author, October 5, 2017.

63 See Jim Stanford, Interview with the author, September 25, 2017.

64 Judy Rebick, Interview with the author, October 16, 2017.

65 Libby Davies, Interview with the author, September 19, 2017.

66 David Meslin, Interview with the author, October 16, 2017.

67 Libby Davies, Interview with the author, September 19, 2017.

68 Libby Davies, Interview with the author, September 19, 2017.

69 Libby Davies, Interview with the author, September 19, 2017.

70 See Jon Weier, Interview with the author, October 18, 2017; and Bill Blaikie, Interview with the author, October 5, 2017.

71 Bill Blaikie, Interview with the author, October 5, 2017; and Jon Weier, Interview with the author, October 18, 2017.

72 Bill Blaikie, Interview with the author, October 5, 2017.

73 Libby Davies, Interview with the author, September 19, 2017.

74 See Jim Stanford, Interview with the author, September 25, 2017.

75 Avi Lewis, Interview with the author, October 26, 2017.

76 Gord Doctorow, Interview with the author, October 18, 2017. See also Harry Kopyto, Interview with the author, October 18, 2017.

77 Aaron Wherry, "The Leap Manifesto and When Celebrities Politic," *Maclean's*, September 15, 2015.

78 Gord Doctorow, Interview with the author, October 18, 2017.

79 Avi Lewis, Interview with the author, October 26, 2017.

80 "The Leap Manifesto: A Call for a Canada Based on Caring for the Earth and One Another," https://leapmanifesto.org/en/the-leap-manifesto/#manifesto-content.

81 Avi Lewis, Interview with the author, October 26, 2017.

82 See Bryan Dale, Interview with the author, October 2, 2017; Avi Lewis, Interview with the author, October 26, 2017; and Joshua Ostroff, "Leap Manifesto Calls on Canada to Change, Well, Everything," *HuffPost Canada*, September 15, 2015.

83 Tristin Hopper, "Leap Manifesto Plan to Overthrow Capitalism Puts Spanner in NDP Plans to Convince Centrist Voters," *National Post*, September 16, 2015.

84 See Hopper, "Leap Manifesto Plan," and Jeff Nagel, "ELECTION 2015: NDP Won't be Guided by Leap Manifesto, Cullen Says," *The Columbia Valley Pioneer*, September 28, 2015.

85 Avi Lewis, Interview with the author, October 26, 2017.

86 "The Leap Manifesto."

87 Harry Kopyto, Interview with the author, October 18, 2017.

88 Craig Scott, Interview with the author, September 26, 2017.

89 See Craig Scott, Interview with the author, September 26, 2017; Janet Solberg, Interview with the author, September 22, 2017; and Avi Lewis, Interview with the author, October 26, 2017.

90 NDP, "Resolutions passed at Convention 2016," http://xfer.ndp.ca/2016/documents/EDM2016-Resolutions-BIL-APP_v1.pdf.

91 Janet Solberg, Interview with the author, September 22, 2017; and Avi Lewis, Interview with the author, October 26, 2017.

92 Avi Lewis, Interview with the author, October 26, 2017.

93 "Tom Mulcair Speaks with Peter Mansbridge Ahead of NDP convention," *The National*, April 6, 2016.

94 Avi Lewis, Interview with the author, October 26, 2017.

95 Craig Scott, Interview with the author, September 26, 2017.

96 "Leap Manifesto: NDP Agrees to Explore Staunch Stance on Fossil Fuels," *CBC News*, April 10, 2016.

97 Bill Stadel, "Leap Manifesto: Alberta NDP 'had nothing to do with this nonsense,'" *CBC News*, April 11, 2016.

98 See Craig Scott, Interview with the author, September 26, 2017; Janet Solberg, Interview with the author, September 22, 2017; and Avi Lewis, Interview with the author, October 26, 2017.

99 Avi Lewis, Interview with the author, October 26, 2017.

100 Janet Solberg, Interview with the author, September 22, 2017.

101 Harry Kopyto, Interview with the author, October 18, 2017.

102 Avi Lewis, Interview with the author, October 26, 2017.

103 Bryan Dale, Interview with the author, October 2, 2017.

104 See Bryan Dale, Interview with the author, October 2, 2017; Craig Scott, Interview with the author, September 26, 2017; Janet Solberg, Interview with the author, September 22, 2017; and Avi Lewis, Interview with the author, October 26, 2017.

105 Avi Lewis, Interview with the author, October 26, 2017.

106 Judy Rebick, Interview with the author, October 16, 2017.

107 Avi Lewis, Interview with the author, October 26, 2017.

108 Jim Stanford, Interview with the author, September 25, 2017.

109 Janet Solberg, Interview with the author, September 22, 2017.

110 Bill Blaikie, Interview with the author, October 5, 2017.

Chapter 12: From Traditional Social Democracy to the Third Way

1 Colin Hay, *The Political Economy of New Labour: Labouring Under False Pretenses* (Manchester: Manchester University Press, 1999), 57.

2 Gerassimos Moschonas, *In the Name of Social Democracy: The Great Transformation, 1945 to the Present* (London: Verso, 2002), 21.

3 Ashley Lavelle, *The Death of Social Democracy: Political Consequences in the 21st Century* (Aldershot, Eng.: Ashgate), 12. See also Thomas I. Palley, "From Keynesianism to Neoliberalism: Shifting Paradigms in Economics," in ed. Alfredo Saad-Filho and Deborah Johnston, *Neoliberalism: A Critical Reader* (Chicago: University of Chicago Press, 2004).

4 Frances Fox Piven, "The Decline of Labor Parties: An Overview," in ed. Frances Fox Piven, *Labor Parties in Postindustrial Societies* (Cambridge, UK: Polity Press, 1991), 7–8; James Cronin, George Ross and James Schoch, "Introduction: The New World of the Center-Left," in ed. Cronin, Ross, and Schoch, *What's Left of the Left: Democrats and Social Democrats in Challenging Times* (Durham, NC: Duke University Press, 2011), 6–8.

5 Anthony Giddens, *The Third Way: The Renewal of Social Democracy* (Cambridge, UK: Polity Press), 26.

6 Sheri Berman, *The Primacy of Politics: Social Democracy and the Making of Europe's Twentieth Century* (Cambridge, UK: Cambridge University Press, 2006), 212; Leo Panitch and Colin Leys, *The End of Parliamentary Socialism: From New Left to New Labour* (London: Verso, 2001), 288.

7 Bryan Evans, "From Protest Movement to Neoliberal Management: Canada's New Democratic Party in the Era of Permanent Austerity," in eds. Bryan Evans and Ingo Schmidt, *Social Democracy After the Cold War* (Edmonton: AU Press, 2012), 48. For internal debates within the party, see for example ed. Z. David Berlin and Howard Aster, *What's Left?: The New Democratic Party in Renewal* (Oakville, ON: Mosaic Press, 2001).

8 Jeffrey Parker and Laura Stephenson, "Who Supports the NDP?" (Paper prepared for presentation at the annual meeting at the Canadian Political Science Association, Vancouver, June 4-6, 2008), 8, http://cpsa-acsp.ca/papers-2008/Parker-Stephenson.pdf.

9 "The Quiet Way," *The Economist*, September 2, 1999, www.economist.com/node/236199.

10 Jim Stanford, "Social Democratic Policy: The Canadian Experience," in eds. Philip Arestis and Malcolm C. Sawyer, *The Economics of the Third Way: Experiences from Around the World* (Cheltenham, UK: Edward Elgar), 87.

11 Lynda Erickson and David Laycock, "Party History and Electoral Fortunes, 1961–2003," in eds. David Laycock and Lynda Erickson, *Reviving Social Democracy: The Near Death and Surprising Rise of the Federal NDP* (Vancouver: University of British Columbia Press, 2015), 32.

12 Murray Cooke, "Layton's Legacy and the NDP Leadership Race," *New Socialist*, September 20, 2011, http://newsocialist.org/laytons-legacy-and-the-ndp-leadership-race.

13 Parker and Stephenson, "Who Supports the NDP?" 5.

14 Alan Whitehorn, "Jack Layton and the NDP: Gains But No Breakthrough," in eds. Jon H. Pammett and Christopher Dornan, *The Canadian General Election of 2004* (Toronto: Dundurn Press, 2004), 118.

15 Brad Lavigne, *Building the Orange Wave: The Inside Story Behind the Historic Rise of Jack Layton and the NDP* (Madeira Park, BC: Douglas and McIntyre), 190–91.

16 New Democratic Party, *Meeting the Challenge: Ed Broadbent and the New Democrats Speak Up for Average Canadians* (Ottawa: New Democratic Party, 1988), n.p., www.poltext.org/

sites/poltext.org/files/plateformes/can1988ndp_plt_en._14112008_181303.pdf.

17 New Democratic Party, *Strategy for a Full Employment Economy: A Jobs Plan for Canada from Canada's New Democrats* (Ottawa: New Democratic Party, 1993), 2.

18 NDP, *Strategy for a Full Employment Economy*, 5.

19 New Democratic Party, *A Framework for Canada's Future: Make Good Jobs the Priority* (Ottawa: New Democratic Party, 1997), n.p., www.poltext.org/sites/poltext.org/files/plateformes/can1997ndp_plt_en._14112008_175711.pdf.

20 New Democratic Party, *The NDP Commitment to Canadians: Think How Much Better Canada Could Be* (Ottawa: New Democratic Party, 2000), 2, www.poltext.org/sites/poltext.org/files/plateformes/can2000ndp_plt_en._14112008_173645.pdf.

21 NDP, *The NDP Commitment to Canadians*, 8.

22 NDP, *The NDP Commitment to Canadians*, 3.

23 New Democratic Party, *Jack Layton NDP: New Energy. A Positive Choice* (Ottawa: New Democratic Party, 2004), 62, www.poltext.org/sites/poltext.org/files/plateformes/can-2004ndp_plt_en._14112008_171856.pdf.

24 New Democratic Party, *Jack Layton: Getting Results for People* (Ottawa: New Democratic Party, 2006), www.poltext.org/sites/poltext.org/files/plateformes/can2006ndp_plt_en._14112008_165642.pdf.

25 New Democratic Party, *Jack Layton and the New Democrats: A Prime Minister on Your Family's Side, for a Change* (Ottawa: New Democratic Party, 2008), 7, www.poltext.org/sites/poltext.org/files/plateformes/can2008ndp_plt_eng._14112008_160417.pdf.

26 NDP, *Jack Layton and the New Democrats*, 11.

27 New Democratic Party, *Giving Your Family a Break: Practical First Steps* (Ottawa: New Democratic Party, 2011), 1, www.poltext.org/sites/poltext.org/files/plateformes/can-2011ndp_plt_en_12072011_114905.pdf.

28 NDP, *Giving Your Family a Break*, 23.

29 NDP, *Meeting the Challenge*, n.p.

30 The Canadian left has commonly opposed sales taxes and argued instead for progressive taxation. Yet this debate often views taxes in isolation from the services they fund and revenue they raise for public services that have a net progressive and redistributive effect. The Scandinavian countries have long relied heavily on sales taxes to pay for their more extensive welfare states. See for example Matt Fodor, "Fueling the Tax Revolt: What's Wrong with the NDP's Anti-HST Campaign," *The Bullet*, September 3, 2010, www.socialistproject.ca/bullet/410.php.

31 NDP, *Strategy for a Full Employment Economy*, 55–56.

32 NDP, *A Framework for Canada's Future*, n.p.

33 Stanford, "Social Democratic Policy," 87.

34 NDP, *The NDP Commitment to Canadians*, 16.

35 NDP, *Jack Layton NDP*, 60–61.

36 NDP, *Jack Layton*, 4.

37 NDP, *Jack Layton and the New Democrats*, 11.

38 NDP, *Giving Your Family a Break*, 9.

39 NDP, *Giving Your Family a Break*, 8.

40 NDP, *Meeting the Challenge*, n.p. However, while free trade did appear in the 1988 platform, the NDP came under heavy criticism for downplaying the free trade issue during the campaign. See for example Janine Brodie, "Comment: The Free Trade Election," *Studies in Political Economy* 28, Spring 1989.

41 NDP, *Strategy for a Full Employment Economy*, 44–45.

42 NDP, *A Framework for Canada's Future*, n.p.

43 NDP, *The NDP Commitment to Canadians*, 8.

44 NDP, *The NDP Commitment to Canadians*, 9.

45 NDP, *The NDP Commitment to Canadians*, 11.

46 NDP, *The NDP Commitment to Canadians*, 13.

47 NDP, *Jack Layton NDP*, 50.

48 NDP, *Jack Layton NDP*, 10, 46–47.

49 NDP, *Jack Layton NDP*, 44–45.

50 NDP, *Jack Layton*, 31.

51 NDP, *Jack Layton*, 28.
52 NDP, *Jack Layton and the New Democrats*, 7.
53 NDP, *Jack Layton and the New Democrats*, 10.
54 NDP, *Jack Layton and the New Democrats*, 17.
55 NDP, *Jack Layton and the New Democrats*, 37.
56 NDP, *Giving Your Family a Break*, 6.
57 NDP, *Meeting the Challenge*, n.p.
58 NDP, *Strategy for a Full Employment Economy*, 11–12.
59 NDP, *A Framework for Canada's Future*, n.p.
60 NDP, *The NDP Commitment to Canadians*, 4.
61 NDP, *The NDP Commitment to Canadians*, 11–12.
62 NDP, *Jack Layton NDP*, 5.
63 NDP, *Jack Layton NDP*, 13–14.
64 NDP, *Jack Layton NDP*, 11.
65 NDP, *Jack Layton NDP*, 51.
66 NDP, *Jack Layton*, 34–35.
67 NDP, *Jack Layton*, 12–14.
68 NDP, *Jack Layton*, 37–38.
69 NDP, *Jack Layton and the New Democrats*, 17–19.
70 NDP, *Jack Layton and the New Democrats*, 20–23.
71 David McGrane, "Political Marketing and the NDP's Historic Breakthrough," in eds. Jon H. Pammett and Christopher Dornan, *The Canadian Federal Election of 2011* (Toronto: Dundurn, 2011), 82.
72 NDP, *Giving Your Family a Break*, 10–11.
73 NDP, *Giving Your Family a Break*, 5–6.
74 McGrane, "Political Marketing," 81.
75 Matt Fodor, "Mulcair's Victory: What Does It Mean?" *The Bullet*, April 6, 2012, www.socialistproject.ca/bullet/613.php.
76 "Thomas Mulcair Promises a Balanced Budget Next Year, Says NDP Won't Run a Deficit to Finance Promises," *National Post*, August 25, 2015, http://nationalpost.com/news/politics/thomas-mulcair-promises-a-balanced-budget-next-year-says-ndp-wont-run-a-deficit-to-finance-promises. Daniel LeBlanc, "Liberals Promise $10-billion Yearly Deficits to Kickstart Economy," *Globe and Mail*, August 27, 2015, http://beta.theglobeandmail.com/news/politics/liberals-propose-modest-deficits-in-order-to-kickstart-the-economy/article26125406/. Ben Spurr, "Mulcair's Vow of Balanced Budget Will Lead to Austerity Measures, Liberals Warn," *Toronto Star*, August 25, 2015, www.thestar.com/news/federal-election/2015/08/26/mulcairs-vow-of-balanced-budget-will-lead-to-austerity-measures-liberals-warn.html.
77 New Democratic Party, *Building the Country of Our Dreams: Tom Mulcair's Plan to Bring Change to Ottawa* (Ottawa: New Democratic Party, 2015), 19, xfer.ndp.ca/2015/2015-Full-Platform-EN.pdf.
78 NDP, *Building the Country*, 2.
79 NDP, *Building the Country*, 6.
80 United Steelworkers, "The NDP Stands on Solid Ground with Tom Mulcair," March 29, 2016, www.usw.ca/news/media-centre/releases/2016/ndp-stands-on-solid-ground-with-mulcair.
81 For instance, the plan for universal drug coverage did not explicitly state that it would extend medicare to include pharmacare—and the cost ($2.6 billion over four years) was significantly less than that of the proposed catastrophic drug plan of 2008 ($4.5 billion). See NDP, *Building the Country*, 64, and New Democratic Party, *Platform 2008 Explanatory Tables* (Ottawa: New Democratic Party, 2008), 6, www.poltext.org/sites/poltext.org/files/plateformes/can2008ndp_table_eng._14112008_163042.pdf.
82 NDP, *Building the Country*, 11.
83 And, hence, the estimated revenue raised was significantly less ($33.7 billion over four years in 2011 vs. $14.8 billion in 2015). See NDP, *Building the Country*, 62, and NDP, *Giving Your Family A Break*, http://xfer.ndp.ca/2011/2011-Platform/NDP2011PlatformSS_web_en.pdf.

84 NDP, *Building the Country*, 59.
85 Maura Forrest and John Ivison, "Jagmeet Singh on Taking on Trudeau, Winning Over Quebec and Now Being 'Sufficiently Electable'," *National Post*, last updated September 28, 2017, http://nationalpost.com/news/politics/jagmeet-singh-on-taking-on-trudeau-winning-over-quebec-and-being-sufficiently-electable.
86 "Tax Fairness Agenda," www.jagmeetsingh.ca/tax_fairness_agenda.
87 Thomas Walkom, "NDP Leadership Rebel Jagmeet Singh Takes Aim at Old Age Security," *Toronto Star,* July 26, 2017, www.thestar.com/opinion/commentary/2017/07/26/ndp-leadership-rebel-jagmeet-singh-takes-aim-at-old-age-security-walkom.html.
88 Gerald Caplan, "Jagmeet Singh Has 'Winner' Written All Over Him," *Globe and Mail*, October 3, 2017, https://beta.theglobeandmail.com/opinion/jagmeet-singh-has-winner-written-all-over-him/article36472291/.

Chapter 14: The CCF/NDP and Populisms of the Left and the Right

1 Christopher Dornan argues that during the 2011 federal election, the NDP soared on "a populist surge in which the party became the magnetic pole for opposition to the Conservatives." In doing so, Dornan highlights Layton's "charismatic" leadership. Christopher Dornan, "From Contempt of Parliament to a Majority Mandate," in eds. Jon H. Pammett and Christopher Dornan, *The Canadian Federal Election of 2011* (Toronto: Dundurn, 2011), 8.
2 Critics, including Michael Laxer, Rick Salutin, and Judy Rebick, described the Ontario NDP as right-wing populists under Horwath's leadership. Michael Laxer, "The Perils of Populism: Andrea Horwath, Taxes, Road Tolls and the 'War on the Car,'" *Rabble*, March 22, 2013. Rick Salutin, "Andrea Horwath's Right-Wing Populism," *Toronto Star*, May 8, 2014. Rebick is quoted in CBC, "Andrea Horwath Campaign Leaves Prominent NDP Supporters 'Deeply Distressed'," *CBC News*, May 23, 2014. Yet, as Salutin later pointed out, the problem wasn't populism *per se*. The concerns were with political drift to the centre or right, of the political spectrum. See Rick Salutin, "What's Wrong with Right-wing Populism Anyway?" *Toronto Star*, June 5, 2014.
3 David Laycock, *Populism and Democratic Thought in the Canadian Prairies, 1910 to 1945* (Toronto: University of Toronto, 1990), 14.
4 For example, Jan-Werner Müller describes populists as "a real danger to democracy." Müller, *What Is Populism?* (Philadelphia: University of Pennsylvania Press, 2016), 103. Some, such as Margaret Canovan, present a qualified defence of populism, while Ernesto Laclau essentially equated populism with democracy. See Margaret Canovan, *The People* (Cambridge: Polity, 2005) and Ernesto Laclau. *On Populist Reason* (London: Verso, 2005).
5 I'm particularly indebted to the work of David Laycock who in turn credits Ernesto Laclau's work. See Laycock, *Populism and Democratic Thought in the Canadian Prairies*; David Laycock, *The New Right and Democracy in Canada: Understanding Reform and the Canadian Alliance* (Toronto: Oxford University Press, 2002); David Laycock, "Populism and the New Right in English Canada," in ed. Francisco Panizza, *Populism and the Mirror of Democracy* (London: Verso, 2005), 172–201. See also Trevor Harrison, *Of Passionate Intensity: Right-Wing Populism and the Reform Party of Canada* (Toronto: University of Toronto Press, 1995); Trevor Harrison, "The Changing Face of Prairie Politics: Populism in Alberta," eds. Todd A. Radenbaugh and Patrick Douaud, *Changing Prairie Landscapes* (Regina: Canadian Plains Research Centre, University of Regina, 2000), 95–108; Trevor Harrison, "Populist and Conservative Christian Evangelical Movements: A Comparison of Canada and the United States," in ed. Miriam Smith, *Group Politics and Social Movements in Canada*, 2nd ed. (Toronto: University of Toronto Press, 2014).
6 As Mudde and Rovira Kaltwasser note, "almost all concepts of populism share the idea that the latter always alludes to a confrontation between 'the people' and 'the establishment'." Cas Mudde and Cristóbal Rovira Kaltwasser, "Populism and (Liberal) Democracy: A Framework for Analysis," in eds. Cas Mudde and Cristóbal Rovira Kaltwasser, *Populism in Europe and the Americas: Threat or Corrective for Democracy?* (Cambridge: Cambridge University Press, 2012), 8.
7 Laycock, *Populism and Democratic Thought in the Canadian Prairies*.

8   On May 26, 1932, at a meeting in William Irvine's Parliament Hill office, the Ginger
      Group MPs passed a motion to create a new party. Kenneth McNaught, *A Prophet in
      Politics: A Biography of J. S. Woodsworth* (Toronto: University of Toronto Press), 259–60.

9   With this diversity of influences, it is important to not reduce the CCF to prairie popu-
      lism. For an excellent analysis of the formation of the CCF and the particular significance
      of the "labour socialists," see James Naylor, *The Fate of Labour Socialism: The Co-operative
      Commonwealth Federation and the Dream of a Working-Class Future* (Toronto: University of
      Toronto Press, 2016).

10   Robert A. J. McDonald, "'Telford Time' and the Populist Origins of the CCF in British
      Columbia," *Labour/Le Travail*, 71 (2013), 88. For a compelling critique of McDonald's
      article that emphasizes the predominance of working-class-based socialism over populism
      in the BC CCF, see James Naylor, "The British Columbia CCF's Working-Class Moment:
      Socialism Not Populism," *Labour/Le Travail*, 71 (2013), 101–21.

11   McDonald, "'Telford Time' and the Populist Origins of the CCF in British Columbia," 94.

12   Laycock, *Populism and Democratic Thought in the Canadian Prairies*, ch. 4.

13   Laycock, *Populism and Democratic Thought in the Canadian Prairies*, 144.

14   S. M. Lipset, *Agrarian Socialism*, revised and expanded edition (Berkeley: University of
      California Press, 1971), 183.

15   Lipset, *Agrarian Socialism*, 181.

16   www.socialisthistory.ca/Docs/CCF/ReginaManifesto.htm.

17   Alvin Finkel, *The Social Credit Phenomenon in Alberta* (Toronto: University of Toronto
      Press, 1989); Laycock, *Populism and Democratic Thought in the Canadian Prairies*, ch. 5;
      Edward Bell, *Social Classes and Social Credit in Alberta* (Montreal and Kingston: McGill-
      Queen's University Press, 1993).

18   Finkel, *The Social Credit Phenomenon in Alberta*, 4. For a discussion of Aberhart's religious
      views, see Clark Banack, *God's Province: Evangelical Christianity, Political Thought, and
      Conservatism in Alberta* (Montreal and Kingston: McGill-Queen's University Press, 2016).
      C. B. Macpherson's classic work, *Democracy in Alberta: The Theory and Practice of a Qua-
      si-Party System* (Toronto: University of Toronto Press, 1953) portrayed Social Credit as
      predominately based on the support of rural independent commodity producers or *petite
      bourgeoisie*. Some subsequent studies have emphasized that initially, Social Credit also had
      urban, including working class, support. See Edward Bell, *Social Classes and Social Credit in
      Alberta*.

19   Finkel, *The Social Credit Phenomenon in Alberta*, 211.

20   Available online via the Bible Bill Historical Foundation website,
      www.aberhartfoundation.ca/PDF%20Documents/Social%20Credit%20Pamplets/SC%20
      1935%20Platform.pdf.

21   David Laycock, *The New Right and Democracy in Canada: Understanding Reform and the
      Canadian Alliance* (Toronto: Oxford University Press, 2002), 10.

22   S. M. Lipset, *Agrarian Socialism*, revised and expanded edition (Berkeley: University of
      California Press, 1971), 139.

23   Thomas H. McLeod and Ian McLeod, *Tommy Douglas: The Road to Jerusalem* (Edmonton:
      Hurtig Publishers, 1987), 61–67.

24   The prevalence of social credit theories within the BC CCF and, in particular, Lyle
      Telford's emphasis on monetary reform, is a central point in McDonald, "'Telford Time'
      and the Populist Origins of the CCF in British Columbia." Edward Bell argued that the
      CCF's Regina Manifesto "is replete with Social Credit phraseology and ideas." Edward
      Bell, *Social Classes and Social Credit in Alberta*, 158.

25   McDonald, "'Telford Time' and the Populist Origins of the CCF in British Columbia," 96.

26   Finkel, *The Social Credit Phenomenon in Alberta*, 3. Lipset made the same point, *Agrarian
      Socialism*, 156, 334.

27   The prevalence of anti-Semitism in the Social Credit movement and the response of the
      Canadian Jewish Congress has been demonstrated by Janine Stingel, *Social Discredit:
      Anti-Semitism, Social Credit, and the Jewish Response* (Montreal and Kingston: McGill-
      Queen's University Press, 2000).

28   That was certainly Lipset's position.

29   Notable examples included R. T. Naylor, "Appendix: The Ideological Foundations of Social

Democracy and Social Credit," in ed. Gary Teeple, *Capitalism and the National Question in Canada* (Toronto: University of Toronto Press, 1972); Peter R. Sinclair, "Class Structure and Populist Protest: The Case of Western Canada," *Canadian Journal of Sociology*, 1 (1975), 1–17; J. F. Conway, "Populism in the United States, Russia, and Canada: Explaining the Roots of Canada's Third Parties," *Canadian Journal of Political Science*, 11, 1 (1978), 99–124; J. F. Conway, "The Prairie Populist Resistance to the National Policy: Some Reconsiderations," *Journal of Canadian Studies*, 13, 3 (1979), 77–91.

30   David Lewis and Frank Scott, *Make This Your Canada: A Review of CCF History and Policy* (Winnipeg: Hybrid Publishers, 2001).

31   Lewis and Scott, *Make This Your Canada*, 81–82.

32   www.socialisthistory.ca/Docs/CCF/Winnipeg.htm.

33   The New Party Declaration also noted that "the economy is effectively in the hands of corporate giants" and spoke of "curbing corporate control." The New Party Declaration is reproduced in Michael S. Cross, *The Decline and Fall of a Good Idea: CCF Manifestoes, 1932 to 1969* (Toronto: New Hogtown Press, 1974), 33–42.

34   Michael S. Cross, *The Decline and Fall of a Good Idea*, 35.

35   According to the Waffle Manifesto presented to the NDP federal convention in 1969, "the achievement of socialism awaits the building of a mass base of socialists, in factories and offices, on farms and campuses." www.socialisthistory.ca/Docs/Waffle/WaffleManifesto. htm. The Waffle Manifesto is also reproduced in Michael S. Cross, *The Decline and Fall of a Good Idea*, 43–45.

36   All quotations come from the Waffle Manifesto as reproduced in Michael S. Cross, *The Decline and Fall of a Good Idea*, 43–45.

37   Bradford and Jenson argue that the emphasis on populist rhetoric served to mask an underlying weakness of social democratic thought and internal divisions within the NDP. Neil Bradford and Jane Jenson, "Facing Economic Restructuring and Constitutional Renewal: Social Democracy Adrift in Canada," in ed. Frances Fox Piven, *Labor Parties in Post-industrial Societies* (Oxford: Polity, 1991).

38   David Lewis, *Louder Voices: The Corporate Welfare Bums* (Toronto: James Lewis & Samuel, 1972), 11.

39   Alan Whitehorn, *Canadian Socialism: Essays on the CCF-NDP* (Toronto: Oxford University Press, 1992), 91.

40   "Standing up for Ordinary Canadians" was the NDP slogan during the 1984 election. On this campaign and Broadbent's depiction of the Liberals and Conservatives as the "Bobbsey Twins of Bay Street," see Desmond Morton, *The New Democrats, 1961–1986: The Politics of Change* (Toronto: Copp Clark Pitman, 1986), 217–220. In the 1988 campaign, the NDP opted for the term "Average Canadians." Whitehorn, *Canadian Socialism*, 215.

41   Whitehorn, *Canadian Socialism*, Ch. 8; Rick Salutin, *Waiting for Democracy: A Citizen's Journey* (Markham: Viking, 1989).

42   David Laycock, "Conceptual Foundations of Continuity and Change in NDP Ideology," in eds. David Laycock and Lynda Erickson, *Reviving Social Democracy: The Near Death and Surprising Rise of the Federal NDP* (Vancouver: University of British Columbia Press, 2015), 133–134.

43   NDP, *Giving Your Family a Break: Practical First Steps* (Ottawa, New Democratic Party, 2011), 1.

44   Steven Weldon, "The 2011 Election and Beyond," in eds. David Laycock and Lynda Erickson, *Reviving Social Democracy: The Near Death and Surprising Rise of the Federal NDP* (Vancouver: University of British Columbia Press, 2015), 290, 292.

45   Michael Kazin, *The Populist Persuasion: An American History* (Ithaca: Cornell University Press, 1998).

46   See Stuart Hall's famous essay, "The Great Moving Right Show," originally published in 1979 and reprinted (among other places) in Stuart Hall, *Selected Political Writings: The Great Moving Right Show and Other Essays* (Durham, NC: Duke University Press, 2017).

47   Whitehorn, *Canadian Socialism*, 81.

48   Maurice Pinard, *The Rise of a Third Party: A Study in Crisis Politics* (Montreal and Kingston: McGill-Queen's University Press, 1975).

49   Michael Adams, "The October 1992 Canadian Constitutional Referendum: The

Socio-Political Context," in eds. Kenneth McRoberts and Patrick J. Monahan, *The Charlottetown Accord, the Referendum, and the Future of Canada* (Toronto: University of Toronto Press, 1993).

50 Cited in Leo Panitch, "A Different Kind of State?" in eds. Gregory Albo, David Langille, and Leo Panitch, *A Different Kind of State? Popular Power and Democratic Administration* (Toronto: Oxford University Press, 1994), 4.

51 Neil Nevitte, *The Decline of Deference: Canadian Value Change in Cross-National Perspective* (Peterborough: Broadview Press, 1996).

52 The NDP struggled to stake out its own social democratic position throughout the constitutional debates from the 1960s to the 1990s. The federal NDP demonstrated a disturbing willingness to embrace the constitutional initiative of the government of the day, whether it was Pierre Trudeau or Brian Mulroney. See Murray Cooke, "Constitutional Confusion on the Left: The NDP's Position in the Constitutional Debates," Paper presented at the Annual Meeting of the Canadian Political Science Association, Winnipeg, June 3–5, 2004, www.cpsa-acsp.ca/papers-2004/Cooke.pdf.

53 Brooke Jeffrey, *Strange Bedfellows, Trying Times: October 1992 and the Defeat of the Powerbrokers* (Toronto: Key Porter, 1993).

54 Jeffrey Simpson, "The Referendum and its Aftermath," eds. Kenneth McRoberts and Patrick J. Monahan, *The Charlottetown Accord, the Referendum, and the Future of Canada* (Toronto: University of Toronto Press, 1993); 194.

55 Mark Lisac, *The Klein Revolution* (Edmonton: NeWest Press, 1995); Kevin Taft, *Shredding the Public Interest: Ralph Klein and 25 Years of One-Party Government* (Edmonton: University of Alberta Press, 1997); Yonatan Reshef and Sandra Rastin, *Unions in the Time of Revolution: Government Restructuring in Alberta and Ontario* (Toronto: University of Toronto Press, 2003); Trevor Harrison, ed. *The Return of the Trojan Horse: Alberta and the New World (Dis)Order* (Montreal: Black Rose, 2005).

56 Steve Patten, "Preston Manning's Populism: Constructing the Common Sense of the Common People," *Studies in Political Economy*, 50 (1996), 95–132.

57 Diana Ralph, André Régimbald, and Nérée St-Amand, eds. *Open for Business/Closed to People: Mike Harris's Ontario* (Halifax: Fernwood, 1997); Sid Noel, ed. *Revolution at Queen's Park: Essays on Governing Ontario* (Toronto: Lorimer, 1997); Stephen Dale, *Lost in the Suburbs: A Political Travelogue* (Toronto: Stoddart, 1999); Reshef and Rastin, *Unions in the Time of Revolution*; Kirsten Kozolanka, *The Power of Persuasion: The Politics of the New Right in Ontario* (Montreal: Black Rose, 2007); Jackie Esmonde, "Criminalizing Poverty: The Criminal Law Power and the Safe Streets Act," *Journal of Law and Social Policy*, 17 (2002), 63–86.

58 Laycock, *The New Right*, ch. 7.

59 Lynda Erickson and David Laycock, "Party History and Electoral Fortunes, 1961–2003," in eds. David Laycock and Lynda Erickson, *Reviving Social Democracy: The Near Death and Surprising Rise of the Federal NDP* (Vancouver: University of British Columbia Press, 2015), 25.

60 James Farney, "Canadian Populism in the Era of the United Right," in ed. James Farney and David Rayside, *Conservatism in Canada*, (Toronto: University of Toronto Press, 2013), 43–58.

61 Tom Flanagan, *Waiting for the Wave: The Reform Party and the Conservative Movement* (Montreal and Kingston: McGill-Queen's University Press, 2009).

62 Clark Banack, "Government for the People, Not by the People: Populism and Parliamentary Governance under Stephen Harper," eds. Teresa Healy and Stuart Trew, *The Harper Record 2008-2015* (Ottawa: Canadian Centre for Policy Alternatives, 2015), 91.

63 Rob Ford's father, Doug Ford Sr., served as a Conservative Member of the Provincial Parliament during the first term of the Mike Harris government. For an analysis that emphasizes the connection between the failure of the left and the rise of Rob Ford, see Todd Gordon, "Rob Ford, Ford Nation and the Suburbs: What's Going On?" New Socialist website, November 25, 2013, www.newsocialist.org/rob-ford-ford-nation-and-the-suburbs-what-s-going-on/.

64 Stefan Kipfer and Parastou Saberi, "From 'Revolution' to Farce? Hard-Right Populism in the Making of Toronto," *Studies in Political Economy*, 93 (2014), 134.

65 Mark P. Thomas and Steven Tufts have looked at the impact of right-wing populism on

the labour movement and the potential for a renewed left populism. Steven Tufts and Mark P. Thomas, "Populist Unionism Confronts Austerity in Canada," *Labor Studies Journal*, 39, 1 (2014), 60–82; Mark P. Thomas and Steven Tufts, "Austerity, Right Populism, and the Crisis of Labour in Canada," *Antipode*, 48, 1 (2015), 212–30.

66 Andrew Jackson, "Census Data Shows Income Inequality Remains a Major Challenge," *Globe and Mail*, October 8, 2017.

67 Former staffers on the Sanders campaign, Becky Bond and Zack Exley, discuss the limitations of the Sanders campaign in terms of anti-racist politics and emphasize the need to make anti-racist politics a central part of left-populist politics. Bond and Exley, *Rules for Revolutionaries: How Big Organizing Could Change Everything* (White River Junction, VT: Chelsea Green Publishing, 2017).

Chapter 15: Medicare and Social Democracy in Canada

1 G. P. Marchildon, "The Three Dimensions of Universality in Canadian Medicare," *Canadian Public Administration* 57, 3 (2014): 362–82 and G. P. Marchildon, "Douglas versus Manning: The Ideological Battle over Medicare in Postwar Canada," *Journal of Canadian Studies*. 50, 1 (2016): 129–49.

2 G. P. Marchildon, "The Three Dimensions of Universality in Canadian Medicare," *Canadian Public Administration* 57, 3 (2014): 362–82.

3 G. Lawson, "The Road Not Taken: The 1945 Health Services Planning Commission Proposals and Physician Remuneration in Saskatchewan," in ed. G. P. Marchildon, *Medicare: Facts, Myths, Problems and Promise* (Toronto: James Lorimer & Company, 2007), pp. 151–82.

4 G. P. Marchildon, "The Douglas Legacy and the Future of Medicare," in eds. B. Campbell and G. P. Marchildon, *Medicare: Facts, Myths, Problems and Promise* (Toronto: James Lorimer & Company, 2007).

5 M. Lux, *Separate Beds: A History of Indian Hospitals in Canada, 1920s–1980s* (Toronto: University of Toronto Press, 2016).

6 J. T. H. Connor, M. G. Kidd, and M. Mathews, "Conceptualizing Health Care in Rural and Remote Pre-Confederation Newfoundland as Ecosystem," *Newfoundland and Labrador Studies,* 30, 1 (2015): 113–38 and G. Lawson, and A. E. Noseworthy, "Newfoundland's Cottage Hospital Systems: 1920–1970," *Canadian Bulletin of Medical History*. 26, 2 (2009): 477–98.

7 D. Gagan and R. Gagan, *For Patients of Moderate Means: A Social History of the Voluntary Public General Hospital in Canada, 1890–1950* (Montreal and Kingston: McGill-Queen's University Press, 2002); W. Feindel and R. Leblanc, *The Wounded Brain Healed: The Golden Age of the Montreal Neurological Institute, 1934–1984* (Montreal and Kingston: McGill-Queens University Press, 2016); and E. Shorter, *Partnership for Excellence: Medicine at the University of Toronto and Academic Hospitals* (Toronto: University of Toronto Press, 2013).

8 E. Dyck and A. Deighton, *Managing Madness: The Weyburn Mental Hospital and Transformations of Psychiatric Care in Canada* (Winnipeg: University of Manitoba Press, 2017).

9 D. E. Chunn, *From Punishment to Doing Good: Family Courts and Socialized Justice in Ontario, 1880–1940* (Toronto: University of Toronto Press, 1992).

10 Lux, *Separate Beds.*

11 Gagan and Gagan, *For Patients of Moderate Means.*

12 C. S. Houston and M. Massie, *36 Steps on the Road to Medicare: How Saskatchewan Led the Way* (Montreal and Kingston: McGill-Queen's University Press, 2013). M. G. Taylor, *Health Insurance and Canadian Public Policy: The Seven Decisions that Created the Canadian Health Insurance System and Their Outcomes* (Montreal and Kingston: McGill-Queen's University Press, 1987).

13 C. D. Naylor, *Private Practice, Public Payment: Canadian Medicine and the Politics of Health Insurance, 1911–1966* (Montreal and Kingston: McGill-Queen's Press, 1986).

14 www.connexions.org/CxLibrary/Docs/CX5373-ReginaManifesto.htm.

15 P. Marier, "A Swedish Welfare State in North America? The Creation and Expansion of the Saskatchewan Welfare State, 1944–1982," *Journal of Policy History,* 25(4): 614–37.

16 A. W. Johnson, *Dream No Little Dreams: A Biography of the Douglas Government of Sas-*

katchewan, 1944–1961 (Toronto: University of Toronto Press, 2004) and Taylor, *Health Insurance and Canadian Public Policy.*

17   Marchildon, "The Douglas Legacy and the Future of Medicare" and Johnson, *Dream No Little Dreams.*

18   Johnson, *Dream No Little Dreams* and T. H. McLeod and I. McLeod, *Tommy Douglas: The Road to Jerusalem* (Edmonton: Hurtig, 1987).

19   J. Duffin, "The Guru and the Godfather: Henry Sigerist, Hugh MacLean, and the Politics of Health Care Reform in 1940s Canada," *Canadian Bulletin of Medical History. 9*, 2 (1992): 191–218.

20   Johnson, *Dream No Little Dreams.*

21   G. P. Marchildon, "Agenda Setting in a Parliamentary Federation: Universal Medicare in Canada" in ed. M. Hill, *Studying Public Policy: An International Approach* (Bristol, UK: Policy Press, 2014).

22   Marchildon, "Douglas versus Manning."

23   For more detailed and in-depth comparisons of the different models in Alberta and Saskatchewan, see especially: Marchildon, "The three dimensions of universality"; Marchildon, "Douglas versus Manning"; G. P. Marchildon and N. C. O'Byrne, "From Bennettcare to Medicare: The Morphing of Medical Care Insurance in British Columbia," *Canadian Bulletin of Medical History, 26*, 2 (2009): 453–75.

24   Marchildon, "Agenda Setting in a Parliamentary Federation."

25   G. P. Marchildon and K. Schrijvers, "Physician Resistance and the Forging of Public Healthcare: A Comparative Analysis of the Doctors' Strikes in Canada and Belgium in the 1960s.," *Medical History, 55*, 2 (2011): 203–22.

26   S. Rands, *Privilege and Policy: A History of Community Clinics in Saskatchewan* (Regina: Canadian Plains Research Centre, 2012).

27   R. F. Badgley and S. Wolfe, *Doctor's Strike: Medical Care and Conflict in Saskatchewan* (New York: Abingdon, 1967) and Johnson, *Dream No Little Dreams.*

28   Rands, *Privilege and Policy.*

29   C. H. Tuohy, *Accidental Logics: The Dynamics of Change in the Health Care Arena in the United States, Britain and Canada* (New York: Oxford University Press, 1999) and G. P. Marchildon, "Legacy of the Doctors' Strike and the Saskatoon Agreement," *Canadian Medical Association Journal* 188, 8 (2016): 676–77.

30   G. Esping-Andersen, *The Three Worlds of Welfare Capitalism* (Princeton: Princeton University Press, 1990).

31   T. Foubister, S. Thomson, E. Mossialos, and A. McGuire, *Private Medical Insurance in the United Kingdom* (Brussels: European Observatory on Health Systems and Policies, 2006).

32   Marchildon, "Legacy of the Doctors' Strike and the Saskatoon Agreement."

33   Esping-Andersen, *Three Worlds of Welfare Capitalism.*

34   Hall Commission, *Royal Commission on Health Care Services, 1961–1964* (Ottawa, 1964); M. Lalond, *A New Perspective on the Health of Canadians: A Working Document* (Ottawa: National Health and Welfare, 1974); *Standing Senate Committee on the Social Affairs, Science and Technology of the State of the Health Care System in Canada* (Ottawa, 2002); and R. Romanow, *Building on Values: The Future of Healthcare in Canada, Final Report.* Commission on the Future of Health Care in Canada (Ottawa, 2002).

INDEX